Modern Language Association of America

Approaches to Teaching World Literature

Joseph Gibaldi, Series Editor

Approaches to Teaching Sterne's
Tristram Shandy

Edited by

Melvyn New

The Modern Language Association of America
New York   1989

Copyright © 1989 by The Modern Language Association of America

Library of Congress Cataloging-in-Publication Data

Approaches to teaching Sterne's Tristram Shandy / edited by Melvyn
   New.
         p.   cm. — (Approaches to teaching world literature : 20)
      Bibliography: p.
      Includes index.
      ISBN 0-87352-515-9   ISBN 0-87352-516-7 (pbk.)
      1. Sterne, Laurence, 1713–1768. Life and opinions of Tristram
   Shandy, gentleman.   2. Sterne, Laurence, 1713–1768—Study and
   teaching.   I. New, Melvyn.   II. Series.
   PR3714.T73A67   1989
   823'.6—dc19   88-28977

Cover illustration of the paperback edition: William Hogarth, illustration for
Tristram Shandy, volume 2, chapter 17, engraving, 1760.

Published by The Modern Language Association of America
10 Astor Place, New York, NY 10003-6981

CONTENTS

PREFACE TO THE SERIES

In *The Art of Teaching* Gilbert Highet wrote, "Bad teaching wastes a great deal of effort, and spoils many lives which might have been full of energy and happiness." All too many teachers have failed in their work, Highet argued, simply "because they have not thought about it." We hope that the Approaches to Teaching World Literature series, sponsored by the Modern Language Association's Committee on Teaching and Related Professional Activities, will not only improve the craft—as well as the art—of teaching but also encourage serious and continuing discussion of the aims and methods of teaching literature.

The principal objective of the series is to collect within each volume different points of view on teaching a specific literary work, a literary tradition, or a writer widely taught at the undergraduate level. The preparation of each volume begins with a wide-ranging survey of instructors, thus enabling us to include in the volume the philosophies and approaches, thoughts and methods of scores of experienced teachers. The result is a sourcebook of material, information, and ideas on teaching the subject of the volume to undergraduates.

The series is intended to serve nonspecialists as well as specialists, inexperienced as well as experienced teachers, graduate students who wish to learn effective ways of teaching as well as senior professors who wish to compare their own approaches with the approaches of colleagues in other schools. Of course, no volume in the series can ever substitute for erudition, intelligence, creativity, and sensitivity in teaching. We hope merely that each book will point readers in useful directions; at most each will offer only a first step in the long journey to successful teaching.

Joseph Gibaldi
Series Editor

PREFACE TO THE VOLUME

Although this preface is at the front of the book—unlike Tristram's, which appears in the middle of the third volume—I believe Laurence Sterne would have appreciated the contents of this collection. To be sure, he could never have imagined that *The Life and Opinions of Tristram Shandy* would two hundred years later be read in classrooms and endorsed by professorial types, but he did yearn for immortality, he did believe he had something important to say, and he did, finally, perceive that a successful literary work must have many different handles. This volume addresses all three ideas. For better or worse, literary immortality today is largely a question of what is taught in the college classroom—what books do instructors pass on to students, one generation after the next? The great political power of canon formation is primarily in the hands of classroom teachers, and no small part of the satisfaction I took in bringing this collection together was the confirmation that *Tristram Shandy* is indeed "swimming down the gutter of time," as Sterne prayed it would. Second, one cannot read the nineteen essays in the collection without realizing that Sterne is an author whose comic wit must be taken seriously; he teaches us, among other things, that reading and writing are the most human, the most life-giving, of our many activities. For modern college students, raised on media blitzes and electronic blips, perhaps no other idea we encounter in literature is as important. And, lastly, Sterne's wonderful sense of the multiplication of meanings manifests itself in a collection of essays centered on one text but hobby-horsical nonetheless, as contributors ride off in their various directions, at times in harmony with one another, at other times in splendid cacophony.

The volume consists of two sections, "Materials" and "Approaches." In "Materials" I have tried to cover some very basic questions: the best text to use, the best primary and secondary materials to consult, the main issues around which commentary on *Tristram Shandy* has revolved. To me the most interesting aspect of this section was my growing conviction that how we teach a work is to a large extent governed by the works we teach before and after it. The clue to this perception, as to most of the recommendations, came from answers to several hundred questionnaires sent to possible instructors of *Tristram Shandy*. I am most grateful to the participants who shared their methods and judgments with us; I relied heavily on the information provided and hope I have represented fairly the many opinions and attitudes expressed in the answers. I want to thank my research assistant for the past two years, Myoung Ah Shin, for helping to compile and organize the responses—and for performing numerous other useful tasks during the editing of the volume.

Section 2, "Approaches," gathers together nineteen essays in which instructors from a broad and useful cross-section of institutions describe their particular emphases and handles. Few will agree with all the approaches, but each may, I think, be read with profit. Sterneans—among whom I consider foremost those gathered together here—will forgive me for acknowledging in my preface one contributor in particular, Arthur H. Cash, the dean of Sterne scholars. His immense knowledge of things Sternean, and even more his generosity and kindness as a reader of Sterne interested above all in helping other readers, could find, I hope, no better platform for acknowledgment than a collection dedicated to improving the classroom presentation of Sterne's greatest fiction.

I thank the MLA Committee on Teaching and Related Professional Activities for its endorsement of the project; the series editor, Joseph Gibaldi, has been the most facilitating editor I have had the pleasure to work with, and I thank him for his many useful suggestions. Finally, I want to acknowledge my eighteenth-century colleagues at the University of Florida—Richard Brantley, Alistair Duckworth, Elizabeth Langland, and Brian McCrea; not one of them reads *Tristram Shandy* the way I do, but precisely for that reason—and the conversation their differences generate—I am most grateful.

MN

Part One

MATERIALS

Melvyn New

Editions

The standard edition of *The Life and Opinions of Tristram Shandy, Gentleman* is the Florida edition in three volumes. The text and textual apparatus, comprising volumes 1 and 2, were prepared by Melvyn New and Joan New and published in 1978; the annotations, 552 pages long, were published in volume 3, edited by Melvyn New, with Richard A. Davies and W. G. Day, in 1984. While the steep price of this scholarly edition prohibits its use as a classroom text, its existence serves several pedagogic purposes: first, it enables instructors to check the accuracy of the text in their selected textbook edition, as well as to trace the textual history of *Tristram Shandy*, since the Florida edition provides a full textual apparatus; second, it enables instructors to answer questions concerning many points of the text that the limited annotations of textbook editions do not address; and, third, it provides those teaching the work or writing about it with a rich repository of first resort. In this regard, the Florida *Tristram* might be compared to the Twickenham edition of Alexander Pope, essential for anyone teaching Pope or writing about him.

Of the annotated textbook editions of *Tristram Shandy* James A. Work's effort in 1940 was the first—and remains the best. Forty-five years after its publication, in fact, twenty-five of our respondents listed it as their first choice, compared to fourteen for its nearest competitor, Ian Watt's edition for Houghton Mifflin. Clearly this is a tribute to the usefulness of Work's book for students as well as to its overall excellence; and, indeed, the editors of the Florida edition single Work out for especial praise:

> There have been several annotated textbook editions of *Tristram* prior to this scholarly edition. The best by far is that by James Aiken Work. . . . Work's annotations are primarily of a historical and pedagogical nature: he identifies historical and contemporary personages mentioned by Sterne, defines "difficult" and foreign words and phrases, and elucidates allusions that a modern student audience could not be expected to grasp. He also identifies, but almost always by citation alone, some of Sterne's major borrowings, particularly those from Rabelais, Burton, and Montaigne. So thorough is his identification of persons that we have chosen to quote his notes directly, wherever we are unable to improve on them. . . . Our admiration for Work's edition is great. . . . Few if any eighteenth-century authors have been better served in being made available to a general reading audience than Sterne has been in James Work's edition. . . . (New, Davies, and Day 30)

Originally published by Odyssey Press, the Work edition has in the last decade passed through several large publishing houses and presently is published by Macmillan. Since Work has died and since in the highly competitive world of modern-day commercial publishing a new edition based on Work seems highly unlikely (because it would be unprofitable), instructors of Sterne are faced with something of a dilemma. After more than forty-five years, Work's introduction is dated, his bibliography is woefully inadequate, and his text is flawed by, among other errors, being set from the second rather than the first edition of volumes 1 and 2. And yet, for a variety of reasons, explored below, none of its successors can present a better alternative.

Ian Watt's Riverside edition (1965) does come close. Most important, its prefatory matter improves on Work's and adequately introduces Sterne's life; the critical issues of sentiment, humor, and learned wit; and questions of form. There are useful chronologies of Sterne's life and of historical events alluded to in *Tristram Shandy* alongside parallel fictional events. There is also a useful glossary of military terms, imitated in the Florida edition, and an appendix discussing military warfare during the War of the Spanish Succession. Like Work, Watt places his notes conveniently for students at the bottom of the page. One further improvement in Watt's text is that, following Sterne's practice, he tries to vary the lengths of Sterne's many dashes, instead of making them uniform, as Work had done.

The drawbacks to the Watt edition include a text flawed, like Work's, by its use of the second edition of volumes 1 and 2; a textual apparatus too selective and too idiosyncratic (why, for example, list variants of the Lynch piracy?) to be of much use, particularly to students; and, finally, a policy of annotation that by its own admission attempts less than Work: "The explanatory notes are aimed at the general reader rather than the scholar, for whom the . . . Work [edition] remains indispensable" (xliii). In addition, the format of the Riverside edition, wherein *Tristram Shandy* is printed in 496 pages, is perhaps less inviting than that of Work's edition, where the text runs to 647 pages; while no modern textbook can afford to re-create the spacious compactness of the original small octavo printing, Work seems to come a bit closer than all others.

Two years after the Riverside edition appeared, Penguin Books published an annotated version edited by Graham Petrie, with an excellent introduction by Christopher Ricks. Again, the text is marred by the use of the second rather than the first edition, as well as by carelessness throughout; Petrie's note on his text makes it clear that no significant attempt to provide an accurate text was undertaken, and indeed many unauthorized readings of the 1780 edition find their way into this edition. The notes are in the back and are primarily reworkings of Work's annotations—few additional notes are added and many of Work's are omitted. Also omitted are Hogarth's illustrations, which Work and Watt both included. There seems no reason to use the Penguin edition in class (although three of our respondents do), except for Ricks's contribution.

The fourth entry in the *Tristram Shandy* textbook sweepstakes is the Norton Critical Edition, edited by Howard Anderson and published in 1980. That once again the first two volumes are set from the second edition is a particularly culpable error at this late date, since Kenneth Monkman's "Bibliography of the Early Editions of *Tristram Shandy*," with its indisputable argument for the primacy of the York first over the London second edition, had been published ten years earlier. The Florida edition had been published two years earlier as well, but Anderson shows no awareness of that. Of all the texts under consideration here, the Norton is the most careless. In addition, the annotations are the most inadequate. What the edition does provide, and what is surely the reason for its preference by a dozen instructors, is a collection of secondary materials, beginning with thirteen pages of contemporary responses, including Boswell's poem to Sterne and comments from well-known figures like Gray, Goldsmith, Burke, and Richardson. The nineteenth-century is represented (in snippets) by Coleridge, Hazlitt, Scott, and Thackeray. The collection of critical essays from the twentieth century runs to one hundred and fifty pages and reprints some of the most important modern essays on *Tristram Shandy*; for example, D. W. Jefferson's "*Tristram Shandy* and the Tradition of Learned Wit," Wayne Booth's "Did Sterne Complete *Tristram Shandy*?," Sigurd Burckhardt's "*Tristram Shandy*'s Law of Gravity," and a selection from Richard A. Lanham's Tristram Shandy: *The Games of Pleasure*. The other selections are less useful, however, and the inclusion of several seems eccentric. It might be noted here that the Norton paperback is poorly bound; the Odyssey (Macmillan), Riverside, and Penguin bindings are a good deal better.

Finally, we arrive at the most recent textbook available, edited by Ian Campbell Ross and published by Oxford in 1983. In an extensive review, entitled "Whim-whams and Flim-flams: The Oxford University Press Edition of *Tristram Shandy*," I wrote: "In truth, the notes are clearly derivative from Work's edition, by way of Petrie. There is hardly one single indication of independent research. Forty-three years of intervening scholarship, if we can believe these notes, have not only produced scant new insights or explanation unavailable in Work, they have not even produced new questions" (1–2). The text, appearing five years after the Florida text, may have been prepared by consulting it or by ignoring it—Ross never says which, although he does use the York first edition as copy-text for volumes 1 and 2 and seems familiar with some of the emendations of the Florida edition. As with the Penguin edition, the notes are at the back and the Hogarth illustrations are omitted; the paperback cover has a fine illustration by Bunbury of Uncle Toby, looking anything but sweet and sentimental—indeed, he looks insane. But Ross's introduction is pedestrian, and there is nothing in the Oxford edition that students would not get more honestly and more accurately elsewhere.

Editions of *Tristram Shandy* are also available from Modern Library, Holt, Everyman, and Signet, but these would serve only those instructors interested in presenting the work without benefit of annotation. The most inexpensive such edition is published by Airmont and is still under two dollars in 1988. The Reynard Library (Harvard Univ. Press) has a volume containing not only *Tristram Shandy* but *A Sentimental Journey* and a selection of sermons and letters (all unannotated); this is a most handy one-volume collection of Sterne's writings, but it has apparently been allowed to go out of print.

Other Primary Materials

While only seven of the fifty respondents who answered the question indicated that they teach *A Sentimental Journey* in the same course with *Tristram Shandy*, instructors (and students) should know that the best scholarly edition of Sterne's second great fiction is that by Gardner D. Stout. Oxford University Press has also published the *Journey*, edited by Ian Jack; it is nowhere near as thorough an edition as Stout's, but the volume also contains *A Political Romance*, Sterne's first attempt to write something besides sermons, and the *Journal to Eliza*. (Oxford reissued this edition in 1983, in paperback, in its World's Classics Series.) A more informative edition of the *Journal* is available in Lewis Perry Curtis's edition of the *Letters*, certainly a major repository for information about Sterne—and about *Tristram Shandy*, for Sterne's letters are particularly rich during the period of its composition. And the *Political Romance* is perhaps best read in the Scolar Press facsimile edition, published with an introduction by Kenneth Monkman. Indeed, it might be suggested that the *Political Romance*, with its satiric reduction of a petty quarrel over ecclesiastical spoils among York clerics, provides a particularly useful approach to the origins of *Tristram Shandy*, one quite different from that usually found in an eighteenth-century novel course, where Sterne follows a novel by Richardson or Fielding. Similarly, Sterne's "Rabelaisian Fragment," two chapters of an aborted satire on sermon writing, readily available in my edition published in *PMLA*, provides a valuable entry into *Tristram Shandy*; this fragment was almost certainly Sterne's first attempt at what became his great fiction. My presentation of the text reproduces a page of Sterne's manuscript; in addition, a glance at the notes can help convince students that Sterne did not write the first word and pray to God for the second, as Tristram suggests. The process of correction is evident on many pages of the holograph, and the notes faithfully record this process.

The Florida edition of Sterne's forty-five sermons is currently in progress, but for now instructors must consult the earlier editions of 1904 (ed. Wilbur L. Cross) or 1926–27 (Shakespeare Head Edition). The Harvard Reynard Library volume, as mentioned earlier, reprints seven sermons; and Marjorie David published a paperback selection in 1973, which is still available. Interestingly, respondents to the MLA questionnaire without exception omitted the *Sermons* from works they might use in teaching *Tristram Shandy*. Insofar as Sterne's canon is relatively quite small and the sermons constitute fully thirty percent of what survives of his writing, perhaps something might be learned from them. Certainly it would puzzle students to know that the author of *Tristram* was also a serious (and quite effective) sermon writer, and from such puzzlements often arise useful insights. The value of the sermons for understanding *Tristram Shandy* is indicated by Mark Loverso's essay "Self-Knowledge and the Lockean 'Self' in *The Sermons*."

Perhaps the most useful primary material that an instructor can bring to the classroom is a copy of the original volumes of *Tristram Shandy*. Few works lose as much of their original flavor in modern format as Sterne's does. Students need some opportunity to grasp the slightness, the serial nature, the readability and pocket-ability of each separate volume; the brilliant coloring of its marbled page; the author's signature on the first page of volumes 5, 7, and 9, protection against the numerous imitations that hounded Sterne; and the appearance of the page with its usual count of fewer than 200 words, much white space, and the dramatic appearance of Sterne's characteristic punctuation mark, the dash. By comparison, the Work edition has some 350 words a page, the Watt edition, 450. If an early edition is not available, I would suggest securing a photocopy—or, indeed, a facsimile edition of any one of several eighteenth-century novels printed in small octavo and now available in such reprint collections as that of Garland Publishing: *Foundations of the Novel: Representative Early Eighteenth-Century Fiction* (1973). By whatever means the instructor uses, students do need to understand that *Tristram Shandy* did not appear to its contemporary audience as an intimidating, closely printed, five-hundred-page tome to be read within the next two weeks.

If one is blessed with a rare-book room—or with a generous budget for facsimile reprints—much can be found that would be of considerable value in teaching *Tristram Shandy*. One might begin with the many imitations of the work, some of which have been conveniently reprinted by Garland Publishing in seven volumes under the title *Sterneiana* (1974). Also useful would be eighteenth-century books on obstetrics and on military warfare, the sorts of books Sterne might have consulted when he wrote about Dr. Slop and Uncle Toby. And of course a collection of Hogarth prints would not only help to set the eighteenth-century mood but might also indicate why Sterne sought so urgently to have that famous illustrator "ornament" his work. Ronald Paulson's *Hogarth: His Life, Art, and Times* is the definitive source for information about the Hogarth illustrations (2: 302–06) as well as a handy repository of Hogarth prints.

For aural effect, one might bring to class a recording of Lillibullero. An entertaining rendition by Paul Clayton is available on a Folkways-Viking recording, *Folk Ballads of the English-Speaking World* (FA 2310).

Secondary Materials

General Studies

Perhaps the single most impressive fact revealed by the survey of instructors of *Tristram Shandy* was the enduring popularity of Ian Watt's *Rise of the Novel*. In answer to the inquiry, "What general studies of the eighteenth century or of fiction would you recommend to the beginning teacher of *Tristram Shandy*?" Watt's 1957 study outdistanced by two to one the next two works cited, A. D. McKillop's *Early Masters of the English Novel* and Wayne Booth's *Rhetoric of Fiction*. While some forty additional titles were offered in answer to this question, quite clearly these three works continue to dominate the presentation of *Tristram Shandy* in the undergraduate classroom in the 1980s.

A second important fact is that in answer to the question instructors almost without exception recommended studies of the novel rather than—if not to the exclusion of—studies of the eighteenth century. Only one work in the latter category, Donald Greene's *Age of Exuberance*, was cited by as many as five respondents—the same number who cited Walter Allen's *English Novel*. Other "historians" of the English novel listed by respondents were Lionel Stevenson, Dorothy Van Ghent, Ernest A. Baker, and Frederick R. Karl; and one respondent still recommends Wilbur Cross's *Development of the English Novel*, first published in 1899. Forster's *Aspects of the Novel* is still used by several instructors; to be sure, Forster does have very interesting things to say about *Tristram Shandy*.

In addition to general histories of the novel, three specialized studies of fiction were recommended: Ronald Paulson's *Satire and the Novel in Eighteenth-Century England*, Robert Alter's *Partial Magic: The Novel as a Self-Conscious Genre*, and John Preston's *Created Self: The Reader's Role in Eighteenth-Century Fiction*. Several respondents also recommended Eric Rothstein's *Systems of Order and Inquiry in Later Eighteenth-Century Fiction*, and several others Martin Price's *To the Palace of Wisdom: Studies in Order and Energy from Dryden to Blake*. One work published after the questionnaires were returned that I would highly recommend is Leopold Damrosch's *God's Plot and Man's Stories: Studies in the Fictional Imagination from Milton to Fielding*, a most useful counterbalance to Watt's *Rise of the Novel*.

Only one respondent mentioned Stuart Tave's *The Amiable Humorist: A Study in the Comic Theory and Criticism of the Eighteenth and Early Nineteenth Centuries*, but it is a most valuable work for establishing a context for the Cervantic elements of *Tristram Shandy*. And although R. F. Brissenden's *Virtue in Distress: Studies in the Novel of Sentiment from Richardson to Sade* was not mentioned at all, it is again a work useful for establishing a context—in this instance the sentimental aspects of Sterne. I have also found English Showalter's *Evolution of the French Novel 1641–1782* extremely helpful for understanding the development of English fiction during the same period. Ioan Williams's edited volume *Novel and Romance, 1700–1800* provides contemporary prefaces, reviews, and commentaries, all useful in establishing the generic context of Sterne's work. And finally, I would suggest Sheldon Sacks's *Fiction and the Shape of Belief* for instructors interested in generic considerations; Sacks does not discuss Sterne specifically, but much that he says about generic distinctiveness seems particularly pertinent to *Tristram Shandy*.

That there is some gulf between critical theory and undergraduate teaching is strongly suggested by the lack of theoretical works recommended by those teaching in the classroom. Erich Auerbach's *Mimesis*, Northrop Frye's *Anatomy of Criticism*, Scholes and Kellogg's *Nature of Narrative*, and Wolfgang Iser's *Implied Reader* were mentioned only once or twice. Most surprising, in view of a theoretical approach that seems tailor-made for *Tristram Shandy* and much eighteenth-century fiction, Mikhail Bakhtin's work was cited only twice. Georg Lukács, Roland Barthes, Paul de Man, Fredric Jameson, and Stanley Fish—to name five writers who seem to dominate present-day discussions about the analysis of fiction—were not mentioned at all. Derrida was mentioned once, but rather unconvincingly. Shlomith Rimmon-Kenan's *Narrative Fiction* was also mentioned once. While possibly the question itself steered respondents in another direction, it does seem evident from the completed questionnaires that tradition plays a powerful role in classroom teaching at the undergraduate level. Most of the titles in present favor are from the 1960s—or earlier. Perhaps instructors are waiting to see whether Lennard J. Davis's *Factual Fictions: The Origins of the English Novel* or Ira Konigsberg's *Narrative Technique in the English Novel*, to take just two examples, pass the test of time; or perhaps, and more likely I am afraid, undergraduates are taught primarily what we learned in graduate school.

There are currently so many "guides" to literary study, whether biographical, bibliographical, or critical, and so many of them are little more than commercial ventures to hold libraries in thrall, that one hesitates to recommend any of them. Two, however, seem to me to have some merit for teachers of *Tristram Shandy*. The first is the two-volume *British Novelists, 1660–1800*, edited by Martin Battestin as volume 39 of the *Dictionary of Literary Biography*. There are substantive biographical and critical entries on almost any eighteenth-century fiction writer an instructor might need to know (and a bibliographical entry as well) and particularly lengthy entries on Defoe, Richardson, Fielding, Smollett, and Sterne; that I wrote the

Sterne entry is, I hope, not the only reason for this recommendation. The second work is Jerry C. Beasley's *English Fiction, 1660–1800: A Guide to Information Sources*, which provides exactly what its title indicates.

Finally, I would add some recommended reading on the eighteenth century as distinct from reading on fiction. George Sherburn and Donald F. Bond's entry in Albert C. Baugh, *A Literary History of England,* is still useful, as is volume 4 of the *Pelican Guide to English Literature,* edited by Boris Ford. W. Jackson Bate, *The Burden of the Past and the English Poet,* says much about the second half of the eighteenth century, as does Paul Fussell, *The Rhetorical World of Augustan Humanism: Ethics and Imagery from Swift to Burke.* J. W. Johnson, *The Formation of English Neo-Classical Thought,* and Lawrence Lipking, *The Ordering of the Arts in Eighteenth-Century England,* might help the instructor place Sterne among his eighteenth-century contemporaries; and certainly one should read Frye, "Towards Defining an Age of Sensibility"; R. S. Crane; Louis I. Bredvold; Greene, "Latitudinarianism"; Leo Braudy; and Jean Hagstrum on sentimentality and sensibility. A. S. Turberville's *Johnson's England: An Account of the Life and Manners of His Age* and M. Dorothy George's *English Social Life in the Eighteenth Century* and *London Life in the Eighteenth Century* should be read alongside the more recent entry in the field, Roy Porter's *English Society in the Eighteenth Century.* A. R. Humphreys's *Augustan World* and J. H. Plumb's *England in the Eighteenth Century* are also recommended as useful background studies. David Chandler has written two very readable books on the campaigns that Toby mimics on the bowling green, *The Art of Warfare in the Age of Marlborough* and *Marlborough as Military Commander.* Kenneth MacLean's *John Locke and English Literature of the Eighteenth Century* is important for obvious reasons and a good place to begin to shape one's own opinion on the single issue that has most dominated Sterne criticism in the past quarter century—Sterne's use of Locke. *The Oxford History of English Literature,* which covers the eighteenth century in two volumes (Butt and Carnall; Dobrée), remains a valuable source of information.

Works about Sterne and Tristram Shandy

Lodwick Hartley's several checklists of Sterne criticism, covering the twentieth century up to 1977, are of great value to instructors and students alike, especially if they are used with sufficient caution. The primary virtue of any checklist is its accuracy of citation; Hartley's first list is quite good in this regard, his second very bad. Unfortunately, that inaccuracy carries over into the introduction and annotations of the second list as well, so that for the period 1965–77 an instructor or student depending on Hartley alone, without doing some personal investigation, will be frequently misled. With this caveat in mind, Hartley is still, obviously, the place to begin one's secondary reading on *Tristram Shandy*. For critical works after 1977, one should consult, of course, the *MLA Bibliography* and *Eighteenth Century: A Current Bibliography*, the 1982 volume of which appeared, somewhat less than "currently," in 1986. My essay "Surviving the Seventies: Sterne, Collins, and Their Recent Critics" is a review-essay that extends Hartley's coverage to 1980, while also commenting on recent trends in Sterne criticism. New criticism on Sterne has been systematically reviewed in the *Scriblerian* since the Autumn 1986 issue.

Sterne has been blessed with two fine biographers in the twentieth century, Wilbur L. Cross and Arthur H. Cash. Cash's *Laurence Sterne: The Early and Middle Years* (1975) finally has its sequel, *Laurence Sterne: The Later Years* (1986); the two volumes replace Cross's *Life and Times of Laurence Sterne*, although Cross is still interesting for those curious about how authors and their works were interwoven by scholars in the first decades of this century. An added dividend in Cash are the many plates, especially those of Sterne himself, as portrayed by Reynolds and other contemporaries. Two less reliable, but readable, biographies are those by Lodwick Hartley, *This Is Lorence*, and David Thomson. In addition, Lewis Perry Curtis, the editor of Sterne's letters, provides in his detailed annotations much documentary information about Sterne's life. Curtis includes the text of Sterne's brief autobiographical sketch, recently made available in a separate edition by Kenneth Monkman (with a newly discovered manuscript of part of it, in facsimile). Instructors who purchase this elegant little volume for their libraries will be able to show students not only an extended example of a Sterne manuscript but also a splendid reproduction of the engraving of Benjamin West's painting of Lydia Sterne with the bust of the author—and will benefit Shandy Hall to boot.

A particularly useful research tool is Alan B. Howes's collection of early critical responses to *Tristram Shandy* in *Sterne: The Critical Heritage*. As with other works in this series, the extracts—from early reviews and from the correspondence and other writings of such major literary figures as Boswell and Voltaire, Coleridge and Goethe—are generously and intelligently selected; in addition to the chronological coverage of English materials up to 1839, there are separate sections devoted to French, German, Dutch, Russian, and Italian commentaries during the same period. Another work that tells us a great deal about the contemporary reception of Sterne is J. C. T. Oates's pamphlet *Shandyism and Sentiment, 1760–1800*. Insofar as *Tristram Shandy*, like all great literature, must in each age be "misread" to satisfy the needs of that age, the "critical heritage" of Sterne is of vital interest; much of the material in these two books can be of immediate interest to instructors and students. A second useful research tool is the concordance of *Tristram Shandy* prepared as a doctoral dissertation at Emory University by Patricia Graves and available through University Microfilms. For instructors and students both, such a tool can be invaluable, especially for tracing Sterne's usage, repetitions, and the presence of certain themes and ideas.

The book-length studies of *Tristram Shandy* most often cited by respondents include works by Henri Fluchère, William Holtz, Richard Lanham, Helene Moglen, Melvyn New, John Stedmond, and John Traugott. Fluchère's work, in the four hundred pages of the condensed translation by Barbara Bray, contains a general survey of attitudes and approaches to Sterne (often without adequate credit given) and some dramatic if not particularly cogent remarks on almost every subject that had been raised about *Tristram* before 1960. His strongest sections are on Sterne's interest in narrative time (although it is A. A. Mendilow's *Time and the Novel* that most respondents single out on this subject, and indeed many of Fluchère's insights stem from that work) and on Sterne's sources, work probably superseded by the Florida *Annotations*.

Holtz approaches Sterne through their mutual interest in Hogarth, Reynolds, and the visual arts in general; well written and interesting throughout, *Image and Immortality* is valuable reading for the instructor and a good place for students to begin to learn how to read criticism. Holtz's chapter on the "limits of language," for example, is a particularly clear exposition of this often discussed approach to *Tristram Shandy*.

Moglen's *Philosophical Irony of Laurence Sterne* has neither the clarity nor interest of Holtz, but it does bring us a little further along the road blazed by John Traugott's highly influential *Tristram Shandy's World*, the single most dominant work of Sterne criticism in the last thirty years. Both authors (and we may add James E. Swearingen's more recent *Reflexivity in Tristram Shandy: An Essay in Phenomenological Criticism*) begin with the notion that *Tristram Shandy* is an analysis of Locke's *Essay concerning Human Understanding*, and while they differ in details they all circle this premise with a prose that would at best prove discouraging to undergraduates and in some instances serve simply as a bad example. Everyone perhaps should read Duke Maskell's essay on Locke and Sterne before entering the thicket, and instructors might also do well to remember the statement on the relationship from the Florida *Tristram*:

> Perhaps the annotator's perspective is simply too limited, but it is worth remembering that few if any literary works in the eighteenth century do not show the influence of Locke's empiricism and sensationalism, especially in fiction; and that few if any problems have more exercised modern critics than that of the relationship between philos-

ophy and literature. That we cannot even settle the most basic problem
of whether Sterne agrees or disagrees with Locke is perhaps a strong
indication that the question has not yet been asked in a manner that
could produce a satisfying answer. (3: 17)

Nonetheless, instructors should be alert to the fact that almost all recent
critical thinking on *Tristram Shandy* has been profoundly affected by Traugott's work, including his belief that Sterne found Locke's ideas concerning
communication limited and that he posited sentiment as a means of more
significant communication than language could provide; and Traugott's further belief that Tristram is positioned on the brink of existential despair
(because human communication seems impossible and the world is rendered
meaningless), to be saved only by the feeling heart. It is far better to encounter these themes in their original statements than in their weaker and
less interesting repetitions; *Tristram Shandy's World* shaped an entire
generation of scholars writing about *Tristram Shandy*, and no instructor
should attempt to teach Sterne without coming to grips with its premises
and conclusions.

Lanham's, Stedmond's, and my own studies have in common their movement away from the philosophical readings of Traugott and his followers and
toward somewhat more formalistic approaches. Stedmond is a sage reader
who returns frequently to the text to demonstrate his assertions; his long
chapter "Tristram as Clown" works volume by volume through the fiction
and provides useful readings of many individual passages that wear extremely
well in classroom discussion. My *Laurence Sterne as Satirist* was often cited
by respondents, indicating that professional politeness is alive and well among
the eighteenth-century specialists polled by the MLA. In fact, however, my
approach to *Tristram Shandy* as a work far more in the Augustan tradition
of satire than in the novel tradition has not been popular among Sterneans.
Only recently have some critics—Swearingen, Mark Loveridge, and Max
Byrd in book-length studies—begun to flirt with the idea that reading Sterne
as an Augustan does have some validity; and Michael Seidel, without reading
very deeply in Sterne criticism, has also been interested in linking Sterne
with satire. Just as recently, however, Martin Battestin (*Providence*), Peter
Conrad, and Leopold Damrosch have found in *Tristram Shandy* a distinct
end of the Augustan era and the beginning of whatever might be said to
have replaced it.

Lanham's approach is through rhetoric and game theory. He is particularly
interesting in his chapter on Sterne's ways with language (ch. 6), a useful
antidote to students who want to confront *Tristram Shandy* with typical
sophomoric lugubriousness.

William Bowman Piper did the Twayne volume on Sterne, a far more readable introduction than usual in that series. One of those most convinced that *Tristram Shandy* should be read in the novel tradition (although the most important chapter actually shows Tristram mediating between tragic and comic outlooks), Piper is useful reading for those inclined to take that approach. A more recent work in a similar series is Max Byrd's *Tristram Shandy* in the Unwin Critical Library. Byrd provides chapters on Sterne's life and literary backgrounds, a discussion of sensibility, and a volume-by-volume reading of *Tristram Shandy*; he also has a brief survey of criticism on *Tristram* and a selected bibliography. While anyone familiar with the critical fortunes of Sterne will find Byrd too evasive by far, he does introduce new readers to some of the critical directions taken toward *Tristram Shandy* in the past quarter century—and he does so with a style geared to the general reader. If an instructor in the past has sent students to the Twayne series, Byrd's volume offers a viable—and more current—alternative.

Three collections of essays on Sterne are available, in addition to the collection in the Norton textbook edition. The first, *The Winged Skull*, edited by Arthur H. Cash and John Stedmond, contains the papers given at the Sterne Bicentenary Conference at Shandy Hall in 1968; while somewhat marred by the urge to celebrate Sterne as "relevant" to the modern age (the conference occurred simultaneously with the Democratic convention in Chicago), the essays nevertheless provide instructors and students with much good material, conveniently gathered. The most valuable effort in the collection is a brief but telling essay, " 'Trusting to Almighty God': Another Look at the Composition of *Tristram Shandy*," by R. F. Brissenden. The volume also contains a selected bibliography of Sterne and some useful illustrations. John Traugott's collection for the Twentieth-Century Views series contains many of the most useful essays written on *Tristram Shandy* before 1968. The most convenient source for certain cornerstone works that everyone dealing with Sterne should read, the volume includes Benjamin H. Lehman, "Of Time, Personality, and the Author"; D. W. Jefferson, "*Tristram Shandy* and the Tradition of Learned Wit"; Viktor Shklovsky, "A Parodying Novel: Sterne's *Tristram Shandy*"; and a portion of W. B. C. Watkins, "Yorick Revisited," reprinted from *Perilous Balance*. Additional essays by McKillop, Mendilow, Jean-Jacques Mayoux, and Traugott himself round out the collection. The third collection, edited by Valerie Grosvenor Myer and part of the Critical Studies Series, contains eleven new essays covering such subjects as sexuality and the double entendre in *Tristram Shandy*; Sterne's relationship to Rabelais, Cervantes, Locke, and Jane Austen; Sterne's borrowings from contemporary science; and such themes as mortality, language, and liberty. Of the three collections, this might be the one to introduce undergraduates to recent Sterne criticism, but that does not necessarily make it the best. Authors represented include myself, Alan

B. Howes, Edward A. Bloom and Lillian D. Bloom, W. G. Day, and Roy Porter, among others. The bibliography, which brings Hartley up to 1983, is purposely selective and for that very reason not as useful as it might have been.

It is one mark of the significance of *Tristram Shandy* in the twentieth century that so much still remains to be listed in this account of only the most important work to be digested by instructors and students hoping to cope with Sterne's complex fiction. Among the essays mentioned by questionnaire respondents, the following must be considered the most important: Robert Alter, "*Tristram Shandy* and the Game of Love," a fine discussion of Sterne's sexual manipulations; Theodore Baird, "The Time-Scheme of *Tristram Shandy* and a Source," the essay that uncovered Sterne's extensive use of Rapin-Thoyras's *History of England*; Wayne Booth, "Did Sterne Complete *Tristram Shandy*?" and "The Self-Conscious Narrator in Comic Fiction before *Tristram Shandy*"; Arthur Cash, "The Lockean Psychology of *Tristram Shandy*" and "The Birth of Tristram Shandy: Sterne and Dr. Burton," a useful and entertaining account of the obstetrical background of *Tristram Shandy* (and, again, Cash provides a set of most useful illustrations); Sigurd Burckhardt, "*Tristram Shandy*'s Law of Gravity," a beautiful essay on Sterne's play with gravity (and graveness) and the center of things; my essays "The Dunce Revisited: Colley Cibber and Tristram Shandy" and "Sterne, Warburton, and the Burden of Exuberant Wit"; Ernest Tuveson, "Locke and Sterne," still one of the best statements on the Locke-Sterne nexus; and, finally, Andrew Wright, "The Artifice of Failure in *Tristram Shandy*." One essay surprisingly not mentioned on anyone's list was Frank Brady's "*Tristram Shandy*: Sexuality, Morality, and Sensibility," which I have always found particularly useful in its balanced view of Sterne's handling of three intertwined and difficult subjects.

Among more recent essays that seem not yet to have come to the attention of our respondents, I would strongly recommend, for instructors and students both, Leland E. Warren, "The Constant Speaker: Aspects of Conversation in *Tristram Shandy*"; Michael Rosenblum, "The Sermon, the King of Bohemia, and the Art of Interpolation in *Tristram Shandy*"; Max Nänny, "Similarity and Contiguity in *Tristram Shandy*"; J. Hillis Miller, "Narrative Middles: A Preliminary Outline" (along with Robert Markley's "translation" of it); Leigh A. Ehlers, "Mrs. Shandy's 'Lint and Basilicon': The Importance of Women in *Tristram Shandy*"; Jonathan Lamb, "Sterne's Use of Montaigne"; and Elizabeth W. Harries, "Sterne's Novels: Gathering Up the Fragments."

Part Two

APPROACHES

INTRODUCTION

The Course

One of the most telling responses we received to the *Tristram* questionnaire was from an instructor who indicated that in her long career she was never "allowed" to teach *Tristram Shandy* because she was the "eighteenth-century" specialist rather than the "novel" specialist. Territorial divisions of this sort bespatter the academic landscape and almost certainly influence our critical commentaries, whether in print or in the classroom. *Tristram Shandy* is a case in point. Overwhelmingly, it is taught in courses in the eighteenth-century novel, where instructors progress with amazing uniformity from Defoe through Fielding and Richardson (or Richardson and Fielding) to Sterne, and then on to Smollett. One eventually becomes known, fairly or unfairly, by the company one keeps. When students encounter *Tristram Shandy* after *Pamela* or *Clarissa*, it is obviously a very different book to them than when they come to the work after *Joseph Andrews*. Their expectations, what they look for, what questions they ask, how they expect characters to behave and stories to unfold—all must be affected by the reading they have done in the immediate past (and, to be sure, over the years as well). How much more, then, would these expectations be changed if *Tristram Shandy* were read immediately after *A Tale of a Tub*, *Gulliver's Travels*, or *The Dunciad*? Or after *Rasselas*, published in the same year as the first two volumes of *Tristram*; or *Candide*, which, even though it *cannot* be taught in a course in *English* literature, was also published in 1759? The year 1759 might be thought of, indeed, as an annus mirabilis of works of fiction that are not very responsive to treatment as "novels."

Surely what students and instructors continue to seek (and therefore find) in eighteenth-century novel courses is the rise and development of the novel, from its rough origins in Defoe to its fulfillment in Austen or (heaven forfend!) Scott. What they want to deal with, what interests them as the connections and interrelations and motifs of the course are questions of plot, of character development, of mimetic realism, and the like. Moreover, these particular expectations from fiction will be reinforced by much that undergraduates read before encountering the eighteenth-century novel, that is, by the realistic fiction that has dominated the literary marketplace for the last two hundred years. It is no wonder, then, that when respondents were asked what their students most disliked about *Tristram Shandy*, the answers had a most uniform ring: the lack of plot, the disruptive time sequences, the digressions, the lack of "interesting" characters, the annoying disorderliness of the narrator. In short, students want a "story," like the other "stories" in a course that traces how stories came to be told in the way most congenial to students' own experiences with fiction. *Tristram Shandy* rarely can be made to satisfy that expectation.

Needless to say, undergraduate curricula and the ordering of English department offerings will not change very quickly, if the past can be taken as any measure of the future. It was encouraging, however, to see from the returned questionnaires that *Tristram Shandy* is occasionally also being taught in eighteenth-century literature courses and in more general courses in fiction and the theory of fiction. In the first instance, one might approach Sterne after reading Dryden, Congreve, Pope, Swift, and perhaps even a bit of Locke and Shaftesbury, Berkeley and Hume; or perhaps one will read him alongside Boswell (a most apt pairing, as Boswell had the genius to recognize), Johnson, Reynolds (Sterne's good friend), and possibly Burke or William Collins. One might even be able to read *Tristram Shandy* in conjunction with *A Sentimental Journey*, something our respondents can rarely do in their novel courses.

More potentially interesting is what might be done with Sterne in a course that is not limited to the English tradition or that uses *Tristram Shandy* to test theoretical hypotheses concerning the enterprise of fiction. Sterne stands to gain much when in the company of Rabelais or Boccaccio or Cervantes or Erasmus. And insofar as it is the function of great literature to undo any critical model, *Tristram Shandy* can hold its own in any course on the theory of fiction. Such courses are bound to be salutary, if only as a check on the tracks and trains we have gotten into, "cluttering like hey-go-mad" over the same road, from which, now that we are in it, "the Devil himself sometimes shall not be able to drive" us. Like Mrs. Shandy and the winding of the clock, the association of *Tristram Shandy* with *Pamela* and *Tom Jones* might well be dispersing the critical energies we bring to our reading and teaching of Sterne.

The Students

Discounting the possibility that undergraduates resist any work over a hundred pages, *Tristram Shandy* does seem to encounter more resistance than almost any other eighteenth-century fiction. Nearly every respondent spoke to this problem. While I have offered one explanation for and possible solution to this resistance, the fact is that *Tristram Shandy* will continue—and should continue—to be taught in courses on eighteenth-century fiction and will continue to follow Defoe, Fielding, and Richardson in the scheme of things, if only because chronologically it did indeed do so. Moreover, teaching *Tristram Shandy* within a different context will in no way necessarily overcome students' resistance but might simply shift the subjects of their discontent. Fortunately, our respondents suggested many useful devices and approaches for engaging student interest in a book that instructors themselves always enjoy; and, equally fortunate, most respondents acknowledge that if the initial resistance can be overcome, good students will find much that delights and instructs them in Sterne's work.

For the sake of coherence I have separated the classroom presentation of *Tristram Shandy* into four categories, all quite arbitrary and overlapping but perhaps useful nonetheless. They are (1) approaches stressing "philosophical" questions, (2) approaches stressing "formal" questions, (3) approaches stressing wit and humor, and (4) approaches stressing comparison and contrast to other fiction. Before discussing each briefly in turn, however, I want to say a few words about the practical problem of class time and the divisibility of *Tristram Shandy*.

While some instructors are forced to cover the work in as few as two class hours, most spend between four and six hours—and a few are in the enviable position of having three weeks (nine hours). As one might expect, *Tristram*'s nine volumes—eight published in pairs and the last published separately—are usually divided into two-volume assignments for each class meeting; often there is either an introductory period at the beginning or a summary period at the conclusion.

A more innovative suggestion is to take up the first period with volume 1 or a small section of it (perhaps even the first chapter), to demonstrate to students in detail all the various games that Sterne will be playing. Several instructors suggest that the first two volumes be read for the first two class sessions, after which larger portions might be more easily managed. What makes the idea particularly valuable is the difficulty most instructors have in doing justice to the later volumes, so dense and complex is the entrance into the Shandy world. By approaching the work slowly and discussing in detail Sterne's progressive and digressive method, students may more readily grasp the remainder of the work.

It is also worth keeping in mind that the last three volumes of the work form a manageable unit, not only because they are approximately the same length as the earlier two-volume units, but also because the subject matter of volumes 8 and 9 is so closely united. But whatever division is accepted, it is surely to be hoped that the work is always read in its entirety. Sterneans have not yet had to deal with such efforts as George Sherburn's well-meaning but damaging condensation of *Clarissa* or Somerset Maugham's effort to read *Tom Jones* for the "story," but as we approach the twenty-first century almost anything is possible. As long books (in the classroom, at any rate) go the way of Greek and Latin, we should try to ensure that *Tristram Shandy* is the last one to disappear.

Classroom Presentation

1. *"Philosophical" questions.* Quite a few instructors approach *Tristram Shandy* through Locke, setting forth the philosophical revolution in epistemology represented by the *Essay concerning Human Understanding* and then working out Sterne's perceived relation to this revolution. This approach need not be as forbidding as it might sound; the major outlines of Locke's theory were commonplace knowledge in the eighteenth century and remain embedded in our own intellectual assumptions. That Locke is easily interpreted in many different ways does not gainsay his universality—Freud and his fate in the twentieth century would be a useful analogy. Concepts such as the association of ideas and "duration and its simple modes" are readily available to students and relevant to them as children of a psychological century. Indeed, it is precisely this predilection to psychological investigation that has made the Locke-Sterne nexus, at least since Traugott, the most important single issue among critics of *Tristram Shandy*.

In what appears to be a quite different direction, several instructors begin with Sterne's absurd world and find in Tristram's "heroic" efforts to establish meaning a forerunner of Sartre and Camus and twentieth-century existentialism. Such a reading usually intersects with a Lockean approach somewhere in the field of language, and from here it should be just a short journey to structuralism and deconstruction. Sterne's interest in impotence and other forms of sexual despair might be found to foreshadow much that is currently being written about love and desire, and once on this path, the instructor can easily move on to Freud, Girard, or Lacan. Indeed, the problem is not so much whether one can uncover Sterne's philosophical implications as it is which philosopher of interest to students one will use as a model to approach his work. Like Cervantes or Shakespeare, Sophocles or Joyce, Sterne will respond to any intelligent model of human behavior and creativity—and will reduce the model to its true proportions rather than be reduced by it. *Tristram Shandy* survived the Victorian age and will certainly survive the psychological-philosophical age as well.

One might suggest under this category the possibility of introducing *Tristram Shandy* through some understanding of Judeo-Christian thought, grounding such an approach in Sterne's own clerical career and the fact that his most substantial body of writing next to *Tristram* is his forty-five surviving sermons. Much here depends on the instructor's predilections and the nature of the course, but if Judeo-Christian thought has been brought to bear on Defoe and Richardson, or on Swift and Johnson, or even on Rabelais and Cervantes, it is just possible that Sterne's work also responds to some familiarity with his traditional religious beliefs. Obviously the place to start would be the "Abuses of Conscience" sermon in volume 2.

2. *Formal questions.* If one pays attention to one's students, it is impossible to avoid questions concerning the form of *Tristram Shandy*, and hence the best strategy may be to confront their concerns at the start. These concerns appear as complaints: There is no story! He keeps jumping around! I can't follow what's happening! While students who have been reading such modern writers as Jorge Luis Borges or John Barth or Thomas Pynchon or Donald Barthelme or Italo Calvino (and let us all pray for undergraduates who do) will find their difficulties lessened, those seeking in *Tristram* the thread of the novel's development from Defoe to Jane Austen or Henry James are likely to be perplexed. Some instructors might want to suggest that the texture of *Tristram Shandy* is indeed more highly "realistic" than what had previously been achieved; others might want to talk about *Tristram Shandy* as an antinovel, an attack on the form of the novel as it was beginning to emerge; still others might want to introduce another genre, and hence other expectations and priorities altogether—the anatomy as defined by Northrop Frye, Menippean satire as defined by Bakhtin, perhaps bricolage as defined by Lévi-Strauss. The idea of *Tristram Shandy* as itself a commentary on the telling of fiction, that is, as metafiction, will certainly find a welcome reception among students fresh from literary criticism courses— and, indeed, it would form a useful text in classes on the theory of fiction, even if one does not agree with Viktor Shklovsky's too-often quoted statement that *Tristram* is the most typical novel ever written. Moreover, in a course on the eighteenth-century novel, the first works of which chronicle the emergence of the realistic mode of story-telling, one will have to deal with the hard wall of Sterne's difference; for many students, the achievements of

Defoe, Fielding, and Richardson might not even become clear until they find in Sterne so dramatic an indifference to what had seemed the only desiderata of all fiction writers.

Another approach to form might stress the internal design of *Tristram Shandy*, beginning with its composition as a serial and its publication over an eight-year period. Or we might equally stress, as one respondent in particular strongly urged, the physical shape of the work (its compact size, large print, easy readability) and then its typographical oddities (the black, marbled, and blank pages; the missing and displaced chapters; the lines of progress at the end of volume 6)—that is, those visual elements of the text that help to distinguish *Tristram Shandy* from almost every other fiction we ever encounter. Still again, attention might be called to the analogical structure many have found in *Tristram Shandy*—or, more simply, students might be asked to draw as many parallels between episodes as they can find. Eventually, some students will stumble on the parallel between Walter's hobbyhorse and Toby's; or between creativity and procreativity, between the start of the homunculus and of the fiction. From there, the instructor might suggest parallels concerning birth, courtship, and death; or parallels in the interpolated matter; or the relation between the interpolated matter ("Slawkenbergius's Tale," for example) and the "story" (Walter's theorizing or Toby's courtship, for example). The high point of such a method would be, of course, for the instructor and the students to work on the relation of volume 7 to the rest of the fiction; students who can articulate some explanation for the volume's presence as part of the whole have at least begun a rewarding relation with *Tristram Shandy*.

Several instructors divide *Tristram Shandy* by having students keep track of three "stories." The first story, which occupies much of volumes 1–5, concerns Tristram's birth on 5 November 1718 and the theories by which Walter attempts to control it and the child's upbringing in the five years immediately following. The second story deals with Toby's battlefields and his courtship of the Widow Wadman, anticipated in the first volumes but not really developed until volumes 6, 8, and 9. This story takes us back in time, covering a period roughly between 1695, when Toby is wounded, and 1713, when the Treaty of Utrecht is signed. The third story is that of Tristram in his study, the narrator as he writes the work from 1759 to 1767, sharing with us his trials, his tribulations, his illness, his impending death. This division has the virtue of separating the different time schemes of the work, one of the major problems first-time readers of *Tristram* seem to experience.

3. *Wit and humor*. The sexual humor of Sterne is certainly one opening to the work, although perhaps the term *sexist humor* might cast a more revealing light on what takes place. Interestingly, Sterne's bawdiness made

the questionnaire's list of both what most interested students and what they found most difficult or uninteresting in *Tristram Shandy*—and in one telling comment a respondent indicated it was the male students who found the sexual humor interesting. In either case, sexual or sexist, Sterne's forthright exhibition of human proclivities can offer the student a fruitful approach to the language of the work, to much of its thematic material (e.g., impotence, creativity, interruption, insinuation, and penetration), and, I at times believe, to much of its fun. In most classrooms, for example, one can point to cracks in the walls, toggle switches for lights, electric outlets, pieces of chalk, and door knobs to show how easily, given a certain mind-set, everything can be turned to a sexual point. As this process continues, the language of the instructor and the class is no longer "safe"; within this very paragraph "opening," "revealing," "place," "fruitful," and "point" have all taken on a certain coloration. From an awareness of how this effect has come about to a richer understanding of the Shandean hobbyhorse is a relatively short step. Students should be encouraged to forage in one of Eric Partridge's collections, *Shakespeare's Bawdy* or *A Dictionary of Slang and Unconventional English*, since it is important they understand Sterne's bawdiness not merely as a phenomenon unique to Sterne but equally the exploitation of a tendency inherent in the use of language.

To be sure, this sexist/sexual humor worries some students; on the one hand, the humor can be seen as directed particularly against women; on the other hand, the bawdiness may be found simply embarrassing by both sexes (despite the permissiveness of the last twenty years, we remain in many ways, not all of them bad, significantly repressed), especially when it is being "shared" with both an "adult" instructor and the opposite sex. One can only admit that Sterne indulges at times in the eighteenth-century equivalent of locker-room humor and perhaps examine the reasons for the persistence of such humor throughout Western civilization. It is certainly worth pointing out that the audience Richardson pictured when he wrote differed dramatically from the one Sterne pictured—and that perhaps no one would be more flabbergasted than Sterne himself to learn that his *Tristram Shandy* was a "classic," being *taught* in colleges and universities to coeducational classes of young adults. As for the humor (or his entire sexual attitude) being culpable, one can only hope for students bright enough to offer the complaint; Sterne's attitudes can be defended, or at least much can be said on both sides of the question, and perhaps no subject will raise more student interest.

An even more difficult aspect of Sterne's wit is what D. W. Jefferson labels "learned wit," the esoteric, encyclopedic graffiti with which Sterne loves to litter his pages. No work that requires footnotes can be easy reading, and for most students *Tristram Shandy*, in terms of its accessibility without annotation, falls somewhere between a Pope poem and a Fielding novel. To suggest that students skip what they cannot understand, that they remain ignorant of the many debts Sterne owes to other writers (including whole sentences and paragraphs), that they try simply to get the gist of the "story" is to provide a limited view of the work. As with Pope, it seems fairer to argue that Sterne has earned a privilege afforded to only a handful of authors—the privilege of insisting that we attempt to re-create portions of his world to help ourselves better to engage his work. Immediate accessibility is a virtue in almost every aspect of modern life, so that this argument is not easily won in any classroom today; it is, however, an argument worth making, and perhaps no small part of Sterne's own meaning is that he weaves the pattern of his work from other writers' threads.

4. *Comparison and contrast.* It would perhaps be worthwhile to introduce *Tristram Shandy* with Wayne Booth's parodic essay "Thomas Mann and Eighteenth-Century Comic Fiction," in which Booth demonstrates that Sterne is the father of all modern literature. In answer to the question "What books do you find most useful to compare with *Tristram Shandy* as part of your classroom presentation?" respondents to the MLA survey cited the following authors and works, arranged here in alphabetical order: Amis, *Lucky Jim*; Austen, *Sense and Sensibility*; Barth, *Lost in the Fun House, Giles Goat Boy*; Beckett; Borges, *Labyrinths*; Brontë, *Jane Eyre*; Calvino; Coover; Crews, *A Childhood*; Dickens; Dostoevsky; Fowles, *The French Lieutenant's Woman*; Joyce, *Portrait of the Artist, Ulysses, Finnegans Wake*; Lawrence; Melville; Nabokov; Proust; Pynchon; Robbins; Shelley, *Frankenstein*; Thackeray, *Vanity Fair*; Vonnegut; Wodehouse; Woolf. Interestingly, no one mentioned Mann, although I have found comparison with *Dr. Faustus* most useful—and, indeed, Mann acknowledges his debt to Sterne in that work and elsewhere. Such lists are of course endless; I introduce this one only to suggest the range of possibilities and the way in which Sterne might profitably be included in a course in world fiction.

Comparisons move in the other direction as well, and *Tristram Shandy* is often compared to earlier works. Naturally enough, the most usual comparison cited by respondents was with Richardson and Fielding, the authors most likely to precede Sterne on the reading list; Defoe and Smollett were also frequently named. Further back, Pope and Swift, most especially Swift, were listed; in fact, several instructors seemed to build their discussions on the similarities and differences between the two. *Don Quixote* was also mentioned by many as a useful comparison, as was Rabelais and Erasmus's *Praise of Folly*. Again, there is no end to this sort of listing, although I will take the liberty of adding two names myself, Petronius and Shakespeare. The *Satyricon* puts much of Sterne's bawdiness into a tradition that helps to justify his humor and perhaps explain his use of impotence as a motif;

and for an author who names his most persistent alter ego Yorick, Shake-speare seems as good an author as any to go to for comparisons. The nurse in *Romeo and Juliet* would be one place to start.

A Word about the Essays

A difficult choice presented to the editors of these MLA volumes is that the editor's independent voice seems subsumed not only by the questionnaires received but by the essays contained in the volume. To gain some freedom in what seemed to me a rather restrictive setting, I decided to complete my discussion of the questionnaires before reading the final versions of the essays. Needless to say, I had some idea of their content, since the MLA and I had to approve the initial proposals. Still, it seemed more appropriate to have my say without the undue influence of others, and that I have had. Now the monologue is over, the heteroglossia can begin, and a most fine one it has turned out to be.

The essays are divided (somewhat arbitrarily, since there are overlapping concerns) into three groups: those that seem to concentrate on a close reading of the text, those that depend on a contextual understanding, and those for whom the contextual approach raises the problematics of context—whether because context can point in different directions or because context is po-litically determined by the critic or simply because, like many great works of literature, *Tristram Shandy* resists categorizations, those of context in-cluded. Hence my division headings, "Text," "Context," and, with a bow to the postmodernists, "Text con Texts," the possible implications of *con* being "with" (e.g., *con amore*), "against," and, perhaps most interesting, "to learn," "to study."

In the collection's first essay, Arthur H. Cash, Sterne's biographer, pro-vides not only some very fundamental hints for getting students started on *Tristram Shandy* but also a most valuable teaching outline for this work that seems to defy all outlines or summaries. Many instructors may want to provide copies for their students.

William Bowman Piper immediately thrusts us into the heart of contro-versy by insisting to his students, pace much of the commentary on *Tristram Shandy*, that while Tristram talks a good deal about the free play of imagi-nation his book affords, Sterne actually guides and controls our reading most forcefully. Piper sees his role in class as that of helping new readers recognize the difference between the appearance of equivocation and the reality of a clearly told story of the Shandy family. Somewhat similarly, Robert D. Spector argues that the best introduction to *Tristram Shandy* might come from an instructor able to show students the work as a whole; more specif-ically, he dwells on the relation between the opening and the closing of the work as they contribute to its unifying themes: "sex, frustration, time, and a failure to communicate." The essence of Spector's approach (and perhaps of all instruction, despite the new grammatology) is to posit for students certain patterns underlying the seemingly chaotic; these structural patterns Spector explores as various manifestations of narrative rhythm, the principles of parallelism, repetition, comparison, contrast, and so on, that we all use to organize (harmonize) our thinking and our writing.

Ira Konigsberg uses the self-reflexivity of *Tristram Shandy* as his key for teaching the work, moving from Joseph Frank's concept of spatiality in fiction to various theories of reading. His discussion emphasizes the distance Sterne creates between the narrative and the reader—and, more broadly, the ways in which Sterne creates the reader he desired. Leland E. Warren takes a similar approach, stressing the conversation that is necessary between Tristram and the reader, the full participation demanded by Sterne. What is most appealing in the two approaches is the occasion provided by *Tristram Shandy* to teach students to read more self-reflexively, that is, to think about the process of reading and about themselves as readers. Surely the lessons learned here will serve them well throughout the curriculum. And what is equally attractive about the two approaches is that they tend to contradict each other, or, at least, to move in very different directions. Konigsberg focuses on what he sees as Sterne's attempt to estrange us from certain comforts of reading (character identification, plot development), while Warren stresses an opposite tendency to engage us in a comic communion; the result in both cases is a student far more aware than previously about how text and reader interact.

I have concluded this section with Betty Rizzo's fine essay because it encapsulates rather well the issues raised by Konigsberg and Warren, while also speaking to Spector's and Piper's approaches. Rizzo balances the various—and often contradictory—challenges of reading *Tristram Shandy*; we are at once seduced and shepherded by Sterne, blindly led to his goals and, with far more independence than readers usually seem to have, left quite abandoned to draw our own conclusions. Most important, Rizzo uses the work to demonstrate to her students the very complex agreement we enter into with all authors, both willingly and despite ourselves, to follow them wherever they want to go.

Section 2, "Contexts," opens with William R. Siebenschuh's discussion of the "coherent vision of our common human nature," which he finds underlying the many paradoxes of *Tristram Shandy*. Counter to the tendency of many students (and instructors?) who see Sterne's vision as particularly modern, Siebenschuh directs them backward toward Pope's "darkly wise, and rudely great," asking them to see in the Shandy family models of human aspirations adrift among human realities. At the same time, however, he directs his students away from Swift's darker vision of this very dichotomy, finding in Sterne a comic sympathy rather than Swiftian contempt. Within this context, Siebenschuh explores in class such issues as the function of reason in the world, Sterne's interest in the uses and abuses of language, and, finally, his bawdiness. The meaning Siebenschuh derives from *Tristram Shandy* is a useful one for our own age: "let us remember who and what we really are . . . and not run mad because of it." Susan Staves takes a similar approach in her class but concentrates on Uncle Toby to highlight the context of sentimentalism out of which she believes he emerged. Most particularly, Staves traces the conflict between goodness and greatness as it culminates in a figure like Toby, in whose portrait the "comedy does not diminish the sentiment, nor does the sentiment annihilate the comedy." Thus, she uses the context of eighteenth-century ideas about militarism to explain the balance Sterne keeps between Toby's "pacific goodness" and his "military enthusiasm"; and she teaches, as does Siebenschuh, that Sterne avoids pressing such contradictions in the interest of learning to live among them.

Sophia B. Blaydes uses a biographical approach in her class, one particularly centered on the contemporary critical reception of *Tristram Shandy*. By focusing her students' attention on how Sterne's audience responded to the eccentricity of his fiction and to the perceived impropriety of his clerical career, she establishes an awareness that many of our attitudes toward a literary work are derived from our notions of morality, decorum, and received opinion and that literary judgments are never independent of social—and political—pressures. Brian McCrea carries this lesson one step further, showing students that in fact the politics of the classroom itself often determines our critical reading of a text. McCrea examines the most common context established by Sterne scholars—Locke's *Essay concerning Human Understanding*—and suggests that the connection "has been imposed on generations of students precisely because it makes it so easy to teach *Tristram Shandy*." McCrea directs attention, then, not to Locke as a valid context for teaching Sterne but rather to the context (especially after Traugott) that gave impetus to the immense popularity of the Locke-Sterne nexus as a key to *Tristram Shandy*. Students, he argues, should be taught to "distinguish the heuristic from the substantial" in the instruction they receive, "to separate stories that should be true from those that are."

Precisely this injunction makes Michael Raymond's essay of especial interest, since it suggests that the difficulty of the work become the occasion for involving students in the various processes of scholarship—the means, still, by which we learn to distinguish between the ephemeral and the substantial. Raymond thus provides, as well, a splendid entrée to the approach taken by Donald Greene, who brings to his suggestions for teaching *Tristram Shandy* a long and distinguished career studying eighteenth-century contexts. Greene concentrates on three specific moments in the text, and from them he develops an energetic reading of *Tristram Shandy* as a work that everywhere condemns "dogmatic rationalism in favor of empirical pragmatism." Most important, however, Greene demonstrates to us, as he must have demonstrated to his students, the vital manner in which good scholarship supports and enriches our teaching.

The opening essay of the final section, "Text con Texts," discusses some problems confronted most especially by female readers (or, perhaps, sensitized readers of both sexes), demonstrating how the traditional sense of context has been expanded to include the context of gender that every author and every reader necessarily bring to a text. I discussed an aspect of this problem in my introductory comments on Sterne's wit and humor, but much more needs to be said in the classroom. Elizabeth W. Harries defines the difficulty of *Tristram Shandy* for her students as primarily "the pattern of sexism and misogyny that runs through the novel"; for herself, however, the systematic stereotyping and denigrating of women that she and her students find do not seem to block her belief that the work is "one of the most important novels ever written." She explores these conflicting attitudes with her students, to avoid, as she writes, having them "dismiss the novel" on the one hand or blinding them to the sexist attitudes of Sterne (or of Sterne's century or of the 200 years of male-dominated interpretation since) on the other. There is no easy path to follow here, but among the many lessons of *Tristram Shandy* one is that reading books is no easy matter. Leigh Ehlers Telotte provides an interesting counterpart to Harries insofar as she confronts the same sexist issue by mounting a stout defense of the role of women in Sterne's fiction. While the subtlety she finds in his exploration of male-female relations may be unexpected in the eighteenth century, she nonetheless leads her students through a cogent reading that locates the misogyny in the Shandy males, but not in Sterne, and that posits a narrator who comes to realizations about the role of women in society that bespeak considerable innovation on Sterne's part. (As a supplement to Ehler's approach, my comments on *A Sentimental Journey* in my *Dictionary of Literary Biography* entry on Sterne provide, in outline, what I hope is plausible as a feminist reading of that work, a reading perhaps applicable to aspects of *Tristram Shandy* as well.)

Elizabeth Kraft and Deborah D. Rogers confront a different complexity of context, namely, that context is often simply the arrangement of a curriculum. Again, I addressed this issue in my introductory section "The Course" and welcome two fine essays that also consider the question. Kraft is one of the few respondents who teaches the work in a Restoration and eighteenth-century survey rather than an eighteenth-century novel course; of particular interest is the manner in which she uses such prior class reading as Pepys and Restoration comedy for comparison with *Tristram Shandy*—a refreshing change from the usual Defoe-Fielding-Richardson preparation. Rogers too teaches the work in the survey course, which she organizes around the useful idea that "the subjective mode" (which in days of yore might have been called pre-Romantic) is a century-long phenomenon, that everywhere "neo-classical" and "subjective" instincts existed side by side. For her, *Tristram Shandy* is the "pinnacle" of the century's play between these tendencies, and she develops her approach by having students ask themselves whether the work is satiric or sentimental.

Maximillian E. Novak confronts the same issue in a somewhat different way, since he avails himself of two classroom opportunities to teach *Tristram Shandy* and takes a different approach in each, depending on whether it is a survey or novel course. In the survey course, he focuses on the satiric models that preceded Sterne, or, more specifically, the satiric target that unifies these models—the pragmatic attack on system makers (whom Greene identifies as dogmatic rationalists). Novak calls his students' attention to the tradition of parodying learned and innovative disquisitions on the nature of the universe and larger questions as a key to understanding the satire in such works as *A Tale of a Tub* and *Tristram Shandy*. In the novel course, however, Novak directs attention to Sterne's realistic re-creation of provincial life and his investigation of the fictional possibilities of that re-creation; the lesson of this approach is found in Sterne's discovery that "incomplete narrative [is] the most realistic form of narrative," insofar as it best captures the fragmentation of experience itself.

In recognition of his dual approach, Novak alludes to *Tristram Shandy* as a *Vexierbild*; Stephen C. Behrendt's classroom approach centers precisely on that visual concept, the capacity of certain visual structures "to suggest almost simultaneously to the perceiver two entirely different 'meanings' " neither of which can be established as correct. In applying this concept to *Tristram*, Behrendt suggests the slipperiness of context, the fact that context is often simply a question of what we place in the light, what in the shade. The approaches gathered in this collection take on a splendid coherence when we realize that Behrendt's essay covers much the same ground as Piper's (and uses many of the same illustrations) and, despite very different avenues of approach, tends toward the same conclusion: "Sterne's multistable texts generate numerous meanings not because the author has carelessly used vague and imprecise language but, rather, because he has carefully and deliberately manipulated exact language to create two or more distinct impressions." In a group of essays in which I have found countless useful hints for presenting *Tristram Shandy* to my students, Behrendt's stands out as one of the most useful.

The final essay in the collection, by Joel Weinsheimer, also discusses the teaching of *Tristram Shandy* in two different contexts, in this instance the traditional course in the eighteenth-century novel and a course in narrative theory. For Weinsheimer, the two should never be at loggerheads as he suspects they have been, and in a series of convincing examples he shows that certain modernist theoretical concepts are repeated in numerous eighteenth-century texts and, from another aspect, that there is no real distinction to be made between "Sterne and Sterne criticism, no antithesis between *Tristram Shandy* and literary theory." It is especially useful, I think, to end this collection with an essay that points to a harmonizing rather than a dichotomizing of approaches and that, interestingly, may cause more consternation by its equation of literature and criticism, history and theory than any other essay in the volume. Behind Weinsheimer's claim, however, we should recognize the indubitable fact behind all the essays and indeed behind this MLA series: great works of literature today (if not always) are *taught* rather than *read*, are institutional rather than personal experiences. We may deplore that fact, but it does help explain why theory and literature are or seem to be one and the same.

And yet. And yet. Surely the diversity of approaches represented by these essays suggests a contrary fact: great works of literature today (if not always) are *read* rather than *taught*, are personal rather than institutional experiences. The essence of teaching any great literary work is ultimately the individual (idiosyncratic) instructor behind the closed door of a classroom filled with individual (and, with luck, idiosyncratic) students. Both instructors and students will agree with some commentators, disagree with others, cover old ground, and perhaps even discover some new. It would be untrue to the life of *Tristram Shandy* in the hands of its "professors" and its "students" to suggest in any way that our approaches can be codified, organized, or contained under a single umbrella, or within a single vision, no matter how extended its reach. "*De gustibus non est disputandum*;—that is, there is no disputing against Hobby-Horses," as Tristram says. Let us hope that in teaching great works of world literature there never will be.

TRISTRAM SHANDY: TEXT

A South West Passage to
the Intellectual World

Arthur H. Cash

A few years ago someone took a poll of graduating college seniors asking them which of the texts assigned during their college careers they most hated. *Tristram Shandy* won. In Sterne's day, such a judgment would have been put down to the shocking double entendres or the even more shocking fact that they were written by a parson and prebendary; but few college students today are that easily disturbed by innuendo or by anything a parson might or might not do. Recently the American Society for Eighteenth-Century Studies held a conference in a hotel where the waiters were moonlighting students. One young woman working in the bar made herself popular with the scholarly nighthawks because she was so delighted to be among her own kind: she was herself an English major. Then she found out that one of us had devoted years to the study of Laurence Sterne. Laurence Sterne! Why? *Tristram Shandy*! Never had she so hated a book. How can that be? we asked. Did she not find Uncle Toby's hobbyhorse amusing? She did not understand what we meant by a hobbyhorse. Did she laugh at the story of the hot chestnut that dropped off the table at the visitation dinner? What, she asked, is a visitation dinner? Were other students laughing? A few—God, yes! And the professor? He loved it! Little wonder she had detested the book, having plowed through nine volumes without ever catching on, reading page after page of jokes that she did not get. This young

33

woman, I fear, typifies modern readers of *Tristram Shandy*. Nor do I speak of this generation only. It should give us pause to think of the fortunes spent in recent years on the study and preservation of Johnson, Boswell, and Walpole, while poor Shandy Hall limps along befriended by not a single millionaire.

Our first obligation in teaching *Tristram Shandy* is to forestall confusion. Because students are ill prepared to deal with Sterne's unorthodox punctuation, comic subdivisions, and digressive method, we must allow more time for reading *Tristram* than we do for other novels. I give them four weeks. I enjoin them never to barge ahead when they are confused but to go back over difficult passages until they get them, or, that failing, to ask me about them at the next meeting. They must mark their books. It is surprising how many students need to be taught how. On the front and back flyleaves, they are to build up an index to things they might want to relocate for purposes of class discussion, an outside paper, or their next examination. I then launch the index by requiring the entire class to keep track of passages that throw light on the question of Uncle Toby's sexual potency. This particular assignment will pay off in time with lively discussions of Toby's and Mrs. Wadman's characters, of plot and narrative strategies, of textual problems and scholarly editing (compare the penultimate paragraph of 9: 21 in the Work edition and the Florida edition), and even of the question whether Sterne completed the novel.

But my most important device for forestalling confusion is my outline of *Tristram Shandy*. I give students a mimeographed copy before they have opened the book, instructing them to lay it on the desk beside the book as they read, consulting it whenever they are in doubt about what is happening. My outline saves a world of pain. I have appended it entire to this article in the hopes that Sir and Madam will find it useful. This particular version is keyed to the Florida edition, but it is no trick to convert it to whatever edition is being used.

There is inevitably an awkward period when students are newly launched upon a novel: they do not yet know enough about the work to carry on much of a discussion. During this period I talk *at* them. I do not think of myself as lecturing; I bring no notes to class except a list of matters I hope to cover. But I bring a lot of visual aids. To give students a sense of Sterne's world, I show them pictures of Shandy Hall, Byland Abbey, St. George's Hanover Square, and the like. I tell them a lot of stories about Sterne's life, his early political career, his activities in York Minster and in the country, his sermons, *A Political Romance*. I describe Sterne's illness and the threat of tragedy that hung over his life, and I show them the newly found letter addressed to Lord Rockingham (included in an appendix of unknown letters in my *Laurence Sterne: The Later Years*) in which Sterne compares himself to

Cervantes and Scarron, writing comedy through pain and anguish. Such devices are especially useful in teaching students the distinction between primary and secondary historical evidence. I hope I can generate in them a critical awareness of the sort of history or biography they are consulting.

I hope, too, to give them an awareness of how a writer of genius transforms his actual experiences into something larger or funnier than life. I describe how the political infighting of the Church of York led to, first, *A Political Romance* and then the story of Parson Yorick in *Tristram Shandy*. I talk about the brutalities of the military life Sterne was exposed to as a child and about his father, Ensign Roger Sterne, and how Sterne transformed these memories into Toby and Trim and their history. But my most striking example is Sterne's transformation of Dr. John Burton of York into Dr. Slop. I show them how Sterne made the identification inevitable when he had Slop deliver Tristram with the wacky forceps invented by Dr. Burton, and I show them slides of the forceps and other instruments in Slop's green-bays bag, convincing them that Sterne's satire of Burton as a physician was justified. But I then point out how Sterne, a Whig and an old political enemy of Burton, a Tory, turned the doctor into a Roman Catholic when in fact Burton was a faithful member of the Church of England. I next read Sterne's description of the man, "a little, squat, uncourtly figure of a Doctor *Slop*, of about four feet and a half perpendicular height, with a breadth of back, and a sesquipedality of belly, which might have done honour to a Serjeant in the Horse-Guards" (2: 9), and then the sworn statement of Cuthbert Davis, collector of the excise for Lancaster, made when Burton's enemies were trying to prove that he had supported the rebellion: the testimony describes him as "a tall well-set gentleman in a light colored coat in boots with a whip under his arm."

When the class is well into the novel, I turn the discussion toward narrative structures and techniques. The outline proves helpful here. How many plots do we find? Usually the class agrees on a "Walter plot" (influenced by *Martinus Scriblerus* and other Augustan satire) and a "Toby plot"—the story of Toby's recovery from his wound, his therapeutic hobby, his failure to regain normalcy when he rejects Mrs. Wadman. But there is no agreement about whether we find a "Yorick plot" or how we are to fit volume 7 into our schemes. Talk about the time frame of these plots leads to a discussion of the historical accuracy of the political and military backdrop and the anachronism of the forceps and medical technology.

Then there is the matter of technique. What, if anything, is the method of Sterne's "digressive method"? Where does Sterne locate his major statements of his methods and purposes? What psychological theories can be evoked to describe this narrator's choices? Does Locke help? Hartley? Freud? In what sense is this a psychological novel? A stream-of-consciousness novel?

Eventually I will assist the class in working out a schematic representation, on the blackboard, of Sterne's narrative point of view.

The third and final part of my teaching of *Tristram Shandy* consists of a discussion of Sterne's themes—any theme at all that students may find, but most especially the themes of time, communication, obsession, and love. Consideration of these will lead, I hope, to a final question for the work, one that has the possibility of pulling together the discussions of several weeks. What is Sterne's attitude toward the distressing problems of communication and love he has revealed, the puzzling psychological phenomena he has brought to our attention? Is he a tragedian, a satirist, a humorist, all of the above, none of the above? I do not care what they answer; I care only that they answer well.

An Outline of *Tristram Shandy*
Volume 1

   I. Conception and factual announcement of birth, 1–9

  II. Backgrounds of the birth—to prepare for the story of "how" Tristram was born, 9–70

     1. Prologue: Tristram states his purposes: life and opinions, self-revelation, friendship, etc., 9–10

     2. The midwife's story—ostensibly—but mostly digressions, 10–40

       a. Digression on hobbyhorses, 12–14

       b. Mock dedication, 14–17

       c. Long digression on the history of Parson Yorick (some missing pieces will be supplied later at the visitation-dinner scene), 17–38

     3. Parents' marriage and marriage contract, 40–46

     4. Mrs. Shandy's false pregnancy of the previous year, which destines Tristram to be born in the country, 46–50

     5. Parents debate whether to have a midwife or man-midwife, finally agreeing to have Dr. Slop in the house in case of emergency; otherwise, the midwife to be in charge, 50–56

       a. The first digression on Tristram's dear Jenny, 56–57

     6. Walter's character as a man of hypotheses, which explains his interest in having a man-midwife present, 57–64

       a. Digression on Madam, the inattentive reader, 64–70

         (1) Includes the memorandum by the doctors of the Sorbonne on the legitimacy of performing baptisms before birth, 67–70

 III. Birth scenes, 70–343

     1. Walter and Toby in the parlor hear the commotion upstairs as Mrs. Shandy's labor begins (the brothers remain together throughout the birth scenes), 70

     2. Uncle Toby's character, part 1: his modesty (the first of three long descriptions of him), 70–82

a. Includes the story of Aunt Dinah, 76–78

b. A digression on digressions, 79–82

3. Uncle Toby's character, part 2: his hobby, the explanation of which involves the history of his wound, his convalescence in Walter's London house, where he begins his military studies in order to explain where and how he was wounded, 82–89

Volume 2

4. Uncle Toby's character, continuation of part 2, his hobby: the story of how Trim suggests a move to Toby's cottage in Yorkshire next to his brother's estate, Shandy Hall, so that they can build model fortifications on the bowling green (this earliest of the campaigns on the bowling green, terminating with the Treaty of Utrecht in 1713, will be taken up in more detail in volumes 6 and 8 [534–72, 664–704]; it is not to be confused with the later campaigns being waged in 1718 when Tristram was born), 93–114

5. Mrs. Shandy's waters break, the midwife is fetched, and Dr. Slop arrives, 114–27

6. Symposium 1 (Walter, Toby, Slop, Trim), 127–216

a. Includes Trim's reading of Sterne's sermon *The Abuses of Conscience, Considered*, terminating in an "advertisement" for a collection of Sterne's sermons, 138–67

b. Includes Walter's theories on the brain and birth, taken largely from the medical works of Dr. John Burton, the model for Dr. Slop, all of which explains why Walter has insisted on Slop's presence during the birth, 169–80

Volume 3

c. Includes Dr. Slop's reading of the anathema of Bishop Ernulph in order to curse Obadiah for so tightly tying up Slop's bag that the doctor has cut his thumb when cutting the knot, 200–16

7. Dr. Slop is called upstairs to deliver the child, 216–21

8. The Shandy brothers fall asleep; Tristram is born while they doze. Tristram the narrator makes use of the situation to present his "Author's Preface," 222–38

9. A squeaking hinge awakens the brothers; they learn of the birth and then of the baby's crushed nose, 239–53

10. Walter Shandy falls on his bed in pain; his brother comforts him; they talk, 254–335

a. Includes a digression on noses in the Shandy family and on misleading words, 256–62

b. Includes a description of Walter Shandy's studies of noses, 262–327

c. Includes an apostrophe to Uncle Toby, 265

d. Includes a digression on learning and reading that concludes with the marbled page, 267–70

Volume 4

    e. Includes the prize item in Walter's collection of nose lore—"Slawken-bergius's Tale," 288–327

11. The brothers rise, come downstairs, talking the while, 335–40
    a. Includes a digression on the making of chapters, 336–38

12. Tristram's dissertation on time in writing and living: he cannot catch himself, 340–43

IV. Baptism scenes, 343–94

  1. Susannah wakes Walter: the child in a fit (convulsions caused by pressure on the cerebellum during delivery) is rushed to the curate and by error baptized with what his father thinks is the worst of all Christian names—Tristram, 343–45
    a. A digression on sleep, 345–47

  2. Walter learns of the error: his "Lamentation," 348–56
    a. A digression on naming: the story of Francis I, 356–59

  3. Tristram's comment on the purpose of his book: wrote against spleen, 359–60

  4. The vain attempt to change the child's name: gathering legal opinion at the visitation dinner (the scene provides missing details in the history of Parson Yorick), 360–94

V. The death of Brother Bobby, 394–444

  1. Walter ponders Bobby's education and its cost, 394–99

  2. The death announced: Tristram becomes heir apparent, 399–400

  3. Tristram explains true Shandeism, 401–02

Volume 5

  4. Tristram on writing and borrowing, 407–09

  5. The "Fragment upon Whiskers," offered as a comment on the instability of words, 409–15

  6. Walter's oration—his response to the news of Bobby's death, 415–26

  7. Mrs. Shandy begins to listen to him from outside the door, 426–27

  8. Trim's oration—the response of the servants in the kitchen, 427–38

  9. Walter concludes his oration, Mrs. Shandy accuses him and learns of her son's death, 438–43

10. Tristram on writing, which is like fiddling, 443–44

VI. Rituals of initiation, puberty, education, 445–533

  1. Walter writes a book on how to educate his son, the *Tristrapœdia*, 445–49

  2. The accidental circumcision of the boy and Walter's reaction, 449–59

  3. Symposium 2 (Walter, Toby, Yorick, Trim, Slop) on education, 459–520
    a. Includes Walter's strictures on rote learning occasioned by Trim's recitation of the catechism, 468–71
    b. Includes Walter's theory that the auxiliary verbs are the Northwest Passage to the intellectual world, 482–87

Volume 6

  c. Susannah and Dr. Slop, having been fighting instead of bandaging Tristram's wound, accuse each other before Walter, 494–96
  d. Includes the "Story of Le Fever," introduced because Le Fever's son has been mentioned as a possible tutor for Tristram, 499–513
  e. Yorick's funeral sermon for Le Fever and the history of Le Fever's son as Uncle Toby's protegé, 513–20
 4. Gossip about the circumcision leads the parents to debate (in the "beds of justice") and then decide on putting Tristram into breeches—a sort of puberty rite, 520–33

VII. Uncle Toby's campaigns on the bowling green—a preparation for the story of his amours with the Widow Wadman (these are the original bowling-green campaigns, chronologically earlier than those that were going on when Tristram was born), 533–72
 1. The progress of the hobby, 533–44
 2. Trim invents a canon that puffs, 544–49
  a. A flash-ahead to the deaths of Trim and Toby, 544–45
 3. Uncle Toby's modesty, 549–50
 4. The Treaty of Utrecht puts an end to the campaigns, 551–52
 5. Uncle Toby's "Apologetical Oration" on military service, 552–57
 6. Tristram tells us how to tell a story, 557–58
 7. A prologue to the commencement of Mrs. Wadman's campaign against Toby, which will be told in volume 8, 558–70
 8. Tristram draws diagrams of his narrative and its digressions, 570–72

Volume 7

VIII. Tristram's flight from death, channel crossing, trip through France, a narrative told chronologically but interspersed with satires on travelers and travel literature and Tristram's musings on life, 575–651
 1. Includes the story of the abbess of Andoüillets and her novice, Margarita, 606–14
 2. Includes the Auxerre scene in which four Tristrams are discoverable, 617–22
 3. Includes the reverie in which Tristram implies that he is sexually impotent, 624–25
 4. Includes the story of the ass and the commissary, 629–38
 5. Includes the story of the lost remarks (i.e., notes), 638–41
 6. Includes the account of dancing with Nannette and the peasants, 649–51

Volume 8

IX. Uncle Toby's amours, part 1: Mrs. Wadman wins Uncle Toby, 655–729
 1. Tristram on love, and on writing and reading about it, 655–63
 2. Mrs. Wadman falls in love, 664–68
 3. Tristram continues to talk about love, 669–72
 4. Mrs. Wadman plans an attack, 673–79

a. Contains a flashback (flash-ahead?) to Symposium 1—Walter and Dr. Slop talk about the blind gut, 674–75

5. Uncle Toby and Trim complete the destruction of Dunkirk in accordance with the Treaty of Utrecht and fall into a conversation, 679–704

    a. Contains the unfinished story "The King of Bohemia and His Seven Castles," 683–93.

    b. Contains Trim's story of the fair Beguine who nursed him, 696–704

6. Mrs. Wadman makes her attack, 704–08

7. Uncle Toby in love; he and Trim prepare a counterattack, 708–16

8. Symposium 3 (Walter, Toby, Yorick, Slop, Mrs. Shandy, Trim), on love, 717–25

9. Walter Shandy writes his brother advising him about love, 725–28

10. Toby and Trim continue preparations for the counterattack, 728–29

Volume 9

X. Uncle Toby's amours, part 2: Mrs. Wadman loses Uncle Toby, 735–809

1. The counterattack—on Mrs. Wadman's house, 735–60

    a. Includes the story of Trim's brother Tom and the Jew's widow and that of the black girl, 742–52

    b. Includes the digression on time, dear Jenny, and the swiftness with which life passes, 754–55

2. Tristram discourses on the need for a balance in fiction of wisdom and folly, 761–67

3. The courtship commences in Mrs. Wadman's parlor, 768–94

    a. Includes two blank chapers, 770–71

    b. Includes a digression on Uncle Toby's potency, 776–78

    c. Includes an "Invocation" to the spirit of Cervantes, which becomes the story of Tristram's meeting mad Maria in France—an "advertisement" for A Sentimental Journey, 780–84

    d. The two blank chapters now supplied, 785–90

4. Mrs. Wadman makes inquiries about Toby's health, 791–94

5. Trim begins his own courtship of Bridget, Mrs. Wadman's maid, and discovers how anxious Mrs. Wadman is about Toby's potency, 795–99

6. Uncle Toby's eyes are opened: he goes to his brother for advice, 800–03

7. Symposium 4 (Walter, Toby, Yorick, Slop, Mrs. Shandy, Trim), also on love, 804–09

Understanding *Tristram Shandy*

William Bowman Piper

In introducing students to *Tristram Shandy* I have found it best to acknowledge emphatically the many and various kinds of interruptions, suspensions, gaps, and, as Tristram calls them, "openings to equivocal strictures" that pervade the development of the narrator's exposition. It has proved to be necessary at the same time, however, emphatically to deny that these openings make the novel impossible to understand or, to give this complaint in its critically respectable form, that they constitute an open invitation to the reader's imagination.

I cope with the ensuing paradox—that, whereas Tristram's discourse is porous, Sterne's novel is invulnerable—first of all by requiring students to read aloud from the novel in class and by urging them to do so even when they study it alone. Reading aloud corrects the modern rate of absorption (which may be appropriate to the *Reader's Digest*) and activates the conversational rhythm and flow that fit Tristram's explicit stylistic intentions. It makes the long sentences, like the very first one, for instance, which might seem intellectually undigestible to an unaided eye, immediately available —available, not as structures, but as developments—and reveals, where they actually occur, the openings to interpretation that the mere sweep of an eye might either neglect or refuse. Reading aloud also forces students at least experimentally to take Tristram's position, assuming some responsibility for what, after all, they themselves are now saying. It thus establishes a climate of committed awareness in which a teacher can effectively oppose both a student's ignorance and the accompanying feeling that this ignorance gives license to set fancy on the wing.

The notion that *Tristram Shandy* has been designed to free its reader's fancy must be especially opposed because it has received impressive sanction from several generations of critics. It has recently been advocated, for instance, by Wolfgang Iser, who pointedly designated *Tristram Shandy* to illustrate his general assertion that "a literary text must . . . be conceived in such a way that it will engage the reader's imagination in the task of working things out for himself." According to Iser, "Sterne's conception of a literary text is that it is something like an arena in which reader and author participate in a game of imagination" ("Reading Process" 280). To support this doctrinal advocacy, not of understanding, but of "imagination," Iser confounds Tristram with Laurence, attributing this statement, not to the Shandy historian, who actually made it, of course, but to his novelistic creator:

> [N]o author, who understands the just boundaries of decorum and good breeding, would presume to think all: The truest respect which

41

you can pay to the reader's understanding, is to halve this matter
amicably, and leave him something to imagine, in his turn, as well as
yourself.

For my own part, I am eternally paying him compliments of this
kind, and do all that lies in my power to keep his imagination as busy
as my own.   (2: 11)

Even if a reader decides that Tristram is as good as his word and has, indeed,
amicably halved his history with his society, allowing "Sir," "Madam," and
the rest fifty percent of the creative responsibility for the story of his life
and the formulation of his opinions, this situation and all its cooperating
participants we must recognize to be the whole conception of Laurence
Sterne. Sterne has created the conversational arena—an arena quite unlike
anything found in any modern English novel—in which Tristram engages
an assembled mixed company of attendants in the deliberate exposition of
his own family history and his own opinions. To help students recognize this
primary aspect of Sterne's creation and see that the novelist has organized,
not a private occasion for the free indulgence of fancy, but a dynamic, public
condition, in which one person confronts a suspicious and censorious society,
is the primary task, or so I believe, for the teacher of *Tristram Shandy*.
Requiring the students to read aloud, once again, which dramatizes the
conversational quality of Tristram's discourse and his continuous social so-
licitation, will greatly help the teacher to accomplish it.

The next task, which the accomplishment of the first makes more manageable, is to show that, despite a few disclaimers, disclaimers he himself
often contradicts, Tristram hardly allows his company half or even a grain
in the composition of his life and opinions. The notorious equivocal openings
provided by Tristram's usage of "nose," "whiskers," and "crevice," for example, are only substantially—not socially—halved. Tristram's discourse
opens before "Sir" and "Madam" and any who identify with them a narrowly
defined choice between each term's conventional meaning and one suggested
by Tristram's conversational context. Even such apparently wide abstractions
as "it" and "thing" Tristram's conversational treatment narrows in the most
pointed and powerful ways. Consider, for instance, the meaning of the term
"thing" in this paragraph, in which Tristram is professedly describing Uncle
Toby's plan for the enjoyment of his military hobbyhorse in the privacy of
his bowling green:

> Never did lover post down to a belov'd mistress with more heat and
> expectation, than my uncle *Toby* did, to enjoy this self-same thing in
> private;—I say in private;—for it was sheltered from the house, as I
> told you, by a tall yew hedge, and was covered on the other three

sides, from mortal sight, by rough holly and thickset flowering shrubs;
—so that the idea of not being seen, did not a little contribute to the
idea of pleasure preconceived in my uncle *Toby*'s mind.—Vain thought!
however thick it was planted about,——or private soever it might
seem,—to think, dear uncle *Toby*, of enjoying a thing which took up
a whole rood and a half of ground,—and not have it known!   (2: 5)

Readers are surely confined to at most two meanings for "thing" here, as in
general with Tristram's equivocal suggestions. If they fail to notice any
"opening" (as they may do, if reading silently) or if they cannot choose
between the two possible meanings, then they are stuck with a single
understanding—in the latter case, that the term is equivocal. It is the readers' responsive understanding, at all events, and not their free imagination
that is at stake—as Tristram often insists.

By considering the explicit call on his reader's understanding that Tristram
makes following the very passage that Iser quotes, one can enforce this point:

'Tis his turn now;—I have given an ample description of Dr. *Slop*'s
sad overthrow, and of his sad appearance in the back parlour;—his
imagination must now go on with it for a while.

Let the reader imagine then, that Dr. *Slop* has told his tale;——
and in what words, and with what aggravations his fancy chooses:——
Let him suppose that *Obadiah* has told his tale also, and with such
rueful looks of affected concern, as he thinks will best contrast the two
figures as they stand by each other: Let him imagine that my father
has stepp'd up stairs to see my mother:—And, to conclude this work
of imagination,—let him imagine the Doctor wash'd,——rubb'd
down,—condoled with,—felicitated,—got into a pair of *Obadiah*'s
pumps, stepping forwards towards the door, upon the very point of
entering upon action.   (2: 11)

The imagination Tristram refers to here is both responsive and intellectual,
not a private flight of fancy: the reader should attempt to conceive, at whatever degree of precision the narrative suggests, the course of the events that
Tristram, the only person who knows them, wishes to share with society. I
sometimes ask my students candidly as we contemplate Tristram's instructions: "Do you in fact think up words or images that suit your own ideas of
this introduction of Dr. Slop—as Tristram seems to allow? Or do you not
take the tale as having been carried this far by Tristram, conceiving both
Slop and Obadiah precisely in the way and precisely to the degree of particularity with which Tristram has presented them—and go on with Tristram's discourse?" Earlier Sterne's narrator directed the members of his

audience, "Imagine to yourself a little, squat, uncourtly figure of a Doctor *Slop*," and went on himself to give a detailed guide of the exact figure in the exact attitude he wished his audience to visualize. This "ample description," which should guide them in responding to the present passage, simply allows them to recall Slop's overthrow, which Tristram extensively described a few pages ago, and to recollect a more general course of events, the details of which are irrelevant to Tristram's purposes, that is, of course, Slop's ablution and introduction to the Shandy quarters, about which Tristram likewise informed them.

In another passage, Tristram has more pointedly indicated the imaginative participation he requires of his readers in the presentation of Dr. Slop and, indeed, throughout the course of his narrative:

> I would go fifty miles on foot, for I have not a horse worth riding on, to kiss the hand of that man whose generous heart will give up the reins of his imagination into his author's hands,——be pleased he knows not why, and cares not wherefore.   (3: 12)

Throughout his discourse with "Sir," "Madam," and the rest, Tristram, as one may amply demonstrate, appeals to and satisfies such a sensitively responsive conduct in his company—whether they are inclined so to render the reins of their imagination into his hands or not. He once insists that a gentleman in the group must have Uncle Toby's bowling green "in his imagination" because, Tristram insists, he has given this gentleman "so minute a description" of it (6: 21). Tristram often denies that a reader could possibly imagine what happened next in the Shandy history—with perfect justification, need I say? He often digresses to explain events no one in his company could have foreseen or understood, always explicitly announcing that he is doing so. He pauses, for example, to explain the confusion Toby and Walter faced when Trim mentioned a "bridge" that needed fixing; to explain why Walter was so determined to employ Dr. Slop in his child's delivery—and even proposed a cesarean section to his wife; to present the peculiar trait that allowed his father to cope with his grief over Bobby Shandy's death; to account for Trim's feelings of guilt over the sash-window accident; and, of course, to illuminate the Widow Wadman's uncertainty about Uncle Toby as a husband, her painful circumstances, and her tragic course of action. Tristram asserts, "It is in vain to leave [any of the peculiar developments in his private history] to the Reader's imagination" (5: 18); however, he expresses the hope that after he has explained them, giving all the Shandy circumstances that curiosity requires and decency will allow, the reader will understand these developments.

"But surely," students may protest, "Tristram leaves a blank for his readers, individually, to fill with any description they choose of the Widow Wadman!" In the first place, as the deliberate reading I advocate makes clear, he leaves this blank only for his masculine readers: "Sit down, Sir, paint her to your own mind." Tristram thus renders the Widow Wadman, by mere virtue of this pointed courtesy, as a figure chiefly interesting as a woman is, not to another woman, but to a man—and hence as a figure of attraction and mystery. Nor is this all: "Paint her," Tristram directs each gentleman in his company, "as like your mistress as you can——as unlike your wife as your conscience will let you" (6: 38). Thus the quality of the portrait, no matter what color of hair or eye, no matter what dimensions of waist or thigh, is firmly fixed. The Widow Wadman must be, as Tristram exclaims on the far side of the apparent gap in his book, "so sweet!—so exquisite!"—the embodiment of romantic feminine attraction as any man understands this. Tristram has simply sacrificed the details to avoid the danger of an argument that might come from his insisting on blue eyes, say, or auburn hair and thus to establish incontrovertibly the figure he will later denominate "a daughter of Eve." Since each man has conjured his own details—(or none?)—some choosing brown eyes and black hair, perhaps— no man can quarrel with this general description. Tristram's courteous with- drawal from details when he first offers the gentlemen this field for their individual fancies—"'tis all one to me"—is thus a device, an equivocation, no truer than his gracious willingness "to halve" the story of Dr. Slop's introduction into Shandy Hall. The precise colors and shapes of the portrait *are* all one to him: they are so, however, because he is determined that every member of his company shall recognize in the widow every man's dream of seduction and romance. Once again, I sometimes ask my students: "Did you in fact fill in the blank that Tristram left *his readers*; or have you not, like me, retained that blank as an actually created part of Sterne's novel?"

"But surely," one may insist, "even if I did honor this gap in Tristram's discourse as a real, actually created element in the total work, I am justified in finding the novel, as many critics assert, generally difficult to follow." This I deny, sometimes challenging my students to show me one hopelessly difficult statement or development. In fact, Tristram's discursive procedures can always be rationally accounted for. He often implores his company to attend closely and seriously to his story. If they do so, they will find that he has accounted economically and yet fully—and as precisely as his social circumstances will allow—for the constricted, tragicomical life he has en- dured. By describing, with all their determining conditions, his conception, his birth, his christening, and a certain early accident, as a brief overview will show, Tristram has explained the total failure, the total lack of normal human chances, that his life, the encroaching end of which he pointedly indicates, has allowed him. One point, the strict biological truth of his potency, I explicitly acknowledge, he has never been able to publish: the social realm, which has come to bound his being and his ambitions, disallows such a precise point of information, not merely on the ground of decency, but also on that of scandal. The principle that inhibits Tristram, a principle the unhappy Widow Wadman would have understood only too well, is that a man cannot effectively declare his sexual potency in public, not, at any rate, once it has become necessary for him to do so. Tristram, nevertheless, as I argue, is able to complete his social communication. Because of his unlucky origins and his sash-window accident—or because of the scandal that came to surround these events—he has been unable to endow society with another generation of Shandys. And since, as he has pointedly explained, his brother died young—before he could enjoy the "free ingress, egress, and regress into foreign parts before marriage" (4: 31) that his father was planning for him—leaving Tristram the Shandy heir, and since Uncle Toby, although personally the best-equipped man ever produced in the course of nature to be a husband and a father, died without issue, Tristram faces in his own imminent death the extinction of his strange and wonderful line. A series of ridiculous but characteristic defeats to his father and his uncle, each of which has been presented much more vividly and much more particularly than any lady or gentleman could have imagined, have terminated in the destruction of the Shandy family. This tragedy Tristram has published, despite the social problems presented by virtually every one of its events, with tremendous clarity and force, thus composing what he himself calls a "tragicomical . . . contexture" (7: 27). There is, then, notwithstanding the incidental demurs by the socially flexible narrator, a complete and, indeed, seamless history made publicly accessible in this novel, a history that, as Tristram boasts, no one could have begun to imagine until he himself brought it forth.

There are, of course, as students quite properly proclaim, gaps of many kinds in the shorter spans of Tristram's discourse, gaps to which a teacher must attend. These "openings to equivocal strictures," which bristle in Tristram's talk, no doubt tease Sir's and Madam's imaginations, as Tristram himself recognizes, and imperil their apprehension of his life and opinions. These openings, however, which constitute a major aspect of Sterne's whole creation, are less open, as I have suggested, less subject to a reader's imaginative intrusion, as a teacher should demonstrate, than they may seem. The teacher, to be effective, must define the quality and extent of these openings in detail.

There are, for one thing, the many gaps asserted by asterisks. Taking from Tristram's book a leaf I have taken before, I ask: "In the passage describing his childhood accident, when Tristram tells his company that 'the chambermaid had left no ******* *** under the bed' and reports to his company that Susannah, who was tending him, had suggested, 'cannot you manage, my dear [while helping him into the window seat], for a single time to **** *** ** *** ******?' (5: 17), do you not know pretty well what words should fill the spaces?" If my students do know, they know; if not, they are left with Tristram's asterisks; and in either case they have a vivid fictional experience, either of Tristram's slyly completed or of his slyly withheld communication. The precise words whispered to the edges of the Shandy world about the extent of Tristram's infant suffering, which the narrator represents with several lines of evenly spaced asterisks, are no doubt, as the disposition of the asterisks suggests, indeterminable; but the general substance of that gossip, as I suggest to my classes, is also available to inference. Beasterisked passages occur throughout Tristram's discourse, and although the degree of the precision with which a reader's responsive awareness fills them varies from passage to passage, one can always, as in the case of Dr. Slop's entrance to Shandy Hall and of Mrs. Wadman's attractions, achieve the particularity of understanding that will allow one to follow Tristram's discourse and his history. Often the degree of precision, although Tristram may tease and delay, is finally absolute. Consider the "****** [six asterisks]" that Dr. Slop produces with a rhetorical flourish from his green baize bag. Tristram admittedly suspends the translation of this figure while he first derives an opinion from Slop's gesture and then fills in some necessary narrative background. During this suspension he experimentally forces a number of terms into the indicated six alphabetical spaces, "a scar, an axe . . . [a] BAMBINO," and, of course, the "*forceps*" Slop had intended to produce. None of these will fit. Finally he presents the six-letter word, "*squirt*," that fits the gap and, of course, his intentions as a portrayer of life and opinions (3: 13–15).

The interpretive suggestions that open in the pauses and suspensions of Tristram's conversation—effects, once again, that reading aloud exposes—require the same detailed pedagogical attention as the asterisks. In this sentence, for instance, "——But for my father's ass [that is to say, Walter's symbolic representation of sexual lust]———oh! mount him—mount him —mount him—(that's three times, is it not?)—mount him not" (8: 31), the reader seems for quite a span to be advised to indulge sexual urges with the utmost energy only to be given at last the exactly contrary advice, that is, to suppress them altogether. In the course of this statement the tripartite repetition of "mount him" is first apparently given to enumerate the stages of the advised activity and then reduced to a device of rhetorical emphasis. At another point Tristram wonders why, considering the qualities of his parents, "I happen to be so lewd myself . . . My mother——madam—— was so at no time, either by nature, by institution, or example" (9: 1). A reader, especially a feminine one (as students of both sexes should be warned), may briefly entertain the deliciously scandalous notion that Tristram's mother was "so," that is, that she was the very opposite of what Tristram finally claims. Nor is this all: the extremely particular modification with which the statement ends allows Madam to continue believing that Mrs. Shandy was "so," if not by nature, institution, or example, yet by some other agency, by association, say, or choice or sheer indifference. Take one last example, this sentence in which Tristram's father is discussing his treatise on infant education, the *Tristrapædia*: "———No,—I think I have advanced nothing, replied my father, making answer to a question which *Yorick* had taken the liberty to put to him,—I have advanced nothing in the *Tristrapædia*, but what is as clear as any one proposition in *Euclid*" (5: 30). It becomes evident eventually that the elder Shandy intended, not to acknowledge modestly (but truly) that he had accomplished nothing with his treatise, but, rather, to defend the clarity of his scholarly exposition. It remains possible, however, for a reader to suspect—and it is with such tentativeness as this that these effects must be recognized—that the son, who interrupted Walter's defense at "nothing" with a considerable amount of narrative explanation and then repeated "nothing," is attacking the actual worth of the *Tristrapædia*. *Tristram Shandy* presents many such openings, to which students should (must) be alerted, many such incidental chances for its readers—in Tristram's words—to choose "a clean road or a dirty one."

With this tissue of public conversation, as students should gradually become aware, Sterne has created both a brilliant social performer and a demanding social environment. For them to benefit from this remarkable creation and enjoy the satire of human society that radiates from it, they must be helped to understand both its clear center and its equivocal outskirts.

Structure as a Starting Point

Robert D. Spector

None of the fictional elements in *Tristram Shandy* is immediately accessible to the undergraduate student. It is difficult for the uninitiated reader to comprehend that there is a narrative line in a fiction that treats time as though it were a game of hopscotch in which the numbers have been placed at random and in which the author intrudes with instructions about composition and reading. What is the novice to make of the advice to skip pages, other than to take advantage of it since concentration has been tried beyond the point of patience? What sense can the innocent and inexperienced student make of digressions and insets that may in themselves offer a plainer narrative development than exists in the main plot? To determine point of view in *Tristram Shandy*, to recognize the unifying factors in the work, and to grasp the details of its characterizations would seem to require a sophistication belonging to mature scholars and critics.

In Tristram Shandy: *The Games of Pleasure*, Richard A. Lanham indicates indeed that the problem of interpreting the novel exists for readers far more sophisticated than most modern undergraduates, and he notes various attempts to grasp a handle that would open a door to a better understanding of Sterne's work. For the eighteenth century it was turning the Tristram handle that exposed "the cleverness, the wit, the freakishness of the novel," permitting readers to admire "its learned wit as never since." In the nineteenth century the Toby handle opened up the "pathos and humor" of the character and the work itself. In the twentieth century, priding themselves on "seeing the novel whole for the first time," critics have, in fact, used the Bobby handle, "one that suits [their] passions, . . . ignorance, or . . . sensibility," one that reveals "a map of the absurd universe, the hobbies, the traps and the pathetic, comic glories of man" (Lanham 15–16).

As Lanham recognizes, the number of handles is far more abundant than his generalization suggests. Within our own time, for example, Melvyn New has presented a reading of *Tristram Shandy* that reinterprets the novel in terms of "locating it in the mainstream of the conservative, moralistic Augustan tradition" and examining it "through the intentions and conventions of the dominant literary form of that tradition, satire" (*Laurence Sterne* 1–2). Lanham himself attempts to unlock the puzzle by grasping the handle of modern game theory, which allows him to observe the manner in which "[w]e see, in *Tristram Shandy*, humor come to represent obsession within the game and with the game sense, the power that discerns separate games and moves with genial tolerance from one to another" (151–52). For William V. Holtz, in *Image and Immortality: A Study of* Tristram Shandy, the appropriate handle is the "tradition of literary pictorialism," an endeavor to uncover "a principle of unity among Sterne's book, his sensibility, and a literary tradition" by using " 'pictorial' relationships in explicating" the work (xi, xiii).

No need to go on, although there are plenty of other approaches, keys or handles, readings or interpretations. These often offer ample information and insights but rarely make the work more accessible to undergraduates confused by a fictional world whose principles remain bewildering at the most elementary level. No more do such other natural approaches to the work—approaches like reader-response theory or deconstructionism—prove helpful at the onset in my classes. To be sure, there is legitimacy in applying either one to *Tristram Shandy*, which clearly invites the reader's participation and seems an ideal paradigm for deconstructive criticism. Still, both theories only further baffle my perplexed and curious students trying simply to comprehend the narrative process of the fiction.

What these students need is to see the work as a whole, to see it as a fictional construction, whose parts belong together within a framework that makes sense. While the structure of *Tristram Shandy* is certainly no more immediately apparent than the other fictional elements are, a demonstration that the opening and conclusion of the work suggest the cyclical and comic character of life itself makes discussion of the book's other characteristics far easier. The sense of randomness and accident, the role of chance, the principles of absurdity, the confusions in communication, the authorial tone and direction—all these follow naturally from the description of a novel whose intention is to create a fictional world that parallels the realities of experience. In these terms *Tristram Shandy* provides an exemplar of Dorothy Van Ghent's useful definition:

> A novel itself is one complex pattern, or Gestalt, made up of component ones. In it inhere such a vast number of traits, all organized in subordinate systems that function under the governance of a single meaningful structure, that the nearest similitude for a novel is a "world."   (6)

Although a more thorough reading ultimately requires consideration of *Tristram Shandy*'s parody, satire, and real-life relationships, Van Ghent's definition of a novel seems a very convenient springboard to the use of structure as a heuristic device in an analysis of Sterne's work. On the basis of this method, structure becomes the framework in which the various fictional elements may be seen to provide the general supports.

The most apparent feature of the structure of any novel, of course, is the beginning and the end. Despite the continuing controversy about whether *Tristram Shandy* was ever completed and whether it belongs to a genre of *non finito*, the novel as it exists presents a clearly related opening and conclusion that offer a valuable heuristic tool. Viewing the connection between the problems of Tristram's birth and those of Obadiah's calf and the Shandy bull and guided by Tristram's initial comments in the last chapter that draw together the procreation of human being and beast, the student discovers a unity suggestive of the novel's major themes: sex, frustration, time, and a failure to communicate. Sterne's fictional world finally takes some shape: the character Tristram has been appropriately reduced in importance to the equivalency of the calf; the Shandean impotency has been extended to the family's animal possessions; Tristram's mother is as confused at the end as at the outset; and the narrator's ironic commentary—the very tone of the novel—has been summarized in Yorick's final statement designating the episode and the novel as a cock-and-bull story, the best ever told.

While linking the beginning and the closure of the work suggests an overall structure to Sterne's fictional world and its ruling principle of absurdity, making that structure meaningful requires a demonstration of the supportive and consistent infrastructure. As A. A. Mendilow argues, "It is only on a cursory reading that *Tristram Shandy* gives the impression of being haphazardly constructed" (168). Nevertheless, few students are likely to discern easily the nature of its form. Sterne's narrative method, his treatment of time, his eschewing of a chronological for an associational development— all pose obstacles to readers accustomed to a straight line of progression, movement dictated by a clock, and causality determined by a simple sequence of events.

Without going into an excessive discussion of Locke that is only likely to confuse the uninitiated reader, Mendilow offers informative discussions of each of these points. He distinguishes nicely the time shifts in the novel: the reader's present, the writer's present, and the events of the book. He explains simply "the discrepancy between duration in terms of chronological and psychological time" (171). Even more significantly, he points to "the naturalness with which . . . chronological dating is worked into the substance of the novel" and to "the accuracy with which the dates, scattered as they are in scores of so-called 'digressions,' are nevertheless made to cohere" (170, 169). In a particularly useful discussion, entitled "Illustrations of Sterne's Use of the Time-Shift," Mendilow, echoing the work of Theodore Baird, examines in detail Sterne's methods for providing specific dates in the novel (188–93).

For all its help, however, Mendilow's analysis is generally limited to a concern for Sterne's narrative technique; it requires extension to incorporate, in particular, the work's overall structure and its creation of a fictional world of the absurd. This would include an explanation of how Sterne's attitude toward, and use of, time reveal an absurdist notion of human experience; how, for example, the narrator's apparent inability to control time in his story reflects a more general lack of control over life's realities. The frustrations Tristram encounters in presenting a straightforward narrative mirror Walter Shandy's frustrated theories about names and noses. The digressive insets remind the reader of the arbitrariness with which events occur in the real world.

The digressive insets are themselves an integral part of the work's structure, important extensions of Sterne's theme and a commentary on the overall narrative technique. At least two--"Slawkenbergius's Tale" and "The Story of the King of Bohemia and His Seven Castles"—are worth looking at closely with students. In the former Sterne demonstrates, with a digression, his ability to offer a straightforward narrative, and its traditional storytelling method comments ironically on the technique he uses in his main narrative. At the same time, despite the discrepancy between the techniques, the inset and the major narrative convey the same themes. The "nose material" in the Slawkenbergian episode cries out for comparison with the Shandean situation: the character's virility in the inset underscores the Shandean impotency, recalling Walter's relationship with Elizabeth, Uncle Toby's wound and the Widow Wadman, the window-sash accident and Tristram's nose. The frustrations concerning names and communication, the play on the relation between the failure of communication and language—these clearly relate the inset to the main narrative and extend the absurdity to the entire world of *Tristram Shandy*. With the "Story of the King of Bohemia" Sterne plays the major narrative technique in a minor key, through the series of interruptions and Trim's inability to relate a story. In Trim's obvious delight in telling a story, which recalls a remark to that effect earlier in the work, Sterne also provides a rhythmic device (repetitiveness) that further contributes to the novel's unity.

This concept of "rhythm" is, in fact, another good approach to the problems of structure and unity amid the apparent chaos of *Tristram Shandy*. As E. K. Brown reminds us, Sterne himself was conscious of the significance of rhythm when in chapter 7 he rebuked his poor woman reader for forgetting what she had read in chapter 6. Brown himself describes "the kinds of repetition with variation" that constitute rhythm in a novel—the development of rhythm in any of the fictional elements, extending from "combinations of words and phrases, sequences of incidents, groupings of character" through "the growth of a symbol as it accretes meaning from a succession of contexts" to the "interweaving" and "interactive relationship" of themes (9). All these are present, of course, in *Tristram Shandy*, and once the student has learned to trace their development, the structure together with the meaning of the work should be more readily accessible.

Even the most intractable of Sterne's eccentricities—his narrative method—yields to better understanding when it is examined as a rhythmic device. The first time that Tristram addresses his readers directly—"Believe me, good folks, this is not so inconsiderable a thing as many of you may think it" (1: 1)—his manner might be attributed to nothing more than quirkiness. As the technique is repeated and repeated, it recalls what has gone on before but takes on additional meanings until his audience has come to understand the relationship of author and readers, the expectations he has of them, the responses he seeks to evoke, and the mind of the persona. Idiosyncracy has given way to familiarity and understanding, and the device has created unity of parts and expansion of knowledge, which, after all, is the function of structure. Similarly, Sterne's associational method moves from oddity to expectancy. Repetition allows the reader to recognize that this element of structure represents a way of expressing epistemology, a manner of evaluating the significance of events, and a means of achieving a reality closer to human experience than that achieved by more conventional novelistic treatments of causality.

For the undergraduate student, perhaps the most accessible and richest use of the concept of rhythm is in its application to the characters of *Tristram Shandy*. This surely is the significance of Coleridge's remark on the work's continuity of characters ("Hence the digressive spirit [is] not wantonness, but the *very form* of his genius. The connection is given by the continuity of the characters" [qtd. in Howes, *Sterne* 356]); clearly, Coleridge is here calling attention to the rhythm of characterization. From Tristram himself through the development of Walter, Mrs. Shandy, Uncle Toby, the Widow Wadman, and Corporal Trim, Sterne's method is to offer some major traits, refer to them throughout the novel, display them in a variety of circumstances that recall earlier usage and expand their meaning. The fundamental traits are there at the character's introduction, and they are not given to change as the novel continues. Rather, their repetition in a new set of circumstances intensifies their significance. Walter Shandy's dependence on authorities— a dependence that dictates his conduct, regardless of outcome—is apparent in the circumstances surrounding Tristram's birth. It is not altered by events, so that the only response Walter can make to Bobby's death is to turn to his reading of Cato, Seneca, and Epictetus. The reliance on authority is no mere whim, as it might appear initially, but, rather, all-consuming, as revealed in the reaction to his loss of a son. Sterne's method throughout the book is to contrast rhythmically his characters—to set up, for example, the confrontation between Walter and Corporal Trim as they grieve for Bobby: "two orators so contrasted by nature and education, haranguing over the same bier," one "a man of deep reading" and the other "of no deeper reading than his muster-roll" (5: 6). In the same way, Sterne establishes the team of Trim and Uncle Toby as descendants of Sancho Panza and Don Quixote and then plays off the corporal's earthy relationship with Susannah against Toby's unproductive courtship by Widow Wadman. Merely examples of

Sterne's technique in using rhythm to develop his characters in *Tristram Shandy*, these serve, at least, to indicate the infrastructure of the work and the manner in which it contributes to the overall structure of the fictional world—a world in which the complex pattern that Van Ghent describes consists of the author's particular way of looking at time, treating character development, and setting forth values.

Approaching *Tristram Shandy* through structure will permit, indeed demand, discussion of narrative technique, style, theme, tone, and characterization. The advantage of the springboard of structure is that it allows the student to dive into the water at a level deep enough to be thoroughly immersed without drowning. Beginning with the Bobby theme (on which this reading of the novel obviously depends) will open the discussion to questions of metaphysics—a subject certain to drown all but the most expert swimmers in a class. Yet ultimately such questions must be dealt with, along with the parody, satire, and sentiment in the work. What, after all, is *Tristram Shandy* without reference to earlier eighteenth-century novels? How can one ignore the way it plays on the genre's dedications, reliance on rules, concern for orderly progression, relation to typography, and genealogical accounts of heroes? Who can overlook the novel's satire that has evoked James Work's abundant notes in the student edition, Melvyn New's insightful commentary, and D. W. Jefferson's "*Tristram Shandy* and the Tradition of Learned Wit"? What would a reading of the novel be without a consideration of the Le Fever and Mad Maria episodes and of the role of sentiment? A proper study of *Tristram Shandy* requires treatment of these topics and more. My approach suggests simply that before being able to deal with such material, the undergraduate must enter into the text and that the most available access is through a sense of its structure.

Tristram Shandy and the Spatial Imagination

Ira Konigsberg

In Raphael's famous fresco *The School of Athens* (1509–10), located in the Stanza della Segnatura in the Vatican, the artist himself stands at the extreme right of the painting, looking out at us. If we are new to the work and unaware of the artist's presence, the painting seems to draw us into its very space so that we momentarily feel the thrill of being amid the great thinkers of antiquity and later times. But once we discover Raphael standing quietly and serenely, observing us from between the faces of Zoroaster and Raphael's fellow artist Sodoma and from over the shoulder of Ptolemy, something radical happens to our perspective of the painting's world—Raphael's outward gaze reestablishes the distance between us and the painting, puts us back in the space of the real world. A peculiar pleasure now arises as we return the gaze, from the interaction between us, standing out here, and the artist, standing in there.

I am obviously suggesting an analogy between Raphael's fresco (mentioned by Sterne in 4: 7) and *Tristram Shandy*, one that serves as a good starting place for a discussion of the novel with students. In *Tristram Shandy* we also have what appears to be the author as a developed figure, a presence in his own created world who gazes out at us, transgressing the space that separates us from his world and, by doing so, also demarcating that space. Raphael's self-portrait amid the figures of *The School of Athens* and Tristram's presence in his very own book as its author add a self-reflexive dimension to their works, make their works in some ways about the relation between the artist and the artist's creations but also about the relation between artist and audience. Of course, the author that we have in the book is Tristram and not the real Laurence Sterne; but certainly Sterne did much to efface the distinction between himself and his character Tristram, both in the way in which he includes in his novel matters from his own life and his own world and in the way in which he sought to project himself as Tristram in his own daily existence; and certainly the artist in the painting, like Tristram in the novel, is as much a creation, a product of the creator's art, as the figures that surround him.

In 1921, Viktor Shklovsky, the Russian formalist, wrote an essay on *Tristram Shandy* in which he made the often cited remark, "*Tristram Shandy* is the most typical novel of world literature." The import of Shklovsky's statement is that Sterne makes us more aware of his novel as a novel than most other novelists do, that we are constantly made to consider the form and "aesthetic laws" of his form (89). To some degree all novels call attention to their specific forms and manners and to the specific interactions they require from their readers, but only on occasion are novelists so consciously aware of these processes that they push them to the forefront of their works.

55

Although *Tristram Shandy* treats such concerns in a manner sufficiently universal to have applicability to all the novels ever written, it does so at a time when the novel had only recently developed as a literary form. The approach I am describing, then, leads to a discussion of time and place with students, to a discussion of the literary and cultural context in which Sterne wrote his extraordinary book. Self-reflexive art tends to come either at the beginning of a development, when form and technique are new enough to elicit a narcissistic fascination with what one is doing, or at its end, when an exhausted form elicits an ironic distancing.

Sterne wrote *Tristram Shandy* with only Richardson, Fielding, and Smollett as his major predecessors as novelists. The novel was new enough, the technique unusual enough to allow endless fascination and play. Equally important, the new fictional form seems so much a product of the period's intellectual climate, so in tune with empirical psychology and Locke's exploration into the mind, for example, that students can learn a great deal about the age by approaching Sterne's work as a self-reflexive fiction in which its author explored ways to erase the line between his characters' minds and his own and between his own and the reader's. Even if one prefers to think of *Tristram Shandy* not as a novel but as a satire, as does Melvyn New, or as an amalgam of older conventions from writers such as Cervantes, Rabelais, and Burton with the new type of fiction, as does John Stedmond, my argument about the book's self-reflexivity and the author's interaction with his readers still serves to help students master its eighteenth-century context.

I must make one further generalization about self-reflexive art that I find useful to explore with students. Since the relation between the created work and reality is a paramount concern for creators of mimetic art, artistic self-consciousness and experimentation seem to come during periods in which conceptions about reality and the individual's relation to reality are changing radically. We are talking now about a novel written by a clergyman who had a remarkable bent for picking up intellectual currents and, by nature both of his clerical position and his own antic disposition, defended against such currents with humor and literary expression. Sterne's novel is about the individual's relation to reality and about art's capacity to deal with that relation; as a result, it is also about the individual's relation to art.

In the context of these remarks, which emphasize the importance of relating *Tristram Shandy* to its time and to art in general, I wish now to develop my approach to teaching the novel. In particular, I wish to suggest the ways in which I extend this idea of the novel's self-reflexivity by amalgamating concepts from spatial criticism and from game theory.

By spatial criticism I mean the type of critical thinking popularized by Joseph Frank in his essay "Spatial Form in Modern Literature" and described in some detail by Joseph A. Kestner in *The Spatiality of the Novel*. Sterne indeed shows in his text a spatial awareness that transcends the mere depiction of external scene and permeates into the very caverns of his narrator's, characters', and readers' minds. Spatiality also abounds in the ways in which Sterne plays with his readers' imaginations and their imaginative interactions with his text. Spatial criticism, of course, brings with it a consideration of time and the mind's capacity to spatialize it, something Sterne considers, in the eighteenth century, in a manner that anticipates such modern writers as Proust and Joyce and, as well, fully challenges the student's own spatial awareness of time as it exists both in and out of the novel.

The description of Dr. Slop's thinking suggests to us the way in which Tristram spatially configures his characters' minds: "the thought floated only in Dr. *Slop*'s mind, without sail or ballast to it, as a simple proposition"; and the similar way in which he perceives his reader's mind: "millions of which, as your worship knows, are every day swiming quietly in the middle of the thin juice of a man's understanding . . ." (3: 9). But Sterne ambitiously and curiously plays with our spatial imagination, not merely our capacity to imagine spatially defined scenes (which Tristram demands throughout the work) but the capacity to hold two or more scenes juxtaposed at once in the imagination: "Is it not a shame to make two chapters of what passed in going down one pair of stairs? for we are got no farther yet than to the first landing . . . and for aught I know, as my father and my uncle *Toby* are in a talking humour, there may be as many chapters as steps . . ." (4: 10). It is this spatial imagination that allows the novelist to break through the severity of chronological time, to create an atemporality by suspending at once in the reader's mind episodes separated even by years: "when a man is telling a story in the strange way I do mine, he is obliged continually to be going backwards and forwards to keep all tight together in the reader's fancy . . ." (6: 33). The technique depends on the reader's capacity to hold in mind the memory of a previously described scene (or several such scenes) while reading another. The culmination of the technique is with the reader's capacity to share Tristram's remarkable triumph over time during his flight from death on the Continent, where he can experience and write about journeys separated in time as if they were happening simultaneously in the present (7: 28). By discussing with students Sterne's interest in pushing his readers toward such experiences, I have found them more willing to exert the energy required to unravel the threads of his narrative, energy they are initially reluctant to spend on a story seemingly without a story.

The concept of game theory has been extensively applied to *Tristram Shandy* by Richard Lanham, who unfortunately limits his argument by claiming that "[t]o make Sterne a prophet of fictional technique seems . . . uncalled for" and also by claiming that Sterne's "relation to us is like his relation to everything else. What fun can be gotten from us?" (100–01, 125). There is something more exhilarating to the work than that, something we can communicate to students that will allow them to realize their own capacities as readers. Sterne wishes to make us experience the possibilities of his narrative form much as he has Tristram experience them in the writing of the book. To do so, Sterne prods us, plays with us, leads us—to do so, he extends the spaces of our minds while making us self-consciously aware that he is doing so. *Tristram Shandy* clearly belongs to a certain type of playful novel described by Elizabeth Bruss as making "one . . . acutely aware of the activity of reading" (153).

In taking such an approach, I find it necessary to go through a certain amount of preliminary work with students and establish with them some basic concepts in narratology that concern readers. I find it useful to begin with Wolfgang Iser's concept of the implied reader as developed from Wayne Booth's remarks about the implied author (*Rhetoric*) and to go forward with refinements on the theory of readers by someone such as W. Daniel Wilson, who has helpfully clarified the distinctions between characterized readers, figures who actually appear in the text; implied, ideal, or virtual readers, for whom the writer writes the text but who themselves must be considered as fictive; and the real reader.

The establishment of such categories is useful in my own approach only to help students understand the way Sterne conducts the game, the way in which he plays off these various readers, one against the other, to push the real reader into certain mental constructs and toward a realization of the reading process in general. Sterne's characterizations of readers, his conversation with these figures, his expectations about what the implied reader can and cannot do, and his creation of specific imaginative experiences in the real reader's mind are all strategies, part of his narrative technique, to make us experience and explore the act of reading itself. For this reason, the distinctions between various types of readers sometimes become very slippery and uncertain in *Tristram Shandy*. Sterne uses both his fictive characterized and fictive implied readers to draw the real readers into the book, to induce the real readers to play their parts and become part of the novel as well as collaborators in its creation: "I am eternally paying him [the reader] compliments of this kind, and do all that lies in my power to keep his imagination as busy as my own" (2: 11).

Raphael's fresco graphically reminds us that a concern of all mimetic art is the distance between the audience and the created world and the process by which that space is transversed. When discussing the spatial world of Tristram's novel, students can easily be made to understand that Tristram himself establishes for us two basic external spatial realities in his novel, the one in which he presently exists, writing his novel, and the one in which his characters exist. With a little further effort they can also be made to see that he establishes a third external spatial reality within his novel, the world in which the reader (characterized, implied, or real) exists when reading the novel: "The reader will be content to wait for a full explanation of these matters till the next year,—when a series of things will be laid open which he little expects" (2: 19). And that awareness is the one, I find, that most interests my students.

But *Tristram Shandy* is also a psychological novel through and through, and it is so in a self-reflexive way unique in literary history for another century and a half. Tristram is interested in more than his characters' minds—he is fascinated with his own mind, which these characters have helped shape and from which they actually originate. In other words, the created reality of Tristram's characters is constantly established for us as part of the reality of Tristram's own mind as it exists at the time of his writing, just the way the reality that surrounds him when he writes is a projection of his mind—both external spaces exist only in the psychological space of his imagination. These ideas are not difficult to communicate to students— Tristram's own discussions of the processes of the mind, his use of Locke, and his specific dramatizations of the mind's operations, several of which I referred to earlier in this essay, will normally make these points.

From the start of the novel Tristram invites us to enter the spaces of his external realities but also the space of his mind—"I have undertaken, you see, to write not only my life, but my opinions also; hoping and expecting that your knowledge of my character, and of what kind of a mortal I am, by the one, would give you a better relish for the other . . ." (1: 6)—but he does so only to pull us up short, to make us aware of our intrusion into that psychological space: "——Fair and softly, gentle reader!——where is thy fancy carrying thee?" (3: 33). Tristram knows exactly where our fancy has been carrying us because his own fancy has been carrying both him and us to exactly the same place. He wants us to be cognizant of the way our minds work when reading his text because this will allow us to understand the way his mind works while writing it—as a writer writing an autobiography of his own mind, he could not ask more from a reader.

The response we develop to the text, then, is ultimately on a cognitive level, an awareness of the way in which Tristram, the supposed author, brings us in and out of the text. But even the type of experience we undergo when lured within the spaces of Tristram's realities—external or internal— are a far cry from experiencing the text in the personal and subjective manner advocated by David Bleich or with the unconscious defense mechanisms defined by Norman Holland. I find a discussion of such approaches with students useful if only to distinguish clearly what Sterne intended with his text. It is fruitful also to show the way Sterne makes sexual sublimation a driving force behind his characters' actions (starting on page 1) and how he brings readers to an awareness of their own prurience when reading the novel—in other words, the way that Sterne makes what we call the "unconscious" into the conscious.

My approach also differs widely from the traditional way of talking about novels in terms of the reader's identification with fictional characters (or, as Georges Poulet suggests, with the author). Identification, association, empathy are all useful concepts to discuss but only to call them into question and to require greater accuracy from the student in understanding the reading process and the reader's response to *Tristram Shandy*. Sterne does elicit identification from the reader, but not in the traditional sense: his intent is to have us identify cognitively with the process of Tristram's mind, not with Tristram's character or his situation.

Sterne's game plan is always to fool the reader into recognition and surprise. He draws us into the world of the novel only to draw us out again so that we can realize how we were thinking when we were in the text. The distance he keeps reestablishing by gazing out at us prevents any type of personal identification with his characters, maintains the proper detachment for our comic appreciation of what takes place within the novel, and constantly returns us to an examination of our responses to his work.

I conclude this discussion of how I teach *Tristram Shandy* by bringing to mind the marbled page in the novel, what Tristram calls the "motly emblem of my work!" (3: 36). But in the text the page actually exists and is not a concept in either Tristram's imagination or the reader's. It exists in the reader's world just as it exists in Tristram's. Like the small, heavy cones, which are images of a divinity, in Borges's short story "Tlön, Uqbar, Orbis Tertius" (17), the page exists as a concrete object transferred from an imaginary world into the real, from imaginary space into actual space. Tristram for the moment turns his gaze from us and together we gaze at the marbled page.

Getting into the Talk:
Tristram Shandy through Conversation

Leland E. Warren

Testimony from a long and various line of good readers suggests that in declaring "writing, when properly managed . . . [to be] but a different name for conversation" (2: 11), Tristram is offering a genuine insight, if not into the way all writing should be carried on, at least into a natural and satisfying way of reading *Tristram Shandy*. William Hazlitt claimed to find in Sterne's writing "the pure essence of English conversational style" (121). In it Virginia Woolf heard the "sound and associations of the speaking voice"; "we are as close to life as we can be" (81). More recently, James Swearingen, in a demanding but valuable phenomenological reading of the novel, attributes to Sterne "an understanding of the language act as rooted in a speaking community. . . . Unlike what happens when a computer is fed information, when reading proceeds like conversation both content and the reader are changed much as the two sides of a metaphor alter one another" (91). Finally, Bruce Stovel argues that Sterne "recreated in his novel the satisfactions found in the familiar, everyday activity of gossiping" and that "the novel's situation, style, and mood recreate that experience" (116, 123). Various as these readers and their critical presuppositions are, all respond to the voice of Tristram in the novel as somehow more engaging, more fully present to the reader than we have reason to expect possible in writing.

Responses from students to whom I have taught *Tristram Shandy* over the past decade attest to Sterne's effectiveness in creating a personal voice that seems to get beyond the written page and seriously to engage even unsophisticated readers in the speaker's personal concerns. But these same readers do not always—in fact, do not usually—find this voice so wholly interesting as the professional writers and readers I have cited above. Part of the problem is that many think they would prefer the novel Sterne doesn't write to the conversation that he does. Why doesn't Tristram get on with the story? Why can't we have more action? Where are beginning, middle, and end? But a more interesting problem is that although Tristram's voice is for most genuinely engaging at times, it also seems to go on too long and finally becomes boring. In the continuation of a passage cited above, Virginia Woolf emphasizes that Sterne's voice conveys "more than talk—after all, the man who *talks* is a bore—it is conversation. And that is a better word than 'rhetoric' to describe what Sterne is after" (81). We know what she means, but for many students Tristram becomes a voice that talks and talks, a bore. He cites or alludes to too many obscure works or names, and he won't even be wholly clear about himself. For such readers Sterne fails because he violates the rules of decorum he himself pays homage to as he

61

identifies writing with conversation: he talks too much and assumes on the part of readers an interest in his trivial concerns that he has not earned.

I should perhaps at this point confess that I consider myself one of the good readers for whom *Tristram Shandy* provides the kinds of pleasures that seem to me very much like those commonly found in conversation (see Warren, "Constant Speaker"). As a teacher of the novel, I consequently find myself in the doubly difficult position, first, of getting students to experience the pleasures I do and, second, of explaining how in this novel these pleasures have a serious—not to say, somber—point. Since this task is rather like urging people to laugh at a joke they didn't find funny in its first telling and then immediately teaching them the joke's moral, I at times feel a bond with Walter Shandy, who also has trouble getting his audiences to enter into the kinds of mental play that give him both sheer delight and the sense that he is on the verge of real understanding. But there is a difference, for unlike Walter, who wants his readers to grasp the ultimate truth of his formulations, I wish only to encourage students to give to Tristram the kinds of attention politeness requires one to give a new acquaintance. When they do so, they often find not only that Tristram is not a bore but that his speech is more than mere talk because it is, even (or especially) when most personal, about matters necessarily interesting to all of us.

When we get students to follow Tristram's directions and to respond to him as to a conversational partner, several consequences should follow as to how they read the novel. First, to keep up their side of the conversation, they must be active. This is no easy matter; decorum demands that they pay strict attention to what Tristram says and try to understand it, but this understanding will necessarily entail—as Tristram warns us—their imagining their share of the matter, and yet they must do so without leaping to unsupported conclusions that would be unfair to Tristram. They must not, in other words, violate the ground rules for conversation. Second, to the extent that they successfully enter into the talk, they will come to realize that the pleasure to be derived from the novel will come from the process of reading itself, rather than from any conclusion we might reach about Sterne's meaning; the effort must be its own reward.

Thus I begin my first lecture on *Tristram Shandy* with a discussion of this contemporary definition of conversation from the sociologist Erving Goffman:

> Conversation . . . might be identified as the talk occurring when a small number of participants come together and settle into what they perceive to be a few moments cut off from (or carried on to the side of) instrumental tasks; a period of idling felt to be an end in itself, during which everyone is accorded the right to talk as well as to listen and without reference to a fixed schedule; everyone is accorded the

status of someone whose overall evaluation of the subject matter at hand—whose editorial comments, as it were—is to be encouraged and treated with respect; and no final agreement or synthesis is demanded, differences of opinion to be treated as unprejudicial to the continuing relationship of the participants.   (14)

This nicely captures the appeal of conversation, or at least of the sorts of ideal private conversations that most of us enjoy from time to time. In such talk we feel at once independent and yet part of a group; we are temporarily free from the demands of daily life, of the need to accomplish something, to reach some end, and yet we feel we are doing something worthwhile. And when we find ourselves involved in such an experience, or, more commonly, when we reflect on the pleasure, it seems to have happened without effort.

But it is not that there has been no effort; rather, the conditions of the conversation have transformed the effort into pleasure. As Goffman's definition suggests, there are two primary factors that go far in determining the success or failure of conversation. First is the nature of the relationships among the participants. For the conversation to succeed, there must be at least temporarily a general feeling of community. Now, although such feelings are easiest to attain when the individuals do know and genuinely respect one another, unless we are to talk always and only to the same small group of people, we must usually work to help create this feeling. The second factor is the subject of the conversation. Students are usually quick to remember cautions they have heard against divisive subjects like politics and religion in conversation and to agree that one should not talk about specialized subjects that others can hardly claim a right to speak on. A modern class will come to sound very much like eighteenth-century guides to conversation: common sense informs both that most talk is badly marred by the unwillingness or inability of the participants to establish mutual regard and to hew to subject lines that make such respect tenable (see Warren, "Turning Reality").

John Preston writes that "if [*Tristram Shandy*] is a conversation, it is a conversation about the failure of conversation," but these failures finally "are the subject of yet another conversation, which is carried on between the readers and the author" (146, 148). This seems true enough when we consider that although Tristram lays down basic rules for conversation, he offers us a variety of reported conversations in which all guidelines are shattered. Riding their hobbyhorses, Walter and Toby have difficulty in comprehending discourse arising outside their obsessions, and this often makes it hard for those to whom they speak to feel they have any status within the exchange. Mrs. Shandy embodies an opposite failure when, in not responding to Walter, she forces him to converse with himself. Even Trim, an accomplished conversationalist, better able than most to understand himself and those to whom he is speaking and therefore capable of knowing when to speak and when to remain silent, "lov'd to advise,—or rather to hear himself talk . . . 'twas easy to keep him silent when you had him so; but set his tongue a-going,—you had no hold of him . . ." (2: 5). Further, among those "readers" who are invited into the talk, many are clearly very bad conversationalists indeed: critics who are far too occupied in finding errors to give any attention to Tristram himself (but for whom Tristram politely provides entertainment by intentionally making errors for them to find [2: 2]) and women who have acquired the "vicious taste . . . of reading straight forwards, more in quest of the adventures, than of the deep erudition and knowledge which a book of this cast, if read over as it should be, would infallibly impart with them" (1: 20) are only the most notable members of this sorry crew. Tristram speaks to us, and much of his speech recounts or elicits examples of apparently failed speaking.

And, of course, Tristram draws from most of us conversational errors as well. Many of my students will readily admit to having been guilty of "reading straight forwards . . . in quest of the adventures." I myself continue to want more certain knowledge of Jenny's relationship with Tristram than decorum justifies my asking (1: 18). And the entire class is implicated when Tristram tut-tuts about his readers who find unclean meanings in words like "noses," "whiskers," and "crevices." But Tristram himself is hardly without blame; certainly he doesn't always make adequate allowances for the limitations of some of his readers, and so they can be excused for feeling left out, without status, and becoming angry. Nor are Tristram's subjects always the most proper; politics, religion, and sex might be expected to alienate some of his company, but death is a sure talk (and, here, print) stopper. Perhaps my recalcitrant students are right; perhaps I am deluding myself when I find any real conversation here.

Instead of yielding to this (for me) unattractive possibility, however, I suggest to them that we consider more closely Preston's comment about failures in conversation being "the subject" of a conversation "between the readers and author." This statement implies that Tristram carries on a successful conversation with us on the subject of unsuccessful conversations. But exactly what constitutes success or the lack of it? Clearly it is a matter for those involved to decide. A nonparticipant is poorly placed to judge accurately, and different participants may make different judgments. But if—taking the license granted us as invited participants of Tristram's fictive conversations—we judge the most hilarious examples of failed communication in the novel according to standards suggested by Goffman's definition, then we might be inclined to pronounce them successful. Certainly Walter,

Toby, Trim, and Yorick find satisfaction most of the time in the talk they carry on with one another. Though this talk rarely leaves any one of them wiser—may, in fact, leave them less so—we have little doubt that something has been gained.

So it is (or should be), I believe, with the talk that goes on between Tristram and my students. Before considering what this something gained is, though, I try to justify to them my speaking of a mutual exchange between Tristram and his readers. I point out that just as Tristram's flight from death in volume 7 brings death to mind, so his various claims to an identity between writing and conversing finally remind us of the unbridgeable gap between them. Conversation does, in a sense, exist in an unrecoverable past; skillful writing may capture something of such talk and allow it to go on giving pleasure long after those who lived it are dead. But the experience itself cannot be preserved any more than Tristram can in his writing give us the true measure of Janatone (7: 9). The relation between print and conversation is like that between print and all other activities of living: print continuously declares how far from life it is.

Tristram cannot, of course, eliminate this gap. What he does instead is make it the subject of the conversation he wishes to have with us in the present of our reading. His success as a polite speaker must depend on the extent to which this subject is capable of involving each of us and on his ability to give us our chance to speak. It seems clear that Tristram avoids the writer's error analogous to "talking all"; he leaves questions unanswered, topics unexhausted. Indeed, this at least apparent openness, inconclusiveness, is the basis for many complaints about the novel; given the chance to speak, students may be very uneasy about what to say. Like Dr. Slop when his discourse on the wonderful progress in obstetrics is interrupted by Uncle Toby's "*I wish . . . you had seen what prodigious armies we had in Flanders*" (3: 1), the reader may at times feel there is no reasonable response possible. Dr. Slop's problem, like that of the Widow Wadman in trying to determine the nature of Toby's wound (9: 26), of Trim in telling of the bridge Dr. Slop is making (3: 23), and of Walter almost every time he speaks to Toby is that the doctor and a conversational partner are talking on different subjects. Instead of a common object or concern that would serve as the meeting point of disparate minds and be the basis for conversation, these speakers confront the difficulties of communion among individuals of various concerns and interests. But these conversations do not stop; instead, spurred by the fact of potential isolation, the speakers somehow move on to new, more nearly common ground and keep talking.

If Tristram is to engage us in conversation, then, he must draw us out of ourselves, not by soliciting our interest in him or urging us to merge our identity with his, but by locating and sketching the outlines of a subject adequate to our conversational needs. As I have suggested above, whether he succeeds in this will necessarily be a question that none of us can finally answer for anyone else. And, since students coming to *Tristram Shandy* for the first time will need to work harder to maintain their side of the conversation than will those who have—through reading, listening to or giving lectures, or writing books and articles—become very comfortable in Tristram's presence, we should not be disappointed if even after our best efforts students do not find Tristram's talk wholly absorbing. But we can help them to see what the subject of this conversation might be and why it might matter.

I have described this subject as the gap between writing and conversation. More accurately, it is the difficulties inherent in the task of bridging this gap, of making the sought-for identification of writing and conversation a reality, of writing a book that is both good and true. Students made aware of this subject can come to see that their confusion and irritation at Tristram's many narrative failings—his digressions, his uncertainty as to what to tell next and what to include and what leave out, his allusiveness—are not errors on their part but are very much what the talk in this book is about. We should not as teachers of the novel try to repress or deny the objections of students who have trouble entering into Tristram's talk; rather we should help them to see how Tristram as narrator speaks to them as readers about exactly these difficulties and by so doing attempts to make them party to the problems he confronts in trying to make writing "but a different name for conversation."

Tristram's text can become for students part of a conversation into which they can enter only if the distance between author and reader disappears as both give attention to the struggle to become good readers. I do agree with Richard Lanham, however, who warns us away from viewing this as a philosophical enterprise with truth as its goal, from reading the novel "as absurdist comedy with sentimental light at the end of the tunnel" (159). Instead, Sterne transforms this struggle into an occasion for pleasure. In *Tristram Shandy* the struggle to read the world is transformed into pleasure because the effort is shared, because it becomes the basis for conversation, for an encounter within which all participants gain a degree of freedom and status rarely found in the routines of life. Our gain as participants in Tristram's good talk should be like that we expect from good conversation, and it is one of the major achievements of *Tristram Shandy* to remind us that such commonplace pleasures are no small thing. The "conversation" among Tristram and his readers does not eliminate or solve the problems that are its subject, but it places them within a social context that makes possible comic communion rather than tragic isolation.

"How could you, Madam, be so inattentive?": Tristram's Relationship with the Reader

Betty Rizzo

For novice readers, one of the many confusing elements in *Tristram Shandy* is the nature of their relationship to Tristram. Other novelists—and if students are reading Sterne, they have probably read Fielding—address their readers directly and toy with them, but Sterne carries the gaming to new extremes and in new directions. In a sense Tristram—one knows it is really Sterne, but for accuracy's sake let us call him Tristram—is playing leader in a game of "follow the leader," in which the readers must at every turn try to follow not only his meaning but his total meaning. So not surprisingly, much of Tristram's effort goes into turning round to shape up his followers. If all proceeds according to his wishes, in the course of his efforts a relationship between Tristram and the reader develops, a relationship that will become intimate. And for some new readers that sort of involvement is a problem. They fail to understand Tristram's advances. They resist putting themselves into his hands. They fail to trust him enough to risk the adventure. In that way, they miss the experience of the book.

If readers do go along with Tristram's game, they must yield to what might, in the modern jargon, be called an ego trip. Tristram insists that readers forget their expectations of simple linear chronological narrative and follow wherever his whims or private associations lead. He deprecates the tendency of modern readers to read for the plot (1: 20). Tristram's system demands a reliance on his leadership, a trust in his choices, that can seem overweening, irritating, demeaning, even perilous—or simply not worth the effort. After some experience readers may begin to understand why Tristram has turned in each new direction, led the way forward (or backward) into yet another strange terrain, but they will never predict beforehand where they will next be led.

But by this time the reader realizes that the game consists of following blindly without map or instructions through each advance, retreat, or digression while at the same time trying to savor fully each jest, double meaning, or allusion; that it means grasping the full import of every remark while at the same time building an understanding of Tristram's general system of belief. Rarely if ever have our students had so many demands placed on them by an author, and it is therefore useful to suggest to them that if entered into wholeheartedly the trip will be a jolly trip, a significant trip, an unforgettable trip, and a trip from which there will be a safe return; in short, that Tristram makes the game, if well played, very worthwhile.

Tristram is skillful at shepherding his flock—one way to think of him is as tour guide, though he sometimes suggests a parson holding forth to his congregation. Often he addresses his aggregate readers. At such times they become readers, good folks, "O my countrymen!," your worships, your reverences. Even more often he addresses his readers singly. The generic reader, whom he addresses as "you," turns out to be, generally, a male: the gentle reader, the penetrating reader, the learned reader, the Christian reader, and, more directly and intimately, Sir, dear Sir, and your worship. Female readers are particularly addressed (usually when Tristram wants to make a point about female hypocrisy or to clarify sensitive or sexual matters about which he assumes women are secretly curious and informed) as Madam, Madams, my fair reader, my dear girl, your ladyships.

His specific remarks to readers help to explicate the rules of the game that until then have had to be taken on trust. Tristram expects to become intimate in time with the faithful reader: "As you proceed further with me, the slight acquaintance which is now beginning betwixt us, will grow into familiarity; and that, unless one of us is in fault, will terminate in friendship.——*O diem præclarum!*" (1: 6). He has no intention of maintaining formal relations and, anticipating intimacy, addresses the reader as "my dear friend and companion"; writer and reader are to laugh together as they jog on; and to forestall the reader's annoyance at not knowing enough, Tristram begs the reader not to get angry: "——only keep your temper" (1: 6).

Readers of *Tristram Shandy* are soon informed, however, that they must decide for themselves such questions as the reason for the singularity of Walter Shandy's notions (1: 19). Readers are not simply to follow blindly but must learn to draw conclusions about their experiences independently. Shortly afterward, a female reader is sent back to retrace some of her travels because she has not come to all the conclusions possible, given the information provided:

> ——How could you, Madam, be so inattentive in reading the last chapter? I told you in it, *That my mother was not a papist.*——Papist! You told me no such thing, Sir. Madam, I beg leave to repeat it over again, That I told you as plain, at least, as words, by direct inference, could tell you such a thing. . . .——Then, I declare, I know nothing at all about the matter.—That, Madam, is the very fault I lay to your charge; and as a punishment for it, I do insist upon it, that you immediately turn back, that is, as soon as you get to the next full stop, and read the whole chapter over again. (1: 20)

Once the lady has departed, Tristram informs the rest of us that he has imposed the penance on her "to rebuke a vicious taste which has crept into thousands besides herself,—of reading straight forwards, more in quest of the adventures, than of the deep erudition and knowledge which a book of this cast, if read over as it should be, would infallibly impart with them." And when "my fair Lady" returns, admitting defeat, he informs her that the clue was in the sentence " 'It was *necessary* I should be born before I was christen'd.' Had my mother, Madam, been a Papist, that consequence did not follow." Madam, like the rest of us, could not have been expected to know the theological profundities that unravel the clue, and Tristram, of course, had not expected her—or his readers—to know what he was talking about. The exercise she has been put through, then, is both to teach her (us) to read this author (perhaps more than his book) with care—for Tristram is sincere in his pious wish at the end of the chapter "that all good people, both male and female, from her example, may be taught to think as well as read"—and, even more significant, to convince her (us) that all efforts notwithstanding, the author is never to be anticipated.

If the reader ever *were* to guess what was in the next page, Tristram says at the end of volume 1, he would blush and tear the page from the book: "I set no small store by myself upon this very account, that my reader has never yet been able to guess at any thing" (1: 25). The reader must yield blindly to Tristram's leadership and must at the same time make unprecedented efforts to comprehend—to "follow"—him.

Tristram all but demands full submission. What sort of reader does he most admire? "I would go fifty miles on foot . . . to kiss the hand of that man whose generous heart will give up the reins of his imagination into his author's hands,——be pleased he knows not why, and cares not wherefore" (3: 12). If Tristram were king, with the powers of a king, he would lead his hearty laughing subjects to be "as WISE as they were MERRY" (4: 32). He scorns to foist off fifty pages of quotations from Rapin: " 'tis enough to have thee in my power——but to make use of the advantage which the fortune of the pen has now gained over thee, would be too much"; the intimate pronoun is now in use, and Tristram commiserates with the powerless reader as "a helpless creature," a "poor soul" (7: 6). Our bondage may be light, but Tristram clearly reminds us from time to time that he is in command.

But although Tristram is a taskmaster, he does sometimes allow his readers their rights. On one occasion, when he wants attention directed to his belief that a gesture makes a greater impression than a word (a perverse theory for a man writing a book!), he bargains with the reader, offering in compensation for attention now his permission to sleep through any other ten pages in the book (5: 7). In the very next chapter he barters a chapter on chambermaids, green gowns, and old hats for a previously promised one on chambermaids and buttonholes, now alas never to be forthcoming. Sometimes, too, Tristram clearly signals the more ambiguous points of the book; he is hopeful that his readers will miss none of the double entendres. Nevertheless, left to themselves, few student readers would grasp half of them, and the instructor may legitimately waver before the task of detailed explication. Toby's confusion over the right end of a woman (2: 7) mirrors the confusion of many readers over numerous passages in *Tristram Shandy*; Tristram's later attempt to clarify the double meaning of *crevice* (3: 31) at the precise moment when he pretends to insist on the single meaning of *nose* suggests that explication may not always be enough.

Because of Tristram's belief that visual impressions are deeper and swifter than the impressions made by words, he presents us with many notable visual images the better to help us understand his characters. The exact stance of Trim as he reads the sermon, Walter's grief-stricken position on his bed, the Widow Wadman's extraction of the tobacco pipe from Toby's hand, Tristram's mother's gentle tapping (remonstrance or confession?) of Walter's hand are only a few examples. They are like instructions to the illustrator; Hogarth indeed did illustrate Trim reading. Such graphics are even better realized, of course, in the blank page, the black page, the marbled page, and perhaps most finely in the flourish of Trim's stick (9: 4), which, if one reproduces the gesture, exactly conveys Trim's meaning and his emotion. But the maps of the terrain we have traveled are perversely provided after we have already struggled through (6: 40). Like explorers in a wilderness, we see the charts of our journeys after returning home again. Furthermore the maps are not fully reliable, for Tristram makes it clear that he is always backtracking and returning to the present, while the maps suggest only a forward movement, a progress through the book without reference to the mental traveler.

To what purpose is Tristram's game with his readers? The more suspicious may eventually begin to suspect designs on their virtue. To what does Tristram's promised intimacy ("*O diem præclarum!*") tend? His work, he tells us at the start, is digressive and progressive too—and at the same time (1: 22). Translated into physical movement this scheme is not so far from the backward and forward motion that is a characteristic motif of the book. The epigraph to volume 3, for instance, postulates a passage from jests to serious matters and back to jests. Using the image of a loom, Tristram tells us "he is obliged continually to be going backwards and forwards to keep all tight together in the reader's fancy" (6: 33). But the backward and forward movement of the head of Ambrose's amanuensis—"like a flail"—was pronounced by Ambrose to be indecent (6: 5). If Ambrose dismissed the amanuensis for it, are we not to be warned that either we do likewise to our narrator or take the consequences? Instead of advancing in his story, Tristram complains, he is, by the impossibility of catching up with the present, constantly thrown back (4: 13). And the reader too is forced backward, forward, and sidewise as Tristram makes excursions into the past and returns to the present. Nor must we forget Madam, forced at the outset to go backward to the preceding chapter and to return no more enlightened than she went. What finally is the implication of this motion, identified as indecent and shared by narrator and reader alike?

But putting such dangerous matters aside, we see also that the promised intimacy between Tristram and the faithful reader has ripened well before the end. The intimate pronoun *thee*, already cited, tells us as much. Perhaps Tristram cannot physically touch us, but through his use of graphics, vivid gesture, the suggestion of an imaginary journey through a real physical terrain arm in arm with our guide, he comes near to doing so. And we know that if reason ties knots (like those around Slop's bag), feeling can dissolve them; a single touch from Tristram causes the knot of Nannette's hair to fall, and, though strangers, it is as if they "had been seven years acquainted" (7: 43). Such a feeling is shared by the faithful, the gentle, the learned, the penetrating reader.

Here is a book in which Tristram demonstrates the unreliability of understanding based on private, personal association; Toby misunderstands Slop's bridge; no one from Mrs. Shandy to the curate can have any idea of the importance (to himself) of Walter Shandy's theories; each person in the Shandy kitchen responds quite differently to the same news of Bobby's death; and Toby and Walter consistently fail to grasp each other's meaning. Yet Tristram has the effrontery to suggest that his readers accompany him through nine volumes (which might have continued while Sterne lived), following a tour of his associations, notably erratic as they are because of the various accidents that befell him in his early years. Evidently he is confident of being a companion and guide of such infinite good humor, wit, and wisdom that his qualities will compensate for all his readers' efforts. And, since obviously for countless readers his confidence has not been misplaced, new readers too may be undeterred by the eccentricity of his terms and be persuaded to begin his acquaintance.

TRISTRAM SHANDY: CONTEXTS

Sterne's Paradoxical Coherence: Some Principles of Unity in *Tristram Shandy*

William R. Siebenschuh

Tristram Shandy offers readers a succession of paradoxes nested like boxes, a steady stream of comic discrepancies between what Sterne's characters say and try and what they actually mean and do. As in all fiction that systematically uses irony and paradox, our pleasure is in proportion to our awareness of the game and its rules.

I usually teach *Tristram Shandy* late in my eighteenth-century novel course, and first-time readers who encounter Sterne after Richardson and Fielding are, not surprisingly, startled. As they can see, the plot of *Tristram Shandy* is certainly not an "action" in an Aristotelian sense. Sterne's characters do not make their ways bravely through a labyrinth of difficult moral decisions and grow as they make each correct choice (à la Pamela and Clarissa). Nor are they easily categorizable as social and moral types (à la Thwackum and Square). Sterne's style, a breathless and apparently whimsical rush of clauses loosely stitched together by dashes and colons, is unlike anything students have read earlier in the course. Though the age valued didactic fiction and operated on the basis of a moral aesthetic, it is hard to find a conventional moral in *Tristram Shandy*, by reputation a notoriously bawdy tale (circumcision by fenestration, noses, placket holes, buttered buns, the

Argumentum Tripodium, crevices, and the right and wrong end of a woman, Madam!). It is a text that can seem to offer little more than what Yorick's concluding phrase suggests: a story about a cock and a bull—"And one of the best of its kind, I ever heard." But this is simply where the paradoxes and the ironies begin.

Though Tristram claims that his book follows no rules (1: 4) and that his pen travels on the wings of whim, caprice, and perhaps Lockean principles of the association of ideas, the novel has always held together quite well. (It most certainly does not read like an essay written by one of Mina Shaughnessy's "basic writers," the people most likely literally to write their first sentence and trust to Almighty God for the next.) Though Tristram constantly asserts his family's originality and proclaims their utter atypicality, the Shandy family is easy to identify and sympathize with. Though Tristram repeatedly asserts his skepticism about language's inadequacy and unreliability, Sterne brilliantly exploits language and reveals its unintended eloquence about our most fundamental desires, motives, and assumptions. And although Tristram repeatedly disparages the seriousness of a book he calls a "careless kind of a civil, nonsensical, good humoured *Shandean* book" (6: 17), the work is easy to take seriously, albeit in distinctly Shandean ways. I had best luck teaching *Tristram Shandy* by concentrating on these paradoxes.

I try to make students see immediately that the Shandys' world is built on paradox, that you can't swing a stick in the book without hitting half a dozen. I begin by focusing on the book's "characters." Walter is a born orator but his primary audience for life is Mrs. Shandy and Toby. They are the well-meaning cakes of soap on which he must shower the sparks of his eloquence ("My mother . . . went out of the world at last without knowing whether it turned *round*, or stood *still*.——My father had officiously told her above a thousand times which way it was,—but she always forgot" [6: 39]). Walter lives to hypothesize, and each of his hypotheses generates a plan that produces exactly the results it was designed to avoid. Uncle Toby, perhaps the sweetest, most genuinely harmless character in English fiction, is happiest when he is thinking about war. Unable to harm a fly, he is fascinated by military strategy and devotes nearly every waking hour to re-creating famous battles in miniature. One of the most instinctively eloquent characters in the book, he can seldom communicate effectively in words. Yorick loves a good horse but rides by choice on a sway-backed brother of Rosinante. He is a clergyman—in charge of a parish of souls—and yet, "with all this sail, poor *Yorick* carried not one ounce of ballast . . . and, at the age of twenty-six, knew just about as well how to steer his course [in the world], as a romping, unsuspicious girl of thirteen" (1: 11).

We then consider what passes for a conventional plot. If anything can be said to stitch the early volumes of *Tristram Shandy* together in a more or less ordinary way, it is the loosely chronological sequence of events that begins with Tristram's begetting, includes his birth and baptism, and ends with his circumcision and putting into breeches. At the begetting, Mrs. Shandy's ill-timed question scatters Walter's animal spirits and Tristram's "whole house"—takes its "turn from the humours and dispositions that were then uppermost . . ." (1: 1). Walter's elaborate negotiations over the marriage settlement—specifically designed to avoid mishap—result in a chain of comic catastrophes: "I was," says Tristram, "doom'd, by marriage articles, to have my nose squeez'd as flat to my face, as if the destinies had actually spun me without one" (1: 15). At the baptism, Walter's hypothesis about names misfires when at the crucial moment he cannot find his breeches and the curate fills the vacuum of Susannah's message by naming Tristram after himself ("There is no *gistus* to it, noodle!—'tis my own name . . ." [4: 14]). Tristram is circumcised by a window sash free to fall because Trim has borrowed the sash weights to use in Toby's miniaturized wars. At this point students have little trouble believing that there is a pattern here.

Though the structure and even the style of Sterne's book may have been influenced by Locke's theory of the association of ideas, Sterne's characters by no means advertise the Age of Reason or represent orthodox versions of Locke's model of the mind. In the world of the Shandys, no one learns much from history or experience, though they invoke both repeatedly to justify their wishes and support their hobbyhorses. A matter of hours before Dr. Slop's state-of-the-art forceps reduce Tristram's nose to something resembling an ace of clubs, Walter has had vivid demonstration of their force: "UPON my honour, Sir, you have tore every bit of the skin quite off the back of both my hands with your forceps, cried my uncle *Toby*,—and you have crush'd all my knuckles into the bargain with them, to a jelly" (3: 16). Here Walter has Othello's ocular proof of the possible danger to his unborn child but only slight misgivings, for "what is the character of a family to an hypothesis?" (1: 21). Ill-fated and misdirected affairs—Aunt Dinah and the coachman, the Shandy mare that gives birth to a mule, the Shandy bull—run through the book like a vein of ore. According to Locke, we learn and grow wiser by reflection on what we experience and what we discover from books. The Shandys' behavior is more consistent with Shakespeare's suggestion that "[a]ll this the world well knows, yet none knows well. . . ."

Book learning and erudition fare no better than history or experience does. Tristram is especially hard on classical wisdom. In an age whose motto still might arguably be said to be Pope's "Be *Homer*'s Works your *Study*, and *Delight*, / Read them by Day, and meditate by Night," Tristram writes a totally "unprecedented" book, and Walter's grave and nearly manic consultations of classical and "learned" authority are pageants of comic irrelevance and irreverence. Learned synods meet to decide that the mother is not kin to her child. Walter consults weighty tomes on circumcision and on trousers and copies whole pages of Obadiah Walker's *Of Education* into his *Tristrapædia*. Authorities (with names like Prignitz, Slawkenbergius, Phutatorius, and Kysarcius) are cited gravely by Walter—and Toby—but always (perhaps one might say, "only") to defend or justify what they want to do or believe anyway. Tristram's father's "way was to force every event in nature into an hypothesis, by which means never man crucified TRUTH at the rate he did . . ." (9: 32).

After we have observed the Shandys in their apparently plotless peregrinations, I have suggested to my students that what we are looking at in *Tristram Shandy* is nothing other than ourselves. This notion too is paradoxical, however, for Tristram claims that he is bent on denying readers precisely this commonest of pleasures—identification. He protests repeatedly that he is unlike any other man's child (1: 3); that nothing in his family is wrought after the common way (2: 4); and that "the hand of the supreme Maker . . . never made or put a family together . . . where the characters of it were cast or contrasted with so dramatic a felicity . . ." (3: 39). He claims he is unique of all biographers.

I argue that the book's uniqueness is more or less all on its surface: the iconoclastic form, the idiosyncratic prose style, the typographical oddities. In truth, the more signals the book sends that it is one of a kind, and the more Tristram formally denies the possibility of our identifying with him and his family, the greater is our pleasure in viewing ourselves in his mirror of comic distortion. The famous Shandy door hinge is the paradigm ("EVERY day for at least ten years together did my father resolve to have it mended,——'tis not mended yet . . ." [3: 21]). The irony of the hinge itself—easy to fix but no one ever does—is what people remember most often, but Sterne's following admonition is arguably the heart of the matter: "Inconsistent soul that man is!—languishing under wounds, which he has the power to heal! —his whole life a contradiction to his knowledge!—his reason, that precious gift of God to him—(instead of pouring in oyl) serving but to sharpen his sensibilities,——to multiply his pains and render him more melancholy and uneasy under them!" (3: 21). As an image, then, not of a foible but of the human predicament itself, the hinge implies the book's unifying idea.

That is to say, I try to convince my students that the principles of unity that bind *Tristram* together are to be found beneath the paradoxes in Sterne's fundamentally coherent vision of our common human nature. The paradoxes reflect that vision. Though the book contains satire on dozens of particular forms of pomposity, hypocrisy, false gravity, self-importance, and self-delusion, each satiric stroke is driven by a perception of the chronic discrepancies between what we know and what we think we know; what we are and what we need to think we are; the real motives for our actions and what we need to believe our motives to be; what we say and what we actually mean—and so on. The illogical procession of episodes, the irrational, routinely self-defeating adventures of the Shandys expand and cumulatively reinforce that vision. The procession of episodes is only illogical to someone who expects books and life to be logical. That sort of person is indeed one of the subjects of Sterne's satire.

Attracted to the apparently experimental aspects of *Tristram Shandy*, my students sometimes want to see Sterne as a modern writer. I argue that in his vision of the human predicament, Sterne is by no means a modern absurdist in disguise. He is not ahead of his time; he is smack in the middle of it. It takes no great stretch of the imagination to see the entire Shandy clan as in Pope's definition of man as "being darkly wise, and rudely great," routinely "in doubt his Mind or Body to prefer" (*Essay on Man*, ep. 2, lines 4, 9). The Shandys are certainly—collectively or individually—a

> Chaos of Thought and Passion, all confus'd;
> Still by [themselves] abus'd, or disabus'd;
> Created half to rise, and half to fall;
> Great lord[s] of all things, yet a prey to all;
> Sole judge[s] of Truth, in endless Error hurl'd:
> The glory, jest, and riddle of the world!
> (*Essay on Man*, ep. 2, lines 13–18)

I never try to argue that the book's charm and staying power derive from any startling originality in Sterne's vision—or even primarily from the effects of his stylistic and structural idiosyncrasies. I believe, rather, it is the essential sanity and humanity of Sterne's humor that give the book its power.

I ask students to compare Sterne's treatment of Walter Shandy's most absurd absurdities with Swift's version of similar behavior in *Gulliver's Travels*, which we also read in the course. At one level, there is no appreciable difference between the silliness and illogic of Walter's comprehensive plans for Tristram's education—the *Tristrapædia* (5: 41–43)—and most of Swift's projectors' schemes in the Academy of Lagado. Walter's plan, grounded on his hypothesis about auxiliary verbs, is surely no less ridiculous, or different in kind, from the plans of Swift's scientists who strive to reverse natural processes, extract sunlight from cucumbers and food from human excrement or develop a new breed of hairless sheep. Yet Swift's irony is relentless and savage. He shows us ourselves flayed, and there is little question that his depiction shockingly alters our appearance for the worse. Sterne gives us our reflection in another kind of mirror. The truths he invites us to see are tempered (not intensified) by his gentler, more balanced humor that mediates and defends: "A WHITE BEAR! Very well. Have I ever seen one? Might I ever have seen one? Am I ever to see one? . . ." (5: 43).

The world Sterne posits is a world only minimally susceptible to reason. Our ability to understand ourselves is intermittent and partial at best. "We live," Tristram cautions,

> amongst riddles and mysteries—the most obvious things, which come in our way, have dark sides, which the quickest sight cannot penetrate into; and even the clearest and most exalted understandings amongst us find ourselves puzzled and at a loss in almost every cranny of nature's works. . . . (4: 17)

In the Shandean universe, the characters' most absurd self-delusions are their attempts to impose reason on a world that can't be reasoned with, their attempts to pretend they know more than they do about their own motives, or that they can consistently control their lives. Yet, the very kind of behavior that aroused Swift's contempt arouses comic sympathy in Sterne. Irrational obsessions keep turning out to be the salvations of his characters, tormenting and preserving them simultaneously.

The Shandys adapt themselves to their situations and to the pressures they face in ways that defy logical analysis. That is part of the point. Toby's fascination with miniaturized war games is comical but also healthy. Nothing makes Toby happier than a trip to the bowling green; no prospect helps so much to heal his wound. As for Walter, his endless hypotheses cause him much pain. They are also his main line of defense against the thousand natural shocks that flesh is heir to. His oratorical eloquence permits him to deal with his son's death; and his wit—producer of much pain and suffering when it is thwarted and unappreciated—compensates and balances: "See here! you rascal, cried my father, pointing to the mule, what you have done!—It was not me, said *Obadiah*.—How do I know that? replied my father" (5: 3). There is more to Walter's manias and obsessions than meets the casual rationalistic eye: "there was a seasoning of wisdom unaccountably mixed up with his strangest whims . . . be wary, Sir, when you imitate him" (5: 42).

Like Samuel Johnson, Sterne assumes a world in which there is much to be endured. Unlike Johnson, however, he assumes that more than a little can be enjoyed as well and that humor can perform a corrective function for both writer and reader. In offering us a comic image of ourselves he seeks not simply to strip us of our illusions. He wants us to see ourselves more clearly and also to be happier with what we see. He wants us to be more aware of the implications of our humanity but more comfortable with them, too. His attitudes are seldom clearer than in his treatment of the uses and misuses of our language, the final paradox I discuss with my students, since a main point in Sterne's work seems to be that language is a wholly inadequate mode of expression.

I have had especially good luck when focusing on Sterne's language. Students unfamiliar with many of the other objects of Sterne's satire (languages and styles they've never read and philosophical positions they've never heard of) feel that his language-centered humor is a game they can play. Much of it derives from Sterne's sense of the comic possibilities of inherent ambiguities, as when Toby earnestly promises the Widow Wadman that she shall put her finger on the very spot where he was wounded. In Sterne's world, the head is opposed to the heart, and words that come from the head confuse, pretend, or deceive. Words from—or to—the heart, the language of the look, the eye, and the gesture, speak volumes. Sterne is notoriously severe on all who use language and style to affect pomposity or parade gravity or who hide behind what today we would term professional jargon. His book contains many parodies of particular forms of "learned wit." Yet there is also an underlying perception of the degree to which our rhetorical practices—our lapses and our pretensions—are linked to motives of which we are sometimes aware—and sometimes not: "To preach, to shew the extent of our reading, or the subtleties of our wit—," says Yorick, "to parade it in the eyes of the vulgar with the beggarly accounts of a little learning, tinseled over with a few words which glitter, but convey little light and less warmth—is . . . dishonest . . ." (4: 26). Dishonest but also extremely common, for, as Sterne well knows, our language reveals us quite eloquently whether we will or no, a fact that leads us directly to Sterne's sexual humor.

My students usually find it hard to believe that Sterne's so-called bawdy has been a matter of controversy. Yet they are quick enough to perceive it. I find that my task is to get them to take it seriously. It is difficult to argue that Sterne has a serious intent behind all his sexual innuendos. I would not want, for instance, to go before a class and defend accounts like that of how Didius "coax'd many of the old licensed matrons in the neighbourhood, to open their faculties afresh, in order to have this whim-wham of his inserted" (1: 7). Eventually, however, I succeed in convincing students that Sterne did indeed use sexual pun and innuendo to make a sophisticated comic statement. For, if some of Sterne's bawdy is simply that—bawdy—much of it is also used comically to remind us of a side of ourselves it has historically been too easy to deny or disguise. Sterne's particular brand of sexual humor makes this postlapsarian side of our nature hard to deny. He knows that what we "may laugh at . . . in the bed-chamber . . . [we will] abuse . . . in the parlour" (7: 20); and—knowing exactly how we are likely to react—he comically dares us to deny (and also dares us to enjoy) the bed-chamber side of our nature. Pointing to the image of Uncle Toby staring at the "bad joint" and refusing to discuss the right and wrong end of a woman, Eugenius exclaims, "Here are two senses." "And here are two roads," Tristram replies, "——a dirty and a clean one,——which shall we take?" (3: 31). When Sterne plies his puns and multiple meanings, he knows exactly which road we will take, and we realize he knows it. He tries to ensure our comfort by consigning all stereotypically prudish responses to the "Madam" whom he baits more or less regularly. But he is master of the art of catching us with our libidinal breeches down and enjoying our humanity, as, for instance, when, with tongue planted firmly in cheek, he declares:

> I define a nose, as follows,——intreating only beforehand, and be-seeching my readers, both male and female, of what age, complexion, and condition soever, for the love of God and their own souls, to guard against the temptations and suggestions of the devil, and suffer him by no art or wile to put any other ideas into their minds, than what I put into my definition.——For by the word *Nose*, throughout all this long chapter of noses, and in every other part of my work, where the word *Nose* occurs,—I declare, by that word I mean a Nose, and nothing more, or less.   (3: 31)

Sterne's sexual humor is as consistent with his comic vision and purpose as are his satiric attacks on false gravity and our other, more intellectual pre-tensions. Let us remember who and what we really are, his book says, and not run mad because of it.

In an opening dedication to Pitt, Sterne says that his book was written "in a bye corner of the kingdom . . . in a constant endeavour to fence against the infirmities of ill health, and other evils of life, by mirth" because, as he writes, "every time a man smiles,—but much more so, when he laughs . . . it adds something to this Fragment of Life." If my classes are at all typical, his book still does have the power to make us laugh and like ourselves a little better than we might otherwise have.

Toby Shandy: Sentiment and the Soldier

Susan Staves

Both *Tristram Shandy* and the history of *Tristram Shandy* are rich in delicious ironies. Now, for many first-time readers, *Tristram* can seem like the eighteenth century's version of *Ulysses* or *Finnegans Wake*: the horribly long, horribly difficult major novel. This view is certainly supported by some recent criticism, including one volume in which we read: ". . . Tristram's way of presenting his life bears comparing with Husserl's central methodological procedure, the phenomenological reduction which consists in exclusion of existential concerns antecedent to reflection" (Swearingen 65). Yet in the first hundred years of its life *Tristram* was a popular book, like Richardson's *Pamela* capable of prompting unauthorized continuations, sequels, and miscellaneous lewd engraftments. Moreover, many earlier readers loved the novel most for its characters of "simplicity," characters like Le Fever, Trim, and—above all—Toby. Indeed, as Sterne entered the popular pantheon of British novelists, his bawdy and his learned wit were apt to be obliterated in favor of tenderer, more simple moments in his writing. Thus, while the entire novel continued to appear in new editions and reprints throughout the eighteenth century, the book most frequently reprinted during the 1780s was *The Beauties of Sterne; Including All His Pathetic Tales, and Most Distinguished Observations on Life, Selected for the Heart of Sensibility* (Howes, *Yorick* 62). The major Romantic critics, who do seem to have read the whole novel, also responded most strongly to these strains of tenderness, simplicity, and pathos. Leigh Hunt, for example, wrote of "exquisite Uncle Toby" as the "prince" of "humour" and declared, "As long as the character of Uncle Toby finds an echo in the heart of man, the heart of man is noble" (qtd. in Howes, *Yorick* 142).

In teaching *Tristram Shandy*, although I do in part follow the usual modern approach of presenting the novel as a text that raises fundamental questions about narrative, I confront its strains of tenderness and simplicity as well. The tenderness and simplicity can be embarrassing, both to me and to students. But I am also trying to help students become decent human beings, and even the most intellectual and ironic among us today do come upon moments when tenderness and simplicity are the only appropriate human responses. Moreover, as I explore with my students, sentiment in the eighteenth century and now had and has both constructive social and political uses and real dangers.

My presentation of *Tristram Shandy* insists that the novel is not a modernist sport mysteriously cropping up in the eighteenth century. I emphasize ways in which Sterne is more intelligible in the literary and intellectual contexts provided by the major writers of the period students know from a survey like that offered by the *Oxford Anthology of English Literature*: Pope,

Fielding, Goldsmith, Johnson, and Gibbon. The character of Toby, I suggest, offers some useful, if at first surprising, ways to relate Sterne to his contemporaries. Since, in fact, *Tristram Shandy* is an extraordinarily selective representation of the world of the 1760s, comparison with these other texts and some discussion of the history of the period highlight for students the nature of that selectivity and allow them to consider whether or not it is troubling.

Toby is a hero of goodness at a historical moment when goodness was coming to be defined as the antithesis of greatness. Our narrator Tristram's enthusiastic blessing of Toby conveniently points to some of the essential elements of this character of goodness:

> Peace and comfort rest for evermore upon thy head!—Thou envied'st no man's comforts,——insulted'st no man's opinions.——Thou blackened'st no man's character,——devoured'st no man's bread: gently with faithful *Trim* behind thee, didst thou amble round the little circle of thy pleasures, jostling no creature in thy way;——for each one's service, thou hadst a tear,——for each man's need, thou hadst a shilling. (3: 34)

The good man here contemplated is good by nature, not by a triumph of repression; devoid of traditional aristocratic magnificence, pride, and aggression; tender and benevolent toward others, not competitive. Far from aspiring to great deeds, public power, or fame, he is content with life in a narrowly circumscribed private sphere.

Greatness, indeed, in the mid-eighteenth century was apt to be attacked as inferior to humble goodness. Greatness was an aristocratic and a pagan ideal, goodness an ideal perhaps more appropriate for Christians and for men and women of the middling sort. Thus, Fielding in *The Life of Mr. Jonathan Wild the Great* (1743) draws a stark contrast between the satirized Jonathan, who aspires to follow Alexander and attain greatness, and Mr. Thomas Heartfree, the bourgeois merchant, "good-natured, friendly, and generous to a great excess" (52; bk. 2, ch. 1). Perhaps the most moving novelistic incarnation of the new type of good-man hero, despite some minor foibles and vanities, is Goldsmith's Vicar of Wakefield (1766). The Vicar's candor, forgiveness, and charity impress when he instantly avows the loss of his fortune, knowing the admission will injure his family; when he begs the Wilmots' forgiveness for the butler who has duped and embarrassed him; and when he sets off to rescue his seduced daughter and then receives her lovingly into his arms.

Eighteenth-century writers were more aware than we are that such celebrations of humble goodness risked bathos. Prophetically, Pope had warned in *Peri Bathous* that bathos was becoming the characteristic trope of modern literature. Greatness and seriousness having earlier been associated with the grand and the large, it was—and probably still is—hard to take seriously a supposedly virtuous person like Uncle Toby said to "amble round the little circle" of his pleasures, jostling no creature in his way. No matter how morally correct Fielding's H. Scriblerus Secundus may be to insist that greatness must be a matter of spiritual quality only, not of physical prowess and size, we have to laugh when he cites Aristotle to defend the reasonableness of a tragedy with a hero, Tom Thumb, so physically diminutive that he dies swallowed by a cow. Hardly any eighteenth-century texts are able to celebrate private goodness and simplicity without either sinking into occasional bathos or using irony to surround purer sentiment so as to achieve some distance from it—the latter, of course, being Sterne's characteristic solution. One of the very few texts that both eschew irony and avoid bathos in praising humble goodness is Johnson's brilliant "On the Death of Dr. Robert Levet" (1783):

> Yet still he fills affection's eye,
>   Obscurely wise, and coarsely kind;
> Nor, letter'd arrogance, deny
>   Thy praise to merit unrefin'd.
>
> . . . .
>
> His virtues walk'd their narrow round,
>   Nor made a pause, nor left a void;
> And sure th' Eternal Master found
>   The single talent well employ'd.   (*Poems* 233–34)

Just as Johnson emphatically recognizes that "obscure wisdom" and "coarse kindness" are paradoxical, so also does virtue limited to a "narrow round" still seem paradoxical to him.

While Sterne does often develop refined ironies to avoid bathos, at crucial points he refuses to ironize Toby's goodness or to permit the laughter of superiority at Toby's expense. Thus, although the narrator provides a protracted account of Toby's assembling a wooing costume from the tattered remnants of his uniform and wig dredged up from his old campaign trunk and although he first entertains the hypothesis that the splenetic might smile at the resulting spectacle, he then firmly reverses field:

> Such it was——or rather such would it have seem'd upon any other brow; but the sweet look of goodness which sat upon my uncle Toby's, assimulated every thing around it so sovereignly to itself, and Nature had moreover wrote GENTLEMAN with so fair a hand in every line of

his countenance, that even his tarnish'd gold-laced hat and huge cockade of flimsy taffeta became him; and though not worth a button in themselves, yet the moment my uncle Toby put them on, they became serious objects, and altogether seem'd to have been picked up by the hand of Science to set him off to advantage.   (9: 2)

The comedy does not diminish the sentiment, nor does the sentiment annihilate the comedy. Contemporaries commented on the oddity of a reading experience that so suddenly oscillates between feeling states conventionally thought mutually exclusive. The *Critical Review* observed in 1762: "The author has contrived to make us laugh at the ludicrous pecularity of Toby, even while we are weeping with tender approbation at his goodness of heart" (qtd. in Tave 225).

Mid-eighteenth century celebrations of goodness, while sometimes bathetic and in many ways problematic, did, I argue, help effect positive social changes. New charities were created to serve unfortunate foundlings, poor children, prostitutes, and slaves (D. Davis; D. Owen; McClure). As a clergyman, Sterne in person applied his rhetorical art for city charity schools that maintained and educated poor children, inspiring a collection of sixty-four pounds for their benefit (Cross, *Life and Times* 90–91). He asked his congregation to imagine that they could see a "disconsolate widow" in "some mournful cottage, where poverty and affliction reign together" and that they could hear her tearful lament "over the infant she knows not how to succour;—'O my child, thou art now left exposed to a wide and vicious world, too full of snares and temptations for thy tender and unpractised age'" ("Case of Elijah" 63). Characteristically, also, Sterne responded to a fan letter from one Ignatius Sancho, a former slave who was touched at the pity for slaves Sterne had expressed in a published sermon. Sterne wrote to Sancho that he was already at work on a "tender tale of the sorrows of a friendless poor negro-girl" (for *Tristram Shandy* 9: 6)—"and my eyes had scarse done smarting with it, when your Letter of recommendation in behalf of so many of her brethren and sisters, came to me——but why *her brethren*?—or your's, Sancho! any more than mine!" (*Letters* 286).

Uncle Toby himself, of course, is neither a clergyman nor a founder nor even a prominent supporter of public charities. That, instead, Toby has had an actual military career as Captain Shandy, shivering in the Irish trenches during King William's wars, is one of Sterne's most profound jokes. What are we supposed to make of the wild incongruity between the character of an English army captain in wartime and the character of the retired suburban gentleman so pacific and tender he refuses to injure a fly? Soldiers, especially common soldiers but officers too, had deservedly shady reputations for brutality and lechery in the Restoration and eighteenth century. Hence the

English horror of a standing army and the American insistence on a Bill of Rights prohibiting the quartering of troops on civilians. Yet the most prestigious classical heroes were military men, and all eighteenth-century gentlemen were educated with the models of Achilles, Hector, Aeneas, and Caesar constantly before them.

Sterne both confronts and avoids fundamental contradictions in eighteenth-century ideas about the usefulness and desirability of military men. He presents his version of the new masculine character—the man of feeling purged of traditional heroic violence, aggression, and sexuality—in the guise of the most stereotypical old hero, the soldier. We are treated to a childhood memory close to the origins of Toby's own efforts to reconcile these contradictions, his memory of his schoolboy responses to *The Iliad*:

> When we read over the siege of *Troy* [the adult Toby says to Walter], . . . was I not as much concerned for the destruction of the *Greeks* and *Trojans* as any boy of the whole school? Had I not three strokes of a ferula given me, two on my right hand and one on my left, for calling *Helena* a bitch for it? Did any one of you shed more tears for *Hector?* And when king *Priam* came to the camp to beg his body, and returned weeping back to *Troy* without it,—you know, brother, I could not eat my dinner.———
>
> ———Did that bespeak me cruel? Or because, brother *Shandy*, my blood flew out into the camp, and my heart panted for war,—was it a proof it could not ache for the distresses of war too?   (6: 32)

Toby's "apologetical oration" in which this childhood memory is embedded appears to be offered by Toby and accepted by Walter as a justification of Toby's regret about the Peace of Utrecht (which brought an end to the War of the Spanish Succession) and a justification of Toby's own military career. His oration contains a remarkable rhetorical question:

> For what is war? what is it, *Yorick*, when fought as ours has been, upon principles of *liberty*, and upon principles of *honour*———what is it, but the getting together of quiet and harmless people, with their swords in their hands, to keep the ambitious and the turbulent within bounds?   (6: 32)

Some students decide that Sterne must have meant to satirize the folly of Toby in this chapter, but such a reading seems to me to ignore other evidence that Sterne as he wrote *Tristram Shandy* shared in the common patriotism and pride of the English over their successes in the Seven Years' War, evidence nicely laid out by Wolfgang Zach.

Nor is it surprising that Sterne should have allowed himself to share in some of the enthusiasm over English success in the Seven Years' War. Expensive as that war was, English military successes on the Continent, in America and Canada, in the West Indies and Africa, and in India were in themselves remarkable accomplishments; moreover, they achieved economic and territorial gains that were crucial in what Stephen Baxter calls "England's rise to greatness" (Baxter; J. Owen 82–93, 126–27). Earlier in the acquisition of empire, Sterne's own father had been a soldier who died young (of a fever) in Jamaica in 1731, where he had been sent when troops were used to help planters deal with rebellious slaves (Cash, *Sterne: Early and Middle Years* 37–39). In the period of the Seven Years' War, English successes in the field aroused patriotic enthusiasms in what might at first seem surprising quarters. Despite his sickly childhood, the young Edward Gibbon volunteered to become an officer in the militia, served as a captain from May 1760 to December 1762, and even tried to become a regular army officer (Craddock 141–64). Like Toby, Gibbon recalled boyhood reading of *The Iliad* (in Pope's translation), recounting how he "tasted the new emotions of terror and pity" reading of the death of Hector and how he "seriously disputed" with his aunt "on the vices and virtues of the heroes of the Trojan war" (Gibbon 61–62). While he was a militia captain, Gibbon spent twenty-one weeks going through the books of *The Iliad* in Greek. "A youth of any spirit," he wrote, "is fired even by the play of arms . . ." (134). And although Gibbon at times found his military service boring and disagreeable, even as the mature author of *The Decline and Fall of the Roman Empire* he still insisted, "my principal obligation to the militia was the making me an Englishman and a soldier" (133).

So, while relishing the comic incongruities between Toby's pacific goodness and his military enthusiasm, Sterne, like almost all his contemporaries, avoided pressing such contradictions as far as they might have been pressed. One of the later continuations of *Tristram*, Isaac Brandon's *Fragments: In the Manner of Sterne* (1797), reveals how that could have been done. Writing as someone who has "learned to feel" from reading and crying over scenes like that of Toby at Le Fever's bedside, this new chronicler of the Shandy family continues the conversations of the various characters into his own time, recording their ideas about issues in the 1790s. Trim raises questions about the morality of the conquest of India in the name of Christianity. Unwilling to be so critical, Toby instructs him: "It is out of our power, Trim . . . to fathom any heart but our own;—it may arise from goodness of intent—and generosity of feeling—as they conceive the light of the Gospel, Trim, as the *only light of happiness*." Trim responds by telling a story he has heard from a brother soldier, one who served in Bengal, about how a quiet Indian landowner had his house and fields forcibly taken from him by the English and then had to watch his family starve, one by one. Three million other Indians are said to have met the same fate. "I would rather have been the Gentoo, Trim—said my uncle Toby—with his starving family about him——than one who had put his profits in his purse, at the expense of the life of a fellow creature" (76). But, of course, when Sterne himself represented Toby at the siege of Limerick, he presented only the sufferings of Toby and Trim, not the sufferings of the native Irish. Similarly, when our pity is asked for the countless old soldier victims of English sentimental fiction, the old soldiers are represented, but the battles they have fought— the battles of empire beyond England itself—and those who have suffered at their hands are not normally represented either. Like *Tristram Shandy* itself, later eighteenth-century comedy and fiction of this age of empire are primarily domestic. Money, like sugar from the West Indies and tea from India, is mysteriously produced from beyond the seas, but soldiers, plantation owners, and other expatriates quickly learned that those at home preferred not to hear the stories of exactly how. Sentiment could be and sometimes was and is cultivated to produce practical ameliorations in the lives of the poor or the enslaved. But I ask my own privileged American students to consider whether sentiment did not and does not all too often also become yet another luxury of the privileged, an item of conspicuous consumption, a sweet feeling to go along with sweet tea?

Sterne and His Early Critics: The Outsider

Sophia B. Blaydes

Students of literature sometimes encounter critical responses to a work that are subsequently reversed by moral responses to its author. Examples abound in survey courses of Restoration and eighteenth-century literature, especially if the readings begin in 1660, end in 1798, and include Laurence Sterne's *Tristram Shandy*. A study of Sterne and his work enables students to examine the critical values of Sterne's society through its aesthetic or literary responses to *Tristram Shandy* and to examine its moral values through its response to Sterne himself. Students' discoveries of the potential differences between literary aesthetics and social ethics will enrich their understanding of the effect of criticism and reputation on writers and their work.

Lest an examination of Sterne's reputation and of criticism of the novel overshadow discussion of *Tristram Shandy* as literature, other writers and works in the course can be used to prepare students for this approach, just as the lessons from Sterne and his novel can become further preparation for writers that follow in the syllabus. For example, the class might consider Jonathan Swift's *Tale of a Tub* (1704) and Samuel Richardson's *Pamela* (1740) not only as literature but also as works that are significant in the history of a developing genre, since neither forces rigidities of structure or tone. Subsequent writers, Sterne among them, could experiment without censure and earn their places in literary history. Similarly, the contradiction between Sterne the clergyman and Sterne the master of double entendres may recall John Wilmot, Earl of Rochester (1648–80), the jester whose satire, philosophy, and dissipation were confounded by his deathbed repentance. The poetry and life of Bernard de Mandeville (1670–1733), the Dutch doctor, and the many volumes of Margaret Lucas Cavendish, duchess of Newcastle (1623?–73), highlight the problems of the outsider, which was Sterne's condition after he became a celebrated writer and a notorious clergyman. Unlike Sterne, Mandeville began as an outsider who dared to mock everyone, especially altruists. Unlike Mandeville, the duchess became an outsider when she wrote poetry, philosophy, drama, and biography and then published it all, trespassing on the male's prerogative. Later in the survey, Sterne and his work might emphasize the dilemma of writers such as Christopher Smart (1722–63), an outsider whose enthusiasm and madness obscured his achievement.

Each of the writers and their works exemplifies some of the problems of aesthetics, reputation, and achievement that confronted Sterne. Like Sterne, Swift and Richardson experimented with form and narrative, developing their own versions of a genre; like Sterne, Rochester shocked society and then derided it, until he repented at his death; Mandeville and the duchess, like Sterne, reinforced their isolation, Mandeville through his caustic satire and the duchess through her ambition and her decision to publish her work during her lifetime; and like Sterne, Smart was charged with enthusiasm, leaving him pitied and his poetry disdained until the twentieth century. By their places in literary history, each of the figures becomes a frame of reference for students as they trace social and aesthetic attitudes that are important to a study of Sterne, his art and life, and his achievement.

Such a biographical and critical approach to *Tristram Shandy* and Sterne emphasizes conditions and qualities that have attracted readers over the centuries: the eccentricity of the novel and the identification of Sterne as an outsider and a madman. The approach also enables the student to consider critical standards applied during the Restoration and eighteenth century, to question them, and, perhaps, to question those applied today. Fortunately, Alan B. Howes has made such an approach available to instructors of *Tristram Shandy* by gathering the necessary contemporary responses in his volume for the Critical Heritage Series.

The reception of *Tristram Shandy* and its author began in 1759 at a high point, with most critics celebrating its wit and invention. The reactions to the first two volumes did not include criticism of Sterne since the author was ostensibly Tristram himself. In an unsigned review, attributed to William Kenrick of the *Monthly Review*, the book's first two volumes and the author, Mr. Shandy, are praised (qtd. in Howes 46–48). Accepting the innovation of the novel in process, the reviewer applauds Shandy's intention "of giving the world two such volumes every year, during the remainder of his life." Yet, he is guarded about Shandy's digressions. He writes:

> [T]o say the truth, we should, for our own parts, be sorry to lose him in that manner [i.e., before he has finished his story]; as we have no reason to think that we shall not be very willing to accompany him to the end of his tale, notwithstanding all his denunciations of prolixity. . . . we have no objection to his telling his story his own way. . . .

The reviewer upholds the writer's freedom of invention: "Every Author, as the present justly observes, has a way of his own, in bringing his points to bear; and every man to his own taste." In particular the reviewer approves the author's decision to include the "excellent moral sermon, into a work of this nature (by which expedient, it will probably be read by many who would peruse a sermon in no other form). . . ." Faulting the "affectation of being immoderately witty," the reviewer excuses it quickly by suggesting it is "perhaps the Author's *manner*." The review concludes with high praise:

> On the whole, we will venture to recommend Mr. Tristram Shandy as a writer infinitely more ingenious and entertaining than any other

of the present race of novelists. His characters are striking and singular, his observations shrewd and pertinent; and, making a few exceptions, his humour is easy and genuine.

More guarded than Kenrick, the reviewer for the *Critical Review* called the first volumes "a humorous performance," but he admits he is "unable to convey any distinct ideas" to his readers and refers them "to the work itself, desiring they will suspend their judgment till they have dipt into the second volume" (qtd. in Howes 52). The *London Magazine*, however, adopted the Shandean style to praise the work, saying that the novel would "be read and admir'd,—Admir'd! by whom? Why, Sir, by the best, if not the most numerous class of mankind" (qtd. in Howes 53). Only the reviewer for the *Royal Female Magazine* hinted at the harsher criticism that would come to the novel and its author, but even here criticism was offered with some praise. According to the reviewer, the novel

> affects (and not unsuccessfully) to please, by a contempt of all the rules observed in other writings, and therefore cannot justly have its merit measured by them. It were to be wished though, that the wantonness of the author's wit had been tempered with a little more regard to delicacy, throughout the greatest part of his work.   (qtd. in Howes 53)

In this brief survey of the critical response to the work's first two volumes, students should also be made aware of the rash of imitations that followed their publication. If imitation is the sincerest form of flattery, then *Tristram Shandy* was admired indeed. Several of these imitations are available in the Garland reprint series called *Sterneiana*, and they are well worth introducing to students. The urge to imitate Sterne's style was the initial reaction of many readers in his own day and probably remains so today. Certainly a glance through any one of the imitations can demonstrate to students just how difficult Sterne's "easy" style is to accomplish, and just how complicated an affair it is to write as if one had no design at all in one's head.

Between volumes 1 and 2 (1760) and the next installment of volumes 3 and 4 (1761), three new editions of the first two volumes were published and so, too, was *The Sermons of Mr. Yorick*. While the multiple editions testify to the popularity of the novel, the publication of *The Sermons* marks the shift in Sterne's reputation. Students might find that a brief look at *The Sermons* and Sterne's preface to the collection is helpful in understanding the collapse of Sterne's critical reputation.

In May, the *Monthly Review* begins its criticisms of *The Sermons*, warning its readers that "[the manner of publishing] these sermons . . . [is] the greatest outrage against Sense and Decency, that has been offered since the first establishment of Christianity—an outrage which would scarce have been tolerated even in the days of paganism" (qtd. in Howes 77). The headnote identifies the title and author of the book: "*The Sermons of Mr. Yorick— Or, Sermons by* Laurence Sterne, A.M. Prebendary of York, and Vicar of Sutton on the Forest, and of Stillington near York." Responding to that, the reviewer continues (in a passage omitted by Howes):

> [H]ad his *first* title-page *only* appeared, we might have had the sat-isfaction to have supposed, that some licentious Layman had presumed to publish these Discourses, under this assumed character, as a ridicule on Religion. But what shall we say to the *second* title-page, in which the *Reverend* and *dignified* Author does not scruple to avow his real name. . . .   (Ruffhead and Rose 422–23)

Then, perhaps for the first time in print, Sterne is criticized for writing *Tristram Shandy*, publishing *The Sermons*, and professing to be a minister:

> Is it possible that a man of such wit and understanding as our Author possesses, should have so little decency and discretion? How can he suppose that the *second title-page* will ease people's minds? Will it not rather disturb them the more, to find a Dignitary of the Church so lost to virtue, and so insensible of shame, as openly to acknowledge himself the Author of so indelicate a Novel; and what is still worse, to use it as a recommendation of works which he publishes in his sacred character.   (Ruffhead and Rose 423)

Paradoxically, the review concludes with a tribute; however, Howes sug-gests that Owen Ruffhead wrote the first portion and William Rose wrote the last two sentences that praise the sermons for their "ease, purity, and elegance" (77).

During the next year, the mixed reception continues, both sides finding strength for their positions in subsequent volumes of the novel and, perhaps more significantly, in explanations and challenges by Sterne himself. Whether students look in Sterne's letters or in the novel itself, they can find ample fuel for the controversy that raged over the clergyman's lack of decorum, his disregard for his clerical function, and his licentious writing and behavior (see Howes 108–18, 135–37). It no longer mattered that his satire was motivated by good intentions: to attack the weak sciences, to satirize ex-tremes of behavior and idea, and, in short, to do good by ridiculing (*Letters* 74, 88–91). By the time his later volumes were read and reviewed, Sterne suffered because more readers found more that was reprehensible in his book. His extended passage on noses, for example, might have amused those who enjoyed satires on learned "blockheads," as Sterne called them (*Letters*

126), but it also upset many who found the extended, and finally graphic, double entendre more than they could accept from a clergyman.

Students may easily see how the critical response changed if they follow its impact on Sterne. By June 1761, Sterne had reached a point where few critics defended him or his work; he writes in a letter, "I care not a curse for the critics" (*Letters* 140). On 21 September 1761, he writes to a friend: "I am scribbling away at my Tristram. These two volumes [5 and 6] are, I think the best.—I shall write as long as I live, 'tis, in fact, my hobby-horse: and so much am I delighted with my uncle Toby's imaginary character, that I am become an enthusiast" (*Letters* 143). The strictures of society, the demands of his profession, and the advice of his friends did not restrain Sterne from continuing *Tristram Shandy* almost to his death. He incorporated in the novel his travel notes and attacks on his critics. On 9 November 1762, Sterne was able to write: "I . . . sport much with my uncle Toby in the volume I am now fabricating for the laughing part of the world—for the melancholy part of it, I have nothing but my prayers—so God help them" (*Letters* 189). Yet, when the prayer was given, Sterne was ill and forced to travel from London to Italy and France.

For the rest of his life, Sterne was followed by criticisms of *Tristram Shandy*'s indecency, its grossness, and its obscenity, all compounded by the writer's clerical collar. Although there are many illustrations, students might profitably read the critical commentary in just one or two of the periodicals. For example, the *Universal Magazine of Knowledge and Pleasure* reviewed volumes 3 and 4 of *Tristram Shandy* in 1761 after Sterne had published his sermons. The review disparages *Tristram Shandy* for its "indecent expressions" and then continues:

> Indecent! did I say? Nay, even downright gross and obscene expressions are frequently to be met with throughout the book. . . . It is generally observable that the playhouses are most crouded, when any thing smutty is to be brought on the stage; and the reverend author of this ingenious performance has no doubt used this method as the most effectual, for making it as universally acceptable as possible. But how far it is excusable in any author, especially one who wears the gown, to gratify and promote a prevailing corrupted taste, either directly or indirectly, let himself and the world judge.   (Rev. 189–90)

The *Monthly Review* also commented again on the novel after volumes 3 and 4 were published that spring. Running fifteen pages, the article explains the reviewer's changed assessment of the novel:

> [I]t is our duty, as Reviewers, to examine books, abstracted from any regard to their Author. But this rule is not without exception: for where

a Writer is publicly known, by his own acknowledgement, it then becomes a part of our duty, to animadvert on any flagrant impropriety of character. What would be venial in the farcical . . . would be highly reprehensible from the pen of a Divine. In short, there is a certain faculty called *Discretion*, which reasonable men will ever esteem; tho' you, the arch *Prebend* Mr. *Yorick*, alias *Tristram Shandy*, have done all in your power to laugh it out of fashion.   (qtd. in Howes 120)

Students can now begin to understand that these early views of Sterne's works influenced critical appraisals for years, undermining almost all future readings of the novel. The lesson of Sterne and his great novel is a difficult one for students to accept. It is easy to find that Sterne was wronged and, therefore, that the age and its critical acumen were faulty, somehow corrupted by an archaic and prudish aesthetic code. The age, after all, disdained the novel's originality after they discovered that a clergyman wrote it. The age openly criticized the novel not because of its strengths or weaknesses but, rather, because of the profession of its writer. The critics insisted that Sterne's profession did not permit him to be eccentric, enthusiastic, licentious, or satiric. In view of the eighteenth century's critical stance, one can simply argue that subsequent ages were deprived of a clear view of Sterne and his novel.

However, from the examples of Rochester, Mandeville, Newcastle, and Smart, outsiders whose works were also judged for the wrong reasons, students may more judiciously place the lot of Sterne in perspective and learn that those who are closest to writers and their works may not be the best critics. Conversely, it would also be unfortunate if students were to leave the study of Sterne with the notion that we are today better critics because we are wiser, more perceptive, and less bound by foolish notions of morality, decorum, and literature. Lest they assume that they are better than those of other ages, students might benefit from comparable lessons of their own time. Teachers might pose for them some questions that would bring the dilemma closer, citing conflicts society has had with writers because of the writers' behavior, beliefs, or professions and not because of the quality or merit of the work. They might ask, for example: "How would you assess the work of a writer who was a traitor during World War II and actively sought the defeat of the Allied forces in Italy?" Ezra Pound presented the mid-twentieth-century American literary establishment with one of its most anguished and embarrassing moments when it seized an award it had bestowed on Pound for his poetic achievement. He won the award for his poetry; he lost it for his politics.

Teachers might ask students about a writer of lesser stature, perhaps a writer of popular novels. For example, they could ask: "How would you assess the work of a priest who writes of problems in the Roman Catholic church, especially the sexuality of those who have taken vows of celibacy?" Andrew Greeley, a Roman Catholic priest who has published many best-selling novels, must respond to criticism within and without the church, facing problems not unlike those that confronted Sterne. Other writers may come to mind who, for reasons other than aesthetic, have been judged harshly and discarded. How should we judge their work? Can we separate their lives from their achievement?

A study of Sterne and his novel will pose questions for students that go beyond the period and touch us all today, questions of the outsider, the enthusiast, and the clergyman. They place in perspective a major problem of literary criticism: To what extent is literary criticism independent of social pressures? There are no easy answers, but there are obviously many examples that raise issues worth considering in a course that includes Laurence Sterne and his work *Tristram Shandy*.

Stories That Should Be True?
Locke, Sterne, and *Tristram Shandy*

Brian McCrea

I will embarrass neither the professor who gave the lecture nor the institution of higher education at which I heard it by naming them—particularly since, in many ways, it was a fine lecture. The subject was the personality of Laurence Sterne, and the goal was to prepare twenty undergraduates to read *Tristram Shandy*, a book that, at first glance, struck me and others as dishearteningly long and annoyingly nonsensical. By the lecture's end, however, I couldn't wait to get at the text. And who wouldn't have been eager to read a book by a man who typified the secularization of the church, by a philanderer and a bawd who was also a priest? We heard John Croft's story about Sterne's leaving his congregation in the lurch while he went partridge hunting. We heard about John Hall-Stevenson and Crazy Castle, and we wondered in what bizarre rites Sterne might have joined with his fellow Demoniacks. And then we heard the last and greatest story, the story that left us laughing so hard that tears came to our eyes even as the bell rang (the lecture was perfectly timed, too): Sterne took as the text for a sermon on the day after his wedding Luke 5.5, "Master, we toiled all night and took nothing."

Of course, the last story is not true, could not be true. Nor are many of the other stories that have given color to studies of Sterne since the nineteenth century, particularly those taken from the suspect account of Croft (Cash, *Laurence Sterne: Early and Middle Years* 85, xx, 145). And yet, as a graduate student, when I discovered the falsity of the story, I felt no diminution in my respect for the teacher who had misled me. Even if he was many years behind in his scholarship, he had sparked my interest. Even if his facts were wrong, he had given us all a sense of Sterne that was intriguing and compelling. The story was so good that I wished it could be true, even while Martin C. Battestin, via Arthur H. Cash, was telling me it was not.

I do not want to argue here for tergiversation. If we know the story about Sterne's postwedding sermon to be false, then we should not retail it, unqualified, to our students. I do want to suggest, however, that the lecture I heard twenty years ago anticipated a major predicament that teachers of Sterne face today and will continue to face: the problem of Sterne's indebtedness (or lack thereof) to the philosophy of John Locke, particularly to his *Essay concerning Human Understanding*. Academic critics have debated for over thirty years the nature and extent of that debt.[1] I do not chart the course of that debate here, but I do note that Kenneth MacLean's once widely accepted attribution of the distinctive formal features of *Tristram*

Shandy to Sterne's Lockeanism—to his lifelong study of the *Essay*—has been sharply challenged. Recent scholars who want to defend this view have, by and large, fought a rearguard action, admitting, for example, that the "principle of the 'association of ideas' which had been thought to account for the erratic structure of the novel, has no prominence in Locke" but then claiming that Sterne is "elaborating an idea implicit in Locke" (Battestin 313–14). Peter Briggs, who also examines the nexus, frankly reminds us, nevertheless, that Sterne wrote most of *Tristram Shandy* in the early 1760s—that is, seventy years after the publication of the *Essay*—and that Sterne was a mere child during the early decades of the eighteenth century when the *Essay* was most discussed and celebrated (495).

We may wonder why so many scholars for so many years have sought to establish a Locke-Sterne connection. I suspect the connection has been imposed on generations of students precisely because it makes it so easy to teach *Tristram Shandy*. It should be true, even if it is not. By taking Sterne to be a Lockean, instructors can produce a full, rich, and satisfying inter-pretation of his otherwise troubling text. But the very sensibleness of the Lockean reading ultimately argues against it; Sterne's motto was, after all, "*Vive la bagatelle.*" Teachers of Sterne, then, must balance the advantages of this reading against doubts that it is true.

Locke helps teachers of Sterne because, once they overemphasize Locke's analysis of the association of ideas (pace Cash, "Lockean Psychology" 125–35), they have found an explanation for both Sterne's comedy and his in-novative plotting. With a distorted version of Locke's *Essay* in place, a fairly standard classroom presentation of *Tristram Shandy* might run like this: Locke's attack on "innate ideas" renders nature subjective and private, not objective and public. Sterne's Tristram, by offering "a history-book . . . of what passes in a man's own mind" (2: 2), provides the first literary portrayal of this new subjectivism. The great theme of the novel is solipsism—the inability of individuals to get outside themselves, to escape their particular associational patterns, to dismount from their hobbyhorses. The hobbyhorse, like the subjectivism it figures, is, however, a mixed blessing. It maims and limits characters, even as it solaces and frees them. Once instructors make the hobbyhorse carry the heavy philosophical weight of associationism, they also clear the way for a reassuring explication of the details of the text. In the lecture I heard as an undergraduate, much was made of the ways in which the hobbyhorses of Walter, Slop, and, most important, Toby harm Tristram. Suddenly, the particulars of the book, instead of being multifarious and confusing, became thematically pointed. It mattered very much that Tristram's involuntary circumcision was owing to Toby's needing window weights for his military toys. Even the most benevolently ridden of hob-byhorses, we could all see, was still selfish.

Of course, Toby's hobbyhorse also saves his life. Without their obsessions, Walter, Toby, even Tristram have nothing. Their hobbyhorses allow them to objectify and place at a distance frightening and complex experiences. Sterne, conveniently placed at the middle of the eighteenth century, can be described as simultaneously relying on and worrying about Locke's epistemology. *Tristram Shandy* becomes a convenient (in the sense of easily identifiable) watershed between the traditional and the modern, between neoclassicism and Romanticism.

Tristram Shandy, perhaps before all else, is a funny book. Because most of Sterne's jokes depend on the misunderstandings to which different associations give rise ("You shall see the very place, Madam; said my uncle Toby" [9: 20]), even his humor becomes philosophical once the instructor and student can feel that they are fitting even the smallest parts (the jokes) into a puzzle already solved—an immensely satisfying experience for both. Even Sterne's bawdy can be seen as one way of dealing with the failures of communication caused by different associational patterns. Here is something to which we all, however shamefacedly, respond. Much the same holds for Sterne's treatment of impotency, with which all the males in the Shandy family, including the bull, seem to be afflicted. While sexual intercourse is a form of communication, an escape from the solipsistic self, the route is blocked for these characters.

Besides helping us to a satisfying account of Sterne's comedy and sexual innuendos, Locke's *Essay* also can rationalize Sterne's plot. Locke's notion of duration, his subjectivization of time, allows a work to be "digressive, and . . . progressive too,—and at the same time" (1: 22). Sterne portrays the passage of time in at least three different ways—two of which depart from standard chronology. In volume 4, chapters 9–13, he takes Toby and Walter one step up a stairway. He breaks the act into four parts (chs. 9–12), showing that what is important in an event is not the chronology but the psychological preoccupations of the characters. The effect here anticipates the cinematic. Tristram slows down the action, stops it, even reverses it. Time briefly seems pliable, subject to the author's control. Throughout these chapters, however, he suggests that the exigencies of standard time persist: "Is it not a shame to make two chapters of what passed in going down one pair of stairs? for we are got no farther yet than to the first landing . . ." (4: 10). In chapter 13 this anxiety culminates in a meditation on the intractability of time. Walter cannot write the *Tristrapædia* fast enough to keep up with his growing son; Tristram, beginning his fourth volume, has "three hundred and sixty-four days more life to write just now, than when I first set out. . . ." Even as Tristram stops his action and calls attention to his deliberate fragmentation and disruption of the event, he also reveals his frustration and anxiety before the superior power of bare chronological time. As with the hobbyhorse, subjectivism (as it here manifests itself in the notion of duration) is a mixed blessing. Despair lurks not too far beneath the whimsy of Tristram's aggressively digressive plotting.

Our Lockean reading of Sterne could (and does) go on. Once associationism renders words equivocal, true communication may be possible only through gesture (Trim's falling hat) and touch (Walter and Toby's various embraces). Sterne's turn to sentimentalism is then seen as a response to the problems created by the new subjectivism. At this point, however, if not earlier, the very neatness of the Lockean reading should begin to tell against it. For, as critics from John Traugott (*Tristram* 15) to Melvyn New (*Laurence Sterne* 104–30) point out, Sterne's most direct literary sources are satiric—Rabelais and Swift, for example—rather than sentimental. Reading Sterne as a Lockean, a generation of literary historians have fit him into the transition from classic to Romantic in which sentimental fiction plays an important part. But the neat fit could be made only if the satiric Sterne was suppressed. Similarly, the grounding of Sterne in Locke could take place only if their differences, particularly in the relative values they assign to wit and judgment (New, *Laurence Sterne* 134–38; Briggs 512–13), were suppressed. Locke, whatever the other complexities of his epistemology, celebrated the potentiality of human reason; Sterne, the putative Lockean, spends much time portraying the failures and the limits of human reasoners.

These suppressions perhaps appear most revealingly in Traugott's *Tristram Shandy's World*, which still holds a central place in Sterne studies over thirty years after its publication, and in his introduction to his collection of essays on Sterne for the Twentieth-Century Views series—one of the volumes to which a nonspecialist preparing to teach Sterne will most likely turn. In both books, Traugott makes a complicated double move—one that has worn well in Sterne criticism but that creates temptations for classroom teachers. On the one hand, Traugott is always ready "to lay the ghost of Locke, that spook said to be back of all the strange happenings of Sterne's works." But, on the other hand, Traugott centers both his book and his introduction on Locke, arguing that Locke provides a "foil" for Sterne, that Sterne "admired" Locke and "fairly destroyed" him (*Laurence Sterne* 13, 14). Traugott willingly admits that Sterne's major literary influences were Rabelais, Swift, and Cervantes, but he devotes most of his discussion to the foil, Locke, rather than to the satiric tradition. This detour through Locke allows Traugott and the generation of teachers (like mine) who followed him to place Sterne at the head of a sentimental tradition rather than in the middle (or at the end) of a satiric one. By only mentioning Rabelais and Swift, Traugott can claim of Sterne, "this is the way he defines the fall—as solipsism, and the way he redeems the fallen—by sentimentalism." Sterne's aesthetic, he maintains, "is founded in sentimentality" (*Laurence Sterne* 4,

10). Tristram, despite all his backward glances at Rabelais and the rest, becomes one of us, anticipating the modern protagonist who must escape from the prison house of language through sentiment, sexuality, or both.

Traugott tempts teachers and students alike to pay little attention to his disclaimers about Locke and instead to accent, as he does, the foil. With an obscure and difficult text to teach, the instructor grasps those features that make it relevant to contemporary experience—that make it "modern." Students, on their part, will resist or find uninteresting a discussion of how and why Sterne varies an older tradition, particularly a tradition with which they are not familiar. But all contemporary students (like students in my mid-1960s generation) have heard lectures, seen movies ("What we have here, Luke boy, is a failure to communicate"), listened to pop songs about communication and its difficulties. From their earliest classes in high school they learn about point of view and different but equal versions of reality. They are much readier for a partial, even distorted reading of *Tristram* than for a full one—one that includes Traugott's first move as well as his second.

So it is convenient to follow Traugott and center Sterne criticism on Locke. But is it valid?

The historical evidence for a Locke-Sterne connection is remarkably slight, for all the attention given to the link. Arthur Cash, in his book *Laurence Sterne: The Early and Middle Years*, shows that Sterne's course work in modern philosophy at Cambridge would have given a "strong emphasis to . . . Locke and Newton" and claims that at Cambridge "Plato was pre-eminent among ancient authors, Locke and Newton among modern" (43, 50). But this is hardly powerful evidence in support of Cash's claim that Sterne "read and reread" the *Essay* "[a]ll of his life" (205). When Cash says that the *Essay* "informed all of his [Sterne's] work" (205), we may guess that he is reading back into history from the perspective of recent interpretations of Sterne. Twentieth-century critics have found Sterne to be a Lockean, so a Lockean he must be. Besides occasional specific references to Locke in *Tristram Shandy* (references outnumbered by those to Rabelais and Cervantes), Sterne's only avowal of Locke's influence comes late in his life and arrives through a foreign intermediary. Much has been made, of course, of Sterne's explanation of his originality to Jean-Baptiste Suard, which gives some credit to a lifelong reading of Locke. But Suard's testimony is at second hand—coming, as it does, in his biography by Dominique-Joseph Garat—and it is not entirely relevant to the composition of *Tristram Shandy*. Moreover, Suard was questioning Sterne at the end of his life, a time when Sterne himself was perhaps trying to find order in (impose order on) the vagaries of his career. As a source for Sterne's particular art Locke, even in Suard's account, finishes a distant third to Sterne's personality and to his reading in the Old and New Testaments (Cash 206–07).

Again, I am trying not to resolve the question of Sterne's debt to Locke but, rather, to define an ethical question that all teachers of Sterne should face. What will we do with those now yellowing pages of our lecture on Locke and Sterne—the lecture that we heard in the fifties and sixties and that, if my experience is typical, still works today. Closely scrutinized, the Locke-Sterne connection seems tenuous enough, or, as Traugott himself puts the matter: "To speak of 'philosophy' in a resolutely nonlogical work such as *Tristram Shandy* is of course a strain" (*Tristram* 4). This is particularly so because *Tristram Shandy* is so rich in literary allusion. Sterne's great ambition seems to have been to stand on a par with Cervantes, Rabelais, and Swift—not to redact Locke. Having said all this, however, we still come up hard against the fact that the Sterne-Locke lecture works and that some evidence, in the text and in the biography of Suard, may justify the connection.

My solution takes me back to the story about Sterne's postwedding sermon. On those occasions when I, now the learned professor, taught *Tristram Shandy* or *A Sentimental Journey*, I always felt that my efforts paled in comparison to the lecture I heard as an undergraduate. I knew more about Sterne than my teacher did, but I could not motivate my students as he had motivated me. Finally, about two years ago, I gave my own "personality of Sterne" lecture, used some of the old undergraduate notes, and awakened and energized some previously somnolent students—students who seemed untroubled when I informed them at the opening of our next meeting that the story of the postwedding sermon could not be true. They, like me years before, felt the story should be true. Similarly, teachers of Sterne can and should use Locke, but that use should be admittedly and explicitly heuristic. While we cannot and probably never will substantiate it, the story of a Locke-Sterne connection, like the story of Sterne's sermon, is too good to pass up, too helpful and too informative not to tell.

Having told the story, however, we at some point must bring our students to see that Sterne is not so much "one of us" as he is a child of the Restoration and eighteenth century—a writer who operates within and contributes to a long-standing satiric tradition. This admission, while perhaps initially difficult, is ultimately in the best interest of Sterne and his teachers. For if, in our lectures on Sterne, we use Locke to make him into a modern, then we no longer can argue that he need be read. For all its seeming appeal the solipsism and prison-house-of-language interpretation directs us not to Sterne, but to Joyce, Woolf, and Ford. Like all easy choices—"Give the students what they want, what they can relate to"—the Locke-Sterne link uncorrected is misguided and harmful. As we teach Sterne, we do best (in presenting Locke as in presenting false but funny stories) diligently to distinguish the heuristic from the substantial, to separate stories that should be true from those that are.

NOTES

[1]For a helpful summary of the debate see Battestin 313–14, particularly the summary of Locke's adding his chapter on the association of ideas only as an "afterthought" to the fourth edition. Associationism belongs to much later philosophers, Hume and Hartley, not to Locke.

[2]For two good examples of readings after Traugott that rely heavily on the connection with Locke see Tuveson, "Locke and Sterne," and Anderson; for an unrelenting attack on the idea of Locke's providing a source for Sterne, see Maskell.

Winding Up the Clock:
Introducing *Tristram Shandy*

Michael Raymond

I teach *Tristram Shandy* in several different courses and usually encounter more than the ordinary opposition of undergraduates to a six-hundred-page work written over two hundred years before 1965—the beginning of time as many modern students view things. They rarely hesitate to express their opinions: the work is boring and tiresome, it lacks a story, it's totally confused and confusing. But even more basic is the single most common complaint I hear, although I always use the Work or Watt edition: "How can we be expected to understand a work that is always talking about books we never read and arguments we don't understand?" Translated into more familiar discourse, the problem is how to teach a highly allusive work of literature to students ill-equipped by education and predilection to deal with so evidently an allusive texture. For while it might be argued that other works— *Pamela*, say, or *Tom Jones*—are in their own ways equally allusive, they give every appearance of being accessible to the reader without additional knowledge; *Tristram Shandy*, to the contrary, appears to students on first encounter a baffling experience.

This bafflement provides me with the particular approach I take to Sterne's work, quite different from my approach to almost any other novel we might read in the same course. With *Pamela*, for example, I feel safe in asking students to write a reaction paper, knowing that they will have grasped the essence of Richardson's intentions and interests with only a little prompting from me. This is not a criticism of *Pamela* but simply an observation—the novel remains readily accessible to my undergraduate readers, if not particularly appreciated by them. Concerning *Tristram*, however, I begin by urging them not to react to the work but to solve it (or, more accurately, to solve the sentence or the paragraph they do not immediately grasp); that is, I encourage them to think about the resources of our library as tools to help them understand what they read. I use *Tristram Shandy* to suggest to them the practice of literary scholarship.

This urging toward scholarship, which undergraduates usually associate with graduate school or professorial drudgery, frequently meets with the same resistance as does *Tristram* itself. But there is in problem solving so immediate a sense of reward that this resistance is much easier to overcome than that to the entire work. One example: few eighteenth-century works offer more rewards to the searcher of the *Oxford English Dictionary* or Partridge's *Dictionary of Slang and Unconventional English* than does *Tristram Shandy*. "Hobby-horse" might be the place to start, but the important point to make is about language itself—how words change their meaning, how the *OED*'s "historical principles" try to track that change, how "slang" is particularly slippery and how its thrust often seems to be sexual. It is not possible to discuss these few ideas about language without, rather evidently, exploring some of the central issues in *Tristram Shandy*; the discussion is, however, much more intelligible to students and much better informed when they have done a little library work on their own.

More broadly, students can begin to investigate the literary allusiveness of the text, starting with the annotations of Work or Watt (the other annotated textbook editions available are not as useful). For example, most students will know about Yorick as a "character" in *Hamlet*, but it is important that they look at the particular passage in the play (and discover that only his skull, not his person, appears) in order to engage in a meaningful discussion of Sterne's allusion. Similarly, a note might inform students that Yorick's horse is derived from Cervantes, but a more comprehensive understanding of *Don Quixote* is required to make sense of the portrait of Yorick that Sterne draws in the opening chapters. Clearly I cannot ask my students to read Cervantes and Rabelais and Burton and Montaigne before they come to class the next day, but at the same time it does little good simply to attempt to fill those gaps for them with capsule digests or my own "interpretation," informed as that might be. Rather, students should be allowed to see for themselves that the texts Sterne depended on create a necessary step in the process of interpretation; even if they only read in Rabelais the paragraph that Sterne borrowed in order to tell us his view of polemical divines, they will see that *Tristram Shandy's* meaning has at least something to do with the author's incorporation of other texts, often verbatim, into his own. For teachers who are trying to help students understand a work that seems to be about intellectual creativity and impotence, creating such an awareness is no insignificant achievement.

Within the limits of a small liberal arts college's library, much can be accomplished along the lines I am suggesting, but of course much is out of reach. One solution is to use *Tristram Shandy* to introduce undergraduates to yet another aspect of scholarship—the learned essay. I specify *essay* because the type of scholarship I like to use probably does not appear on most instructors' reading lists. I have always suspected the Twayne series, the collections of essays, and the introductory book-length study, which usually head reserve-reading lists for undergraduates, and indeed I steer my students away from them. I send them instead to Theodore Baird's essay on the time scheme in *Tristram Shandy*, not because of his comments on that time scheme but because of his skillful demonstration of how the discovery of a source can help open a difficult text to interpretation. R. F. Brissenden's essay "Sterne and Painting" is useful for the same reason; having read Brissenden on the painters' scale, one can return to a very particular page in *Tristram* with the strong sense of having solved its meaning—or at least one cannot claim to have no idea what's going on. In short, even within the limited number of journals and scholarly books in a small library (compared to the library of a graduate institution), there are numerous examples of literary scholarship to further literary understanding. Before students can learn to dance to the tunes of modern critical theories, they need to learn something about walking; baffled as they seem to be when they first encounter *Tristram Shandy*, they are particularly receptive to the idea that our understanding of any worthwhile literary text is built through the slow accumulation of knowledge and information. And when students have begun their own process of accumulation, a discussion of the difference between Shandy pedantry and real learning is all the more readily conducted.

The notes to *Tristram Shandy* in the third volume of the Florida Sterne makes my approach at once easier and more difficult. On the one hand, students can, within a single source, discover many of the ways in which they must be informed if they are to begin to understand the work. On the other hand, the availability of so much information in one volume works against my desire to have them ferret out answers for themselves. Still, much remains for them to do. The Florida *Notes* provides sufficient bibliographic data for them to locate sources and to read further in the borrowed materials. Second, they will often find teasing discussions of the allusions, not enough to enable them to "interpret" the passage, but enough to set their minds turning toward a plausible reading. Third, students will note scores of allusions surrounding the ones they were able to spot. This is a humbling experience, but also an enriching one. And finally, students may discover that the connections made by scholars are not very different from those they make, when similar information is available to them. Students who calculate that Mrs. Shandy carried Tristram eight months and not nine will be gratified to see that scholars have learnedly debated over the same observation. Such early gratification has made many a literary scholar out of undergraduate English majors.

Tristram begins his life and opinions with the commonplace notion that the "conditions of conception determine the future of the child" (*Notes* 39); the conditions under which *Tristram Shandy* is introduced to students seem similarly crucial. Like Mrs. Shandy, I believe it is important to wind up the clock, even if other things are happening at the same time. Our students are usually in a great rush—they want to "finish" this work and get on to the next and the next, and then to final exams and then to graduation. Students—as well as their instructors—might profit by taking some time to consider process, in this instance, the process of learning enough to write *Tristram Shandy* or to read it. To pretend that it is a work of immediate accessibility flies in the face of our students' experience. It seems much more appropriate to admit the truth of their first impressions and to show students how the process of scholarly investigation and research can help them over-come intellectual difficulties. To wind the clock in this manner might just create a class more willing to expand their critical approaches, more willing to value scholarship and the library that is central to its practice, more appreciative of the broad, historical liberal arts tradition that has been the outcome of scholarly pursuits in both the arts and the sciences. Careful attention to the initial conception of *Tristram Shandy* can result in a "happy formation" for teachers and students alike.

Pragmatism versus Dogmatism:
The Ideology of *Tristram Shandy*

Donald Greene

Like, I suppose, most readers, I first came to *Tristram Shandy* under the impression that it was sui generis, an amusing curiosity, a sport. Many had earlier expressed that opinion. An anonymous reviewer of 1761 thus accounted for its supposed temporary popularity: "ODDITY was the bait that hooked in the gaping multitude. . . . *Oddity* in the book, which, certainly resembles nothing that ever was, or ever will be, which is without any design moral or immoral, and is no more, indeed, than a combination of notions, facts, and circumstances, that terminate in—*nothing*" (Howes, *Critical Heritage* 134). At least two famous critics, whose judgments I normally respected, likewise dismissed it: Samuel Johnson with "Nothing odd will do long. *Tristram Shandy* did not last" (Boswell 2: 449) and F. R. Leavis as "irresponsible (and nasty) trifling" (2). Many commentators have called attention to Sterne's innumerable borrowings from writers in the tradition of "learned wit"—Rabelais, Montaigne, Burton, Cervantes, Swift—but have arrived at no very definite conclusions about the reasons for such borrowing, except mere amusement.

Only after much time spent in reading and pondering the work, and in trying to interest students in it—willing as the better students were to be amused, they found it difficult to become deeply involved with an oddity that terminated in nothing—did it begin to come together for me. Three related passages seemed to me to provide particularly significant clues, and I have found it most helpful to call attention to them when students first tackle the book.

The first of these is the epigraph, from Epictetus's *Encheiridion*. I give it here transliterated into the Roman alphabet:

> Tarassei tous Anthrōpous ou ta Pragmata,
> alla ta peri tōn Pragmatōn Dogmata.[1]

In editions of the novel it usually has some such translation as "It is not things that disturb men but their judgments about those things." The context is a discussion of death. In good Stoic fashion, Epictetus tells us that death itself is not terrible: it is only our irrational view of it that causes it to perturb us—and no self-respecting Stoic should be perturbed by external things. The passage occurs only a few sentences after the notorious advice, "If you kiss your child, or your wife, [remember] that you kiss a being subject to the accidents of humanity; and thus you will not be disturbed if either of them dies" (260). It is hard to imagine Sterne, or most of his contemporaries, subscribing to this view—the Sterne of Le Fever and the dead ass or Johnson in chapter 18 of *Rasselas* or Fielding in book 4, chapter 8, of *Joseph Andrews* or Voltaire in *Les deux consolés*. Walter Shandy is at his most contemptible when, on receiving news of his son Bobby's death, he launches into an elaborate Stoic oration, in which "the pleasure of the harangue was as *ten*, and the pain of the misfortune but as *five*," and eventually he is "smiling, for he had absolutely forgot my brother *Bobby*" (5: 3). The imperturbability of Johnson's, Fielding's, and Voltaire's would-be Stoics breaks down at the death of a child; Walter's is made of sterner stuff.

If it is impossible to believe that Sterne is telling us, in his epigraph, that his book is designed to inculcate Epictetan (or Walter Shandean) Stoicism, what are we to make of the quotation? The usual translation is no doubt how an Attic Greek might have read it. But by Sterne's time *dogmata* and *pragmata* and their derivatives in other languages had a wide spectrum of connotation. As borrowed by Latin (and English), *dogma* is generally defined as "philosophical tenet" or "doctrine." *Pragmata* at once suggests "practical," and one signification of it given in Liddell and Scott's *Greek-English Lexicon* is "reality"—things as they are. It seems to me that the epigraph will be closer to what Sterne wanted us to read if we give it a more modern rendering: what is needed is pragmatism, not dogmatism; it is not reality that causes most trouble for the human race but far-fetched, thin-spun, rigidly held theories imposed on reality by pride in the human capacity for ratiocination.

This reading places the work squarely in the midst of the great antirationalist, antidogmatic, empiricist tradition that runs from at least the Renaissance (Rabelais, Bacon) through the eighteenth century (Locke, Hume, and beyond). The representatives of this view rejected Aristotelian and scholastic worship of the "divinely bestowed" human *nous* ("reason") and its supposed power to arrive at knowledge by manipulation of words (an exclusive possession of the human race) without resort to observation by the senses (see Greene, *Age*, ch. 3). Walter Shandy is one of the great satiric creations of this tradition, in the same class as Swift's Lagadoan scientists and Voltaire's Pangloss. He is an inveterate syllogizer; he is convinced that "there is a North west passage to the intellectual world; and that the soul of man has shorter ways of going to work, in furnishing itself with knowledge and instruction, than we generally take with it" (5: 42); he believes that there is "a strange kind of magick bias, which good or bad names, as he called them, irresistibly impress'd upon our characters and conduct" (1: 19); he "was a great motive-monger, and consequently a very dangerous person for a man to sit by, either laughing or crying,—for he [like some modern dogmatic psychiatrists] generally knew your motive for doing both, much better than you knew it yourself" (6: 31); "he was systematical, and, like all systematick reasoners, he would move both heaven and earth, and twist and torture every thing in nature to support his hypothesis" (1: 19). Of course, there are many other characters in the work who believe in the magic power of words: Bishop Ernulphus, the lawyers who draw up Mrs. Shandy's marriage settlement, the logicians of Strasburg, the Abbess of Andoüillets and her novice. Students enjoy tracking them down.

Dogmatists like Walter Shandy are still with us, of course, some having much more power to do harm to the human race than he; he is far less dangerous than Swift's Grub-Street Hack, not to mention the dictatorial enforcers of various -isms in twentieth-century Europe and elsewhere. Indeed, Uncle Toby's hobbyhorse, a milder obsessive version of dogmatism —though even for Uncle Toby, " 'Twas not by ideas . . . his life was put in jeopardy by words" (2: 2)[2]—causes more immediate damage to Tristram, effecting his unexpected circumcision through the removal of the counterweight of the window to make cannon for Toby's great model of Namur. "A great MORAL might be picked handsomly out of this," says Tristram (5: 19) —a moral that might dwell not only on Toby's and Trim's ignoring the practical consequences of their passion for lead but also on Walter's being so busy working out, in the *Tristrapædia*, the theory of how best to ensure Tristram's welfare that it does not occur to the father to take a few minutes off to nail down the defective window (5: 26). Walter's chief damage to his son, however, is the burden of the name Tristram, the sad. Not of course that the name in itself has any magic power—there have been quite happy-go-lucky girls named Dolores. But Walter's dogmatic belief in the power of names and his particular dislike of the name Tristram must have communicated itself to the boy. Whatever suspicions his eight-months gestation may arouse, there is no question that Tristram is Walter's son.

The second passage I discuss with students is closely connected to the first. This is simply Tristram's bald statement of what the work is about: "If 'tis wrote against any thing,——'tis wrote, an' please your worships, against the spleen" (4: 22). One at once remembers that Swift (in his poem "The Author upon Himself") called *A Tale of a Tub* a "treatise writ against the spleen" (*Poems* 196). Spleen (or melancholy or neurosis or half a dozen other names) is the creation of needless unhappiness for oneself and those one comes into contact with (see Greene, "From Accidie to Neurosis"). It is a commonplace among Bacon and his followers that the life of the rationalist is emotionally and morally unhealthy. The most famous such denunciation is that of Swift's Aesop in *The Battle of the Books*; for students who have read Swift before coming to Sterne, the connections are readily apparent. Aesop, they recall, berates the dogmatizing spider (the imagery comes from Bacon), of whose theories, *"if the materials be nothing but Dirt, spun out of your own Entrails . . . the Edifice will conclude at last in a* Cobweb. . . . *For any thing* else . . . *the* Moderns *may pretend to, I cannot recollect;*

unless it be a large Vein of Wrangling and Satyr, much of a Nature and Substance with the Spider's *Poison.*" By contrast, whatever the pragmatic and empiricist bee has got "*has been by infinite Labour, and search, and ranging thro' every Corner of Nature: The Difference is, that instead of* Dirt *and* Poison, *we have rather chose to fill our Hives with* Honey *and* Wax, *thus furnishing Mankind with the two Noblest of Things, which are* Sweetness [of the spirit] *and* Light [of the intellect]" (*Tale* 235).

There is little sweetness and light in Walter Shandy. A fine account of spleen caused by egocentric rationalism is Walter's great problem with his squeaking parlor door. "EVERY day for at least ten years together did my father resolve to have it mended . . . his [dogmatic] rhetoric and [pragmatic] conduct were at perpetual handy-cuffs.——Never did the parlour-door open—but his philosophy or his principles fell a victim to it;——three drops of oyl with a feather, and a smart stroke of a hammer, had saved his honour for ever" (3: 21). There follows a wonderfully funny melancholic self-pitying rhapsody: "Inconsistent soul that man is!—languishing under wounds, which he has the power to heal!—his whole life a contradiction to his knowledge!—his reason, that precious gift of God to him—(instead of pouring in oyl) serving but to sharpen his sensibilities . . ." and so on. It hardly needs pointing out that one of the remedies for spleen is laughter, which Rabelais, Cervantes, Swift, and Sterne were so adept at provoking and which critics still find somewhat suspect—is there ever a hint of humor in the voluminous writings of F. R. Leavis, who dismissed Sterne as trifling? Sterne added to the second edition of his volume 5 an epigraph from a decree of the Second Council of Carthage, which may be translated, "If any cleric or monk engages in jesting words, exciting laughter, let him be anathema."[3] What the Reverend Laurence Sterne, one of whose anti-Shandean characters is Agelastes, the unlaughing, thought of that anathematizing is evident.

Finally, I call students' attention to a third passage, Tristram's opinion that, while angels ratiocinate and syllogize by intuition and human beings by the rules of Aristotelian logic, inferior beings "syllogize by their noses: though there is an island swimming in the sea [Britain] . . . whose inhabitants . . . are so wonderfully gifted, as to syllogize after the same fashion, and ofttimes to make very well out too . . ." (3: 40).

Noses of course are penises, as ears are in *A Tale of a Tub*. Are this and other not very recondite allusions to sexual matters merely an excuse for Sterne to indulge in irrelevant obscenity for his own amusement and that of his more dirty-minded readers? There is more to it than that, I think, and students should be encouraged to look beyond Sterne's bawdy surface to its implications. It is significant that Sterne chose to end his book (and his doing so supports the theory that the end we know *is* the end) with the story of a seemingly fraudulent bull, which impresses Walter Shandy by his appearance and manner but which fails to produce any offspring. James A.

Work comments wittily on the suspicion of "sexual impotence that hovers like a dubious halo over the head of every Shandy male, including the bull" (lx), though it must be said in fairness to the bull that he was not impotent—he "went through the business with a grave face" (9: 33)—but merely sterile and the Florida annotators leave a glimmer of doubt even about that (*Florida Edition* 3: 551–52).

Bacon wrote of the Greek and scholastic philosophers, "Assuredly they have that which is the characteristic of boys: they are prompt to prattle, but cannot generate, for their wisdom abounds in words but is barren of works" (*Novum Organum*, aphorism 71). The claim of the New Philosophy of Bacon and the Royal Society (and Bacon's and Swift's bee) was that it would be productive of something useful to the human race instead of sterile logomachy. It is appropriate, and perhaps not unintended, that *Tristram Shandy*, having begun with an account of Walter's loftily rational approach to the sexual act, should end—as well as with the episode of the unsatisfactory bull—with his tirade against the indignity to "the race of so great, so exalted and godlike a Being as man" of having to procreate the species by the same vulgar method as four-footed beasts (9: 33).

It is surely time that the charge of pointless lubricity against Sterne be dropped. Sterne writes about human sexuality because, unlike Walter Shandy, he approves of it, as Joyce, speaking through Molly Bloom, approves of it: it is something desirable and indispensable in human life. Is this a shocking attitude for an ordained clergyman? Sterne would often have conducted the office of Holy Matrimony of the Church of England—a quite down-to-earth document (before it was bowdlerized in the nineteenth century) in which the new husband swears to his wife, "With my body I thee worship"—and would have had no such qualms as Walter's about the sexual act's being beneath the dignity "of so great, so exalted and godlike a Being as man." As a sound Augustinian Christian, like his fellow priests Donne and Swift, he knew that human beings are no such thing.

Does being aware of the presence of such "controlling ideas" in *Tristram Shandy* make it less an enjoyable novel than a philosophic treatise? I think not: on the contrary, it gives a focus, perhaps hitherto missing, to the emotional relationships among, in particular, the three principal characters— Walter, the dedicated rationalist and dogmatist; Toby, far less inhuman than his brother, yet obsessed with the abstruse doctrines of fortification and ballistics (to be sure, an obsession with a large mixture of nostalgia); and Tristram, respectful and fond of his elders, able to see and appreciate what is good in them, yet bewildered and saddened by their too evident follies. Even the peripheral characters Trim, Dr. Slop, Yorick, and Obadiah seem to become more alive when viewed in relation to the controlling ideas manifested by the others.

And yet—. If, as I have suggested, the main thrust of the work is the condemnation of dogmatic rationalism in favor of empirical pragmatism, does the work leave us with the conviction that if the world were peopled exclusively by such unswerving devotees of pragmatism as Mrs. Shandy and the Widow Wadman (though there may be a touch of the romantic as well as the practical in her pursuit of Uncle Toby), it would be the ideal place to live in? The mind recoils from such a prospect.

Perhaps there is a parallel in Johnson's *Rasselas*, written at the same time Sterne was writing the first volume of *Tristram Shandy*. One of the later chapters in Johnson's book bears the title "The Dangerous Prevalence of Imagination"—"prevalence" meaning domination—and one can easily suppose that if Walter Shandy had had access to an astronomical observatory, he too might have ended by controlling the weather and the movements of the heavenly bodies. Yet it was "that hunger of imagination that preys incessantly upon life and must be appeased" (*Rasselas*, ch. 32) that impelled the young Prince to escape from the stultification of the Happy Valley, where all material wants are satisfied and no one is happy—though Mrs. Shandy might have felt comfortable there. What is the solution, if any? The question might well be put to students who have read Sterne's great work thoughtfully.

NOTES

[1]To help those unfamiliar with Greek to follow the syntax, I give a rearranged text with an interlinear translation:

Ou	ta	Pragmata	tarassei	tous	Anthrōpous,
Not		practicalities	trouble		human beings,

alla	ta	Dogmata	peri	tōn	Pragmatōn.
but		dogmas	concerning		practicalities.

Ta, tous, and *tōn* are forms of the definite article, required (as in French) with nouns used collectively.

[2]Sterne probably uses *ideas* in the sense of Locke's "simple ideas"—that is, sense impressions, primarily visual. The word derives from the Greek verb meaning "to see," cognate with Latin *video*.

[3]Interestingly, in Umberto Eco's popular novel *The Name of the Rose* the plot concerns a fanatic monk who rails against laughter, citing authorities similar to this decree; murders those whom he suspects of trying to get access to his carefully hidden unique manuscript of the supposed second book of Aristotle's *Poetics*, an apologia for comedy; and ends by destroying it and himself.

TRISTRAM SHANDY: TEXT CON TEXTS

The Sorrows and Confessions of a Cross-Eyed "Female-Reader" of Sterne

Elizabeth W. Harries

Tristram Shandy is first and foremost a novel about reading and readers. Tristram as narrator cajoles, teases, insults, confuses the various readers who emerge in his text: Sir, Madam, your worships, the learned hypercritics, my dear, dear Jenny. Many of his chapters—chapter 20 of volume 1, for example—are comic exercises in good reading. But how do our late twentieth-century students read (or fail to read) the work? And how can recent theories of reading illuminate the ways we teach (or fail to teach) it?

Let me begin with a confession: I have taught *Tristram Shandy* close to ten times, to a total of close to five hundred students, most of them women (usually in a lecture course on the earlier English novel). And I'm afraid that, of these hundreds, not more than twenty enjoyed reading Sterne's work or will ever return to it. (Perhaps the usual pessimism of jaded English teachers has entered into this mournful estimate, but normally I incline to optimism.) My students moan but end up being drawn into and even admiring *Moll Flanders, Pamela, Clarissa,* and *Tom Jones*. But *Tristram Shandy* seems a closed book; the other pages turn out to be almost as impenetrable as the "marbled page (motly emblem of my work!)" that Sterne flaunts before his unlearned reader in volume 3, chapter 36. What makes this novel about

111

reading so difficult for my students to read? Or—perhaps another way of asking the same question—what makes it so difficult for me to teach?

Much of the difficulty is of course built into the narrative strategy of the book. Sterne is determined to make it impossible for his readers to read "straight forwards . . . in quest of the adventures" (1: 20). The techniques, habits, and expectations that students have found adequate for most of their TV watching, moviegoing, and reading—the linear reading that can tell them what happens; the suspense of a gradually but clearly unfolding plot; the satisfactions of tension and resolution, of symmetry and closure—all turn out to be useless here. Or worse than useless, for it is precisely these techniques, habits, and expectations (at least as characteristic of twentieth-century readers as of eighteenth-century readers) that Sterne challenges. He refuses to give his readers the rewards of "story." Rather, like Trim's story of the King of Bohemia in volume 8, the story somehow is lost in the whirligig of digression and narration about narration.

A second difficulty (certainly more acute for twentieth-century readers than for eighteenth-century ones) is the "learned wit" of the fiction. Few of my students have read Rabelais or Cervantes, to say nothing of Swift, Burton, Locke, Quintilian, or the Bible. The Work edition I've been using seems to them to bristle with forbidding footnotes that prevent their direct contact with the text. Some discussion of the kind of learning and pedantry that Sterne is mocking and the kind of fiction he's taken as his model can help; I've occasionally begun the course with *Don Quixote*, à la Dorothy van Ghent. But still the learned wit seems remote and musty to students, and probably pointless as well.

Another difficulty (again more acute for twentieth-century readers than for their eighteenth-century counterparts) is the babble of competing voices and tones that make up the curious texture of *Tristram Shandy*. Speed-reading is not the technique to use here; but even after we've read passages aloud together, emphasizing the dramatic cacophony of Sterne's style, my students want the work to be a monologue. Reading the text is difficult enough; hearing it comes even more slowly, if at all.

The central difficulty for my students, though—and for me as well—is the pattern of sexism and misogyny that runs through the novel.[1] In Tristram Shandy's world, there is hardly any room for women:

> all the SHANDY FAMILY were of an original character throughout;——
> I mean the males,—the females had no character at all,—except,
> indeed, my great aunt DINAH. . . .   (1: 21)

Tristram is both frightened and contemptuous of them, echoing his uncle Toby's terror and his father's disdain as well as Pope's "Epistle to a Lady."

And his great-aunt Dinah has only distinguished herself by being "married and got with child by the coachman"; the passive voice underlines the helplessness that characterizes many of the women of the novel.

Women are presented either as passive, asexual nonentities or as threatening adversaries in sexual combat. The Widow Wadman is a figure for woman as sexual predator, her "venereal" eye (8: 25) carefully contrasted with Tristram's mother's "thin, blue, chill, pellucid chrystal" (9: 1). Susannah, the fair Beguine, even the foolish fat scullion scrubbing the fish kettle (probably a sexual symbol)—all play minor roles in the conflict between the sexes. The impotence that seems to trouble most of the males in the book (including the Shandy bull) is implicitly attributed to the aggressive sexuality of woman. Walter Shandy explicitly associates the Widow Wadman with Eve:

> My father . . . was demonstrating to Yorick, notwithstanding my
> mother was sitting by——not only, "That the devil was in women,
> and that the whole of the affair was lust;" but that every evil and
> disorder in the world of what kind or nature soever, from the first fall
> of Adam, down to my uncle Toby's (inclusive) was owing one way or
> other to the same unruly appetite.   (9: 32)

Like most of Walter Shandy's hypotheses, this mythic one is presented as questionable; both Yorick and Uncle Toby, in their different ways, are prepared to argue against it as the book ends. But the image of woman as Eve, the eternal temptress and source of evil, is always latent in the novel. Women remain the other, "sitting by." Their questions, often inopportune, and interpretations, often mocked, mark the deep chasm between their trivial, yet threatening, interests and man's higher sphere.

The book's jokes, too, are part of the sexist pattern, from the central joke about the first Sunday night of the month to the promised chapters on green gowns, buttonholes, chambermaids, whiskers, and noses. As Coleridge says, "We have only to suppose society *innocent*—and [this sort of wit] is equal to a stone that falls in snow; it makes no sound because it excites no resistance" (Howes, *Sterne* 354). Coleridge is certainly right that Sterne is counting on the smutty resistance of his readers' imaginations; but the resistance that permits us to interpret his innuendo may lead, in some modern readers, to another kind of resistance—a resistance to being bamboozled into participating in jokes one doesn't really find funny.

Poor "Madam" is a case in point. Throughout the novel Sterne is hard on all his "inside readers," the mock readers who surface in the text to ask questions, usually not quite to the point ("Pray, what was your father saying?" [1: 1]), and to be abused for their poor reading. But Madam is most often in trouble. Tristram carefully plays her up as an example of female "honesty" and innocence, stressing "that female nicety . . . and inward cleanliness of mind and fancy" that make the female sex "so much the awe" of the male sex (1: 21), while at the same time making it clear that she is alert to his every off-color suggestion. (Wayne Booth once called her a "lecherous prude," an apt phrase for the figure Sterne has invented.) And it is Madam who is castigated, half seriously, for her inattentive reading early in the book, for not drawing the inference that Tristram's mother *"was not a Papist"* (1: 20). At the end of that chapter Tristram makes an observation that goes to the center of my problem—and of my students' problem as well:

> I wish the male-reader has not pass'd by many a one, as quaint and curious as this one, in which the female-reader has been detected. I wish it may have its effects;—and that all good people, both male and female, from her example, may be taught to think as well as read.

This almost looks as if Sterne were carefully separating the reactions of "female-readers" from those of "male-readers." But in fact he is pressing here for a similarity of response, working toward one reading style for all "good people." Madam, the stalking horse (possibly an unfortunate term if we fit it into Tristram's lexicon) for many of Tristram's jokes, is also a figure for all bad readers, male or female, who cannot follow his eccentric logic or narrative curves. Madam as "example" is also an example of women being maneuvered into reading like men. The comedy of her failure to do so too easily obscures the assumptions that lie behind it.

So far I've drawn up what must look like a one-sided indictment of the novel and its relegation of women to one restricted corner of existence. Perhaps it's time for a second confession: though I am acutely aware of the ways *Tristram Shandy* systematically stereotypes and denigrates women (if we can say anything in the work is systematic), I will never stop reading and marvelling over the book. How can I explain my continuing pleasure in it, almost undiminished by my consciousness of its serious limitations? How can I communicate that continuing pleasure and my reasons for it more effectively to my students, making them better readers of Sterne in the process?

What I must wrestle with is the conflict between my growing commitment to feminist analysis and my abiding belief that *Tristram Shandy* is a book everyone should read, one of the most important novels ever written. This conflict is one that many critics today, most of them women, feel, more or less consciously, when they try to deal with established canonical texts. As readers, teachers, and critics, we tend to look at literature cross-eyed, one eye zeroing in on the patriarchal bias of the text, the other shooting off in another direction, noting form and structure, creative ambiguity, intertextuality, and all its other canonical beauties. If we do not retreat exclusively into separatist "gynocritics" (Elaine Showalter's term for women writing about women writing—a nice Shandean regress), we must somehow find an approach to literature that permits us to reconcile our critical view of the tradition with our appreciation of it.

A few years ago Wayne Booth reexamined his reactions to Rabelais and his evaluation of Bakhtin in the light of feminist criticism, showing how both writers, in works that emphasize polyphony, omit or suppress the feminine voice. (Think of Walter Shandy arguing with the voices of a Christian, heathen, husband, father, patriot, and man, and then think of Mrs. Shandy left with only one still, small voice, arguing "only like a woman" [1: 18]). Here is part of Booth's conclusion:

> [I]f what I have been doing here has any legitimacy at all, then most of the world's classics are indeed placed into a controversy that will never be easily resolved. Not thrown out, not censored, not burned, but thrown into controversy. In short, I finally accept what many feminist critics have been saying all along: our various canons have been established by men, reading books written mostly by men for men, with women as eavesdroppers, and now is the time for men to join women in working at the vast project of reeducating our imaginations. ("Freedom" 74)

"With women as eavesdroppers": this is literally, comically true in the Shandy world—Tristram's mother poised at the crack in the parlor door, the Widow Wadman listening to Trim and Uncle Toby from her thickset arbor. In a deeper sense Booth's sketch of our literary traditions is also true of the problems *Tristram Shandy* presents for me as reader and teacher. In saying that such books are "thrown into controversy," however, Booth is only describing the current state of things. What he does not tell us—and perhaps no one can—is how to present that controversy to one another and to our students, how to avoid the schizophrenic or cross-eyed approach, how our reeducated imaginations will ultimately reread, reconstruct, or reinvent the works we have been taught to consider classics.

The puzzle of the reader's construction of the work is of course a puzzle that fascinated Sterne as well. He is constantly inviting participation in the making of his book, calling on the reader to draw a portrait of the Widow Wadman in the blank space he provides (6: 38) or to imagine a scene or conversation. (It is probably significant that Madam is rarely appealed to in this way. "Sir" must paint the Widow Wadman "as like your mistress as you can——as unlike your wife as your conscience will let you"; and Tristram leaves the reader "something to imagine, in *his* turn" [2: 11; my italics].) *Tristram Shandy* is, among many other things, a comic anticipation of much current reader-response criticism that attempts to place the meaning of the work somewhere in the interaction of reader and text.[2] And, like Sterne (even when he is poking fun at Madam), most reader-response critics habitually assume that the actual reader is a neutral, sexless, competent one with "universal" prejudices, reactions, and feelings—or, in other words, essentially male. Even the recent attempts to "en-gender" response theory, however, seem baffled when faced by the question I'm worrying here: What happens when readers must reject some of the roles a novel asks them to play, while still accepting and enjoying others?[3]

Or, to put the problem in its most concrete form, how should I go about teaching the following passage about Locke's *Essay*?

> [A]s I write to instruct, I will tell you in three words what the book is.—It is a history.—A history! of who? what? where? when? Don't hurry yourself.——It is a history-book, Sir, (which may possibly recommend it to the world) of what passes in a man's own mind. . . .
> (2: 2)

Ten years ago I approached this passage by talking about the dialogue with the mock or inside reader ("Sir"), the implications of Tristram's "writing to instruct," the comic literalization of a corner of Locke's theory for Sterne's description of the workings of the mind, the significance of the word *history* in this context and in relation to the rising novel and to *Tristram Shandy* itself. Today I would certainly want to be more specific about the dialogue with the inside reader (Why is it "Sir," not "Madam"? What do his questions show?) and then to linger over "what passes in a man's own mind." (Can we take "man" as universal, as identical with "human"? What pictures does Sterne give us of minds in this book? Are there any female minds? What about the Widow Wadman's in 9: 21?)

But even the order in which I discuss these topics will be important. If I begin by pointing out the sexist assumptions behind the passage, then move on to other topics, I may seem to be dismissing that perspective, treating it as secondary. If I begin as a general reader, then move on to become a "female-reader," I run the danger of leading my students to dismiss the novel, to throw out the baby with the very dirty bathwater. Though it's possible to start with either approach and perhaps to return to it later, it is very hard to find a satisfactory balance between the two.

This practical problem only hints at the larger questions that loom behind it, questions I cannot yet answer. What is the relationship between the novel's sexist bias and its self-conscious, fragmented, digressive narration? How are we to understand—and teach—a text that, while undermining conventional expectations about narrative and language, at the same time shores up many prejudices and cultural myths about gender?

My current, temporary, jerry-built solution is to begin my discussion of the novel by making the same confessions to my students that I have made here, to acknowledge my difficulties and my cross-eyed reading of the text. So far, this approach has seemed to make them more willing to wrestle with the text themselves, to experiment with different ways of reading the novel, to begin to transform themselves into readers who can both respond to and resist the invitations of the text. But I hope someday that I'll understand the relation between the ways I see the text and be able to show my students a fuller way to approach it: "any one is welcome to take my pen, and go on with the story for me that will—I see the difficulties of the descriptions I'm going to give—and feel my want of powers" (9: 24).[4]

NOTES

[1]I don't want to imply that my students fall on the book the way the Bacchantes did on Pentheus, screaming for vengeance and ripping it to shreds. What I'm talking about here is an instinctive resistance to some of the book's basic assumptions. Even in this age of raised consciousness and in a women's college, many of my students seem to repeat my old inarticulate feeling, when reading Rabelais or D. H. Lawrence in college or graduate school, that there was something about those books that I could not name or argue about but that both excluded and repelled me. My literary training may have "immasculated" me (see Fetterley; Schweickart), but it had not prevented a deep uneasiness about certain canonical texts.

[2]See the useful anthologies edited by Jane Tompkins, and by Susan Suleiman and Inge Crosman. For a good summary and evaluation of various theories of reading, including "reading as a woman," see Jonathan Culler, *On Deconstruction* 31–83.

[3]Perhaps the most persuasive explanation of this phenomenon so far is Patrocinio P. Schweickart's. She argues that we can identify with or appreciate the "utopian" moment of a text while rejecting its "ideological" moment. This seems, however, to become a matter of partial identification with heroes like Birkin in Lawrence's *Women in Love*. For different approaches to the same problem, see the essays by Annette Kolodny and Nina Auerbach.

[4]Some of my colleagues have already begun to "go on with the story"; I want to thank Joan Garrett-Goodyear, Ann R. Jones, William A. Oram, Thalia Pandiri, Susan Van Dyne, and Elizabeth von Klemperer for their prompt and challenging suggestions. And thanks to my research assistant, Laura Brewer, who at the last minute saved me from some sins of omission and commission. For a recent article that ties *Tristram Shandy* to the Western topos of the bad "female-reader," see Noakes.

"Fire, Water, Women, Wind":
Tristram Shandy in the Classroom

Leigh Ehlers Telotte

One of the many attractions of teaching *Tristram Shandy* is that it readily opens so many paths for teacher and student to explore. Part of the fun of the book, though, is that along those paths are numerous obstacles and pitfalls. For example, the sudden graphics—the black, marbled, and blank pages; the diagrams of progress made; Trim's flourish—all undermine any attempt to deal with *Tristram Shandy* as a usual narrative. The digressions and self-referential elements also take readers out of the common road of storytelling. Similarly, Sterne's fiction seems to offer a formidable array of antifeminine commentary that might elicit immediate objections from readers sensitive to such issues. Too often, of course, it does not, in part because students tend to identify too closely with the Shandy males, in part because the work appears to put women at so comic a disadvantage that no serious response seems appropriate. At the same time, some students will indeed turn hostile, but often mistakenly, because they perceive no distance at all between Sterne and the Shandys. Confronting the many pitfalls of the role of women in *Tristram Shandy*, particularly the role of Mrs. Shandy, is an excellent way to open a discussion of the work, to challenge naive readings, and to balance certain satiric elements with a discussion of Sterne's redemptive elements, significantly associated with the women characters.

In a quest for male disparagement of women, the zealous student can find many examples. The Shandy males are forever telling us how victimized they are, especially by women. In even the most cursory of readings, certain events in which women are blamed, accused, maligned, and otherwise denigrated stand out. The work opens with a dirty joke that seems to be at Mrs. Shandy's expense. During the entire birthing story, extending over several volumes, Walter Shandy repeatedly finds fault—with the expense of Mrs. Shandy's previously unfruitful trip to London and with her choice of delivery method (normal rather than cesarean) and attendant (the midwife, significantly, rather than Dr. Slop). Complaining about the commotion in the house, he says, "[w]e shall have a devilish month of it . . . fire, water, women, wind" (4: 16). Uncle Toby, despite his kind words for his sister-in-law, remains alienated from women and suffers his romantic misadventures with the Widow Wadman, who asks too many pointed (and legitimate) questions about the wound on his groin. Tristram suffers a physical misadventure at the window sash, a near castration that gives specious cause to his embracing of the masculine at the expense of the feminine; Tristram's accident occurs, at first blush, through the carelessness of Susannah, who "did not consider that nothing was well hung in our family" (5: 17).

Beginning a class discussion with such scenes allows for the posing of a

larger question: How justified are the Shandy males in their self-proclaimed
sufferings at the hands of women? The goal here is to help students realize
that in these and similar episodes the onus lies with the male accusers, not
with the women, and thus that Sterne prompts his readers, in effect, to
question the characters—and especially the hobbyhorses—of the Shandy
males. Certainly, Walter's problems with the clock arise from the rigidity
of his own systematic nature; his limiting of "family concernments" to the
first Sunday of the month inevitably leads Mrs. Shandy to her "unhappy
association of ideas" (1: 4). Similarly, his dissatisfaction with the plans for
Tristram's delivery stems from his foolish obsession with protecting the "seat
of the soul," in total disregard of Mrs. Shandy's welfare. It is important to
point out to students, who no doubt take cesarean deliveries for granted,
that in the middle of the eighteenth century the operation was always fatal
to the mother. And again, Walter's begrudging Mrs. Shandy's trip to London
is directly connected to his invocation of the political philosophy of Robert
Filmer; students need to know that Filmer's patriarchal schemes had been
effectively exploded by Locke more than half a century earlier and that
Sterne's readers would have easily recognized that Sterne was ridiculing
Walter's old-fashioned, reactionary ideas.

Early in any discussion of *Tristram Shandy*, students should be able to
see that they cannot simply accept without question the statements of Shandy
males concerning women. Tristram, Walter, Toby do not speak for Sterne
on the issue of women; quite the contrary, Sterne carefully undercuts many
if not all of their attitudes. Tristram is, however, a more complex creation
than Walter or Toby. Sterne treats Walter almost exclusively as an object
of satire; Toby, though praised for goodness of heart, is associated with a
sterile sentimentalism that Sterne clearly finds wanting in the encounter
with the Widow Wadman. But Tristram is more complex because at times
he is barely distinguishable from Sterne while at other times he is a direct
and vulnerable target.

One of Sterne's satiric devices, not readily accessible to students, is the
contrasts he draws by learned allusions. To demonstrate this, I trace patterns
of simple allusions to Greek and Egyptian myths, reinforced by associations
with Christian thought. In this context, Mrs. Shandy is clearly associated
with procreative and restorative powers. Sterne implies that his characters
should strive to balance male and female roles, and when the male Shandys
fail to do so, Sterne's allusions point to impotence, destruction, and death.
All is not lost for Tristram, however, since some hope of restoration appears
at the work's end. It might be said that I try to provide not so much a feminist
reading of *Tristram Shandy* as a reading that illustrates Sterne's sympathy
with feminine interests.

The allusions to mythology that I rely on appear first in Walter's theory of Christian names. Desiring a name that has a "magic bias" strong enough to compensate for his infant son's crushed nose, Walter chooses "Trismegistus" (4: 8). Hermes Trismegistus, the supposed author of the hermetic books of ancient knowledge, was traditionally identified with Thoth, "the Egyptian god of wisdom, inventor of arts and sciences" (Work 279–80). But the name carries further implications, unrecognized by Walter and Tristram but known to eighteenth-century readers of classical literature. Thoth is a healing figure, linked with the Isis-Osiris resurrection and vegetation myth. After the murder and dismemberment of Osiris, Isis collects the body parts and must supply an image of Osiris's phallus; with the aid of Thoth, Isis then restores life to Osiris. Thoth's powers of healing and knowledge are thus exercised in the service of a goddess-mother figure who alone has the power to restore the emasculated male.

These materials for an archetypal reading allow me to identify Mrs. Shandy with Isis, in that she too attempts a restoration after Tristram's circumcision/castration. Students most likely will focus on Tristram's reactions in this episode, but I ask them to contrast the parents' reactions as well. While Walter sends for arcane books to research the subject, Elizabeth Shandy, acting in a helpful, motherly fashion, goes off for "lint and basilicon" to dress the wound (5: 27). Her attempts to restore the wounded male are further reflected by her practical concern with breeches. Tristram, misunderstanding her attitude, sneers at her lack of interest in the Shandean trip to the Continent: "my mother, who being taken up with a project of knitting my father a pair of large worsted breeches . . . staid at home . . . to keep things right during the expedition" (7: 27). Elizabeth's knitting represents love and care and is emblematic of her attempt to restore order and creativity to a house visited by death (brother Bobby's) and declining potency (Walter's, Toby's, Tristram's). Sterne's point is that she represents a necessary balance for this world. To the male Shandys' "masculinity" (reason, science), she joins an instinctive, restorative femininity, and we should not despise her because she is "not a woman of science" (6: 39).

Sterne also provides a Christian context for this mythic pattern of the restorative mother. In one episode, Elizabeth, Toby, and Parson Yorick listen to Walter deliver a Platonic discourse on the difference between philosophical love, which he prefers, and physical love, which he rejects. Yorick refutes Walter, saying, "I think the procreation of children as beneficial to the world . . . as the finding out the longitude," and Elizabeth picks up the thread: "*love* keeps peace in the world" (8: 33). Toby, too, rejects Walter's Platonic argument: "what has a man who believes in God to do with this?" Christian love should combine both the physical and the spiritual and lead from replenishing the earth to finding ultimate love and salvation in heaven. Walter, unfortunately, does not understand this position; for him, physical love is a misfortune to which he "would never submit . . . like a christian" (8: 26). It is at this point quite obvious to students that Sterne has discredited whatever attitudes toward women Walter might express.

The consequence of the male Shandys' failure to deal with their sexuality (and Toby and Tristram are implicated equally with Walter) is that they are cut off from women and cannot benefit from their creative and restorative powers. Again, I focus discussion on Sterne's pattern of allusions, this time those evoking loss, impotence, and death. The most obvious instance students might note is Walter's wonderful argument that *"the mother is not of kin to her child"* (4: 29). Sterne's footnotes refer to an actual sixteenth-century legal decision, but the idea can be traced at least as far back as Aeschylus's *Oresteia*. Apollo posits just such a defense for Orestes, who, having killed his mother to avenge his father's murder, is charged with matricide by the Furies. The resolution to this conflict provides a useful ironic contrast to Shandy Hall; the goddess Athena recognizes the need to honor both male and female, the patriarchal Olympian pantheon and the matriarchal rule of the Furies. Walter's interest in a one-sided Apollonian resolution echoes the Shandean endorsement of the homunculus theory of reproduction, which in effect reduces the mother to a passive role, nothing more than a "venter" (4: 29). Sterne uses Yorick to refute Walter on grounds of common sense and by implication on grounds of violating the Christian commandment to honor both parents. I like to point out to students not only Trim's exposition of that commandment later in the work but the fact that Locke's attack on Filmer makes great rhetorical play with Filmer's consistent dropping of "and mother" in his many citations of the fifth commandment as the basis for patriarchy.

Again, the consequence of the Shandy males' attempt to glorify the father and exclude the mother is twofold: the males are alienated from women and suffer an all but irreversible split between mind and body, intellect and procreation. And again, Sterne uses a classical allusion to make his point. Toby, despite his whimsical sentimentality (or perhaps because of it) and respect for Elizabeth Shandy, echoes a longstanding tradition of misogyny. Concerned with the glories of male militarism, Toby as a schoolboy reacts to Homer: "was I not as much concerned for the destruction of the *Greeks* and *Trojans* as any boy . . . ? Had I not three strokes of a ferula given me . . . for calling *Helena* a bitch for it?" (6: 32). Toby's punishment is, of course, his failed amours with Mrs. Wadman, his alienation from women and by extension from life itself. Tristram's punishment is just as devastating; he suffers a divided existence, alternating between his intellectual hobbyhorse, the compulsion to write his life and opinions, and his physical infirmities, particularly his impotence with Jenny (7: 29).

The last scene of *Tristram Shandy* helps me to tie these various threads together. Although Walter laments that his bull "might have done for Europa herself in purer times" (9: 33), he fails to recognize the implications of his bull's seeming impotence. Given the context of all the allusions that have gone before, I suggest that the Shandean world is lacking the magic associated with Trismegistus and that therefore the bull (associated in myth with Osiris) cannot impregnate the cow (associated with Isis). In the fallen world of Shandy Hall, women are despised and civilization itself is in peril. As an earlier allusion tells us, the Greek poet Hesiod argued that civilization begins with "a man,—a woman—and a bull" (5: 31; Hesiod actually said an ox, so that Walter's misquotation is particularly interesting). The Shandys are doomed to cultural decline and impotence as long as they pursue patriarchal power at the expense of love and respect for women.

Although Walter seems a lost cause, some hope remains for the Shandy family. Both Mrs. Shandy and Parson Yorick are present at the end of the novel to provide the final lines. Tristram at the end still shares some of his father's negative attitudes toward women and cannot yet, like Trim, honor both his father *and* his mother. The point I make in class is that in Tristram's relationship with Jenny, with his various flirtations in volume 7, and with Maria in volume 9, a new attitude might be discernible. Surely students recognize by this time that they have been guided by Sterne toward rejecting Walter's attitudes and Toby's failures as the unhealthy manifestations of inadequate sexual understanding; how much Tristram is able, as a commentator on Walter and Toby rather than an offspring of them both, to overcome their influence is one of the many puzzles of *Tristram Shandy* with which I like to leave the class. What I do try to make clear, however, is that Sterne's satire on the shortcomings of the Shandy males has as one of its measures an ideal of an equal, respectful relationship between men and women. Mrs. Shandy is really the heart of Shandy Hall; the family cannot function or survive without her, a fact that Tristram does not fully understand. What he does seem to comprehend, however, is that human life is a search not for explanatory theories but for harmony, perhaps a harmonious household in which the man and woman coexist in love and respect. Sterne had often preached much the same message about marriage from the pulpit, but for our modern students we perhaps need say nothing more than that we should not label such messages from the past as necessarily or inherently sexist. Sterne deserves a more careful reading.

Tristram Shandy and the Age That Begot Him

Elizabeth Kraft

In 1760 Laurence Sterne wrote to his friend Mrs. Fenton: "I have just finished one volume of Shandy, and I want to read it to some one who I know can taste and rellish humour" (*Letters* 120). When we as teachers introduce our students to this novel that we love, we too would like assurance; we want to assign it to those we know will value it. So we create the audience Sterne sought. In some ways this task is not difficult. Many students quite unfamiliar with the heroic couplet, the via media, or the difference between wit and judgment will nonetheless enjoy the tale and the telling. Yet knowing the literary traditions within and against which Sterne wrote his eccentric masterpiece certainly enriches a reading of the novel and can make the difference between enjoyment and, as Sterne would have it, relish.

As part of an upper-division course in Restoration and eighteenth-century British literature, the reading of *Tristram Shandy* benefits from contact with ideas, tensions, and techniques that begin with Dryden, Pepys, and the restoration of Charles ii and that culminate in the novels of Fielding, Richardson, and Smollett, the vision of William Blake, and the upheaval of the French and American revolutions. And just as *Tristram Shandy* gains from the course, so the course profits from the novel. Taught late in the term, following a chronological sequence, *Tristram Shandy* can serve to draw together the varying thematic strands introduced earlier and help foster a proper appreciation of the vitality and variety of eighteenth-century literature.

> BOSWELL.   But, then one must be very well instructed.
>
> ROUSSEAU.   Ah, sure enough. You must have a well furnished head.

On the first day of class, I distribute a syllabus glossed by this quotation from Boswell's *Private Papers* (Tillotson, Fussell, and Waingrow 1138; this anthology is the primary text for my course). The primary purpose of the citation is to commend the students for endeavoring to furnish their own heads; but in addition the exchange serves as an effective point of reference for an introductory lecture outlining the main concerns of the course.

I direct the students' attention first to voice: Boswell's passive voice places the burden of instruction on instructors; Rousseau's active voice has the opposite effect. More generally, Boswell's language suggests a confidence in external authority while Rousseau's language supports a turning from the external to the internal for authorization and definition. Together the statements epitomize the struggle between the individual and the figures of authority that characterizes the thought of the Restoration and eighteenth century on every level—in governmental, religious, domestic, and literary realms. It is a tension students should learn to recognize early on.

Next we consider pronouns. While Boswell says "one," Rousseau says "you," and again, together, they represent a central paradox of eighteenth-century thought. The tendency to universalize is, of course, the dominant impulse of the period, but students should be alerted to the interest in the personal and idiosyncratic that begins at the century's onset as curiosity about the aberrant and unusual and that by century's end has become a celebration of the individual and distinctive.

To conclude our discussion, I note the significance of Boswell's presenting his observation in dialogue. I elicit from the students the various other options the author might have used: "Rousseau told me that . . . ," "I believe and my friend Rousseau agrees that . . . ," "It is held that . . . ," and so on. Most revisions will tend to shift the focus toward Boswell alone, though some, like "It is held that," will impersonalize the remark. Any revision will deemphasize the sociability inherent in dialogue. We remark that Boswell's chosen mode of expression reveals a concept of thought that assumes the response of a listener, and I point out that this concept is characteristic of Restoration and eighteenth-century literature in general. Finally, I mention that later in the term the students will again find the furnishings of one head an occasion for sociability as they are drawn by conversation into a relationship with Tristram and the Shandy household.

As the semester progresses, I continue to emphasize the dialectic of Restoration and eighteenth-century literature. The oppositions defined by the major Augustans themselves—passion versus reason, wit versus judgment, particular versus general—I present as part of a more general tension between autonomy and authority, in political terms, and the new and the traditional, in aesthetic terms. Throughout the semester I lecture on, and encourage students to explore for themselves, these various tensions and their resolutions through journal entries, essays, and exams focused on such topics as Dryden's defense and qualification of monarchical prerogative in *Absalom and Achitophel*; Mary Astell's claim for a woman's right to choice between a dependent role in a traditional marriage and an independence achieved through education; the reliance on and modification of ancient forms in the mock epic and the verse of imitation; and the development of new modes of expression, particularly the novel. When my students encounter *Tristram Shandy* in the ninth week of the semester, then, they are prepared to understand Shandyism as a dialectic in which antitheses, like Walter and Toby, are posited and reconciled. For they see that although *Tristram Shandy* rarely achieves the logical synthesis of classical balance, the mind of Tristram unites all the oppositions of his world both in the very act of perceiving them and, as Toby and Walter themselves often achieve synthesis, in an affection that abides when reason fails.

I begin our two-week study of *Tristram Shandy* with a very general lecture on the novel as genre, pointing to its distinctive interest in the individual life from Defoe to Sterne. I discuss the novel's claims to historicity and suggest that in a sense those claims were valid, for characters like Clarissa, Parson Adams, Captain Trunnion, and Yorick attained a level of reality for their first readers denied to their living models and to their authors. I point out that the novelists themselves were aware of the propensity of their characters to take on a certain autonomy and that much eighteenth-century fiction can be read in terms of a friendly struggle between the author-narrator and the characters of a work for control of both the text and the reader. We look at some selected passages from *Tom Jones* as the best example of a balanced relationship between narrator and character and at excerpts from *Clarissa* as the best example of a character's (Lovelace's) surprising victory over authorial intent. In *Tristram Shandy*, I point out, the narrator's struggle to tell his story *is* his story; the narrator is himself the character that he cannot control.

After the initial lecture the remainder of our time with *Tristram* is spent in guided discussions in which I try to follow a general movement from theme to form to theme once more. I begin by focusing on volumes 1–5 since the students are not required to complete their reading of the novel until the end of the first week. I introduce, first, the topic of Tristram's parenting and education, a topic that has the double virtue of intersecting one of the large thematic rubrics of the course: the relation of the individual to authority. Walter will remind the class of the meddling guardians of Wycherley, Etherege, and Congreve, but students will find his efforts to shape his son's life much less ominous than those of Lady Woodvill and Old Bellair because his schemes are repeatedly and therefore predictably thwarted. I point out that in a sense, however, Walter's obsession with his plans is probably more damaging to Tristram than their implementation would be, and I cite as the obvious example the elder Shandy's immersion in his *Tristrapædia*, the great scheme of his son's education that preempts that education. We discuss Tristram as the victim of an authoritative irresponsibility that denies him the guidance he needs and forces him into a noble but chaotic attempt to structure his own experience.

At the end of the first week and throughout the second, our discussions move from topical concerns to considerations focused more strictly on the eighteenth century. At this time I point to Yorick's sermon as of central importance in defining the novel's relation to the period as a whole. I remind students of Pope's definition of reason as "the *God* within the *Mind*" and of Locke's explanation that reason is "natural *Revelation*, whereby the eternal Father of Light, and Fountain of all Knowledge communicates to Mankind that portion of Truth, which he has laid within the reach of their natural

Faculties" (Tillotson et al. 642, 197). At the same time, we recall that the major writers and thinkers of the period were acutely aware that any "*Ignis fatuus*, in the *Mind*"—to quote Rochester (Tillotson et al. 33)—could be touted as a manifestation of reason, and as a result conservative writers argued that individual enlightenment must test itself against the extrinsic measures of law, scripture, or tradition. So although Yorick's sermon begins with a sneer that suggests heresy, after a close analysis of the logic of the argument students recognize that Yorick's conclusion falls within the mainstream of Augustan thought:[1]

> [Y]our conscience is not a law:--No, God and reason made the law, and have placed conscience within you to determine;—not like an *Asiatick* Cadi, according to the ebbs and flows of his own passions,— but like a *British* judge in this land of liberty and good sense, who makes no new law, but faithfully declares that law which he knows already written. (2: 17)

Yorick, like other writers of the period from Locke to Burke, would have us govern our lives by what he styles as the formally codified and perfectly if precariously balanced collaborations of human being and God. Yet, I ask the students, is there not a paradox in his insisting that human beings typically abuse their powers of self-direction and in his assigning reason such a central role as coauthor of the law? Why does Yorick grant reason a privileged position in the fundamental instance and question its ability in incidental affairs? Could not a law made by "God and reason" be repealed or revised by "God and reason"? What is the difference between the abuse of conscience that Yorick describes and the right use of reason? And, finally, if we take Yorick's dictum itself as law, a rule by which we measure the thought and behavior of ourselves and others, how are we then to respond to Toby, Walter, and especially Tristram, each of whose hobbyhorsical reasoning is as self-justifying as any other abuse of conscience could be?

As we explore these questions, I guide the discussion to Sterne's and the period's preoccupation with the nature of individual consciousness. We talk about our own understanding of the difference between consciousness, conscience, and reasoning; and we note that often, by Sterne's definition and by our own, consciousness is in effect an abuse of conscience or a state of false reasoning. Yet Sterne, like others of his time and ours, is interested in the processes of the mind, as well as in the moral status of its final products. I point out to the students that Tristram designates his story a "history-book of what passes in a man's own mind," and I remind them of works we studied earlier in the semester that include sympathetic accounts of states of mind seemingly precluded by reason. We come to *Tristram Shandy* with the memory of Pepys and his wife quaking in bed, convinced that the noise of a chimney sweep is a ghost (Tillotson et al. 65); we remember Pope's Eloisa, who surrenders herself completely to ideas that compound her grief, fantasies that sharpen her emotional pain. Yet we also recall the satire of the Scriblerians that condemns the aberrant state of mind by demonstrating the way it works. In many ways, I suggest, *Tristram Shandy* is very like this satire; Sterne's use of rising and falling imagery, graphics, and particularly the unreliable, self-implicating narrator begs us to make the connection and to read the novel as we read *A Tale of a Tub*, as criticism of its own form and matter.[2]

Many passages would serve to illustrate this point, but I favor Tristram's explanation of his digressive art of progression (1: 22) for the bridge it provides between the thematic concerns we are now discussing and the formal concerns we will consider later. In his comment, Tristram sounds very like the *Tale of a Tub*'s hack; in fact, as the notes to the Florida edition of *Tristram Shandy* point out, there is an exact parallel between what Tristram says of the origin of his art and the hack's response to a challenge from the Royal Society to "compare their books by weight and number with those of the 'Grub-street' Brotherhood' " (3: 117). Both Tristram and the *Tale*'s putative author cite the movement of the earth as on the one hand the "trifling hint" that inspires method and on the other the "small affair" that buttresses opinion. Both narrators are clearly possessed of an inflated sense of their own worth, for the notions that the earth might really move with the jolting irregularity of Tristram's work and might truly sit as lightly on the scales as the productions of Grub Street are preposterous notions indeed. I suggest to my students that in such Scriblerian passages Tristram has become so enamored of his power as maker—maker of his life and of his story—that he has lost all sense of his place in the world; he has in fact become his own world as we all tend to do if we allow ourselves to be too self-concerned and self-consumed, too much interested in the processes of our thought. Is not Sterne's novel, then, very like Swift's satire, I ask the students, a mirror in which we should see our distorted images and learn to avoid the excesses reflected there? If their answer is yes (which it undoubtedly will be, considering the way I have presented the question), what then, I ask, is the difference between Sterne's novel and Swift's satire or between the novel and satire in general?

I ask the question to make my students think, not to suggest we can (or should) draw a fast and definitive distinction, for the novel, particularly the comic novel, has made use of satiric conventions from Cervantes's *Don Quixote* to John Kennedy Toole's *Confederacy of Dunces*. If there is a distinction to be made, however, it resides in character, and I tell my students that in spite of the traits Tristram shares with Swift's hack I tend to respond to him and all the Shandys as I respond to Pepys and Eloisa; I like them with or without Sterne's consent because his narrative, with its focus on character, will not allow me finally the objective judgment and rejection that satire invites. To illustrate my point briefly, I ask the students, as my own teacher John Sitter once asked me, to imagine how Swift would have rendered Toby's rationalization of humanistic militarism. The difference is, I think, that between Shandyism and what T.S. Eliot called Swiftian disgust, between a novelistic interest in various states of mind and a satiric exposé of various kinds of false reasoning.

I conclude this particular discussion by saying that *Tristram Shandy* is involved in a self-dialectic, enticing us into the mind and world of a likable narrator on the one hand and providing us extrinsic standards by which to judge him and find him lacking on the other. We reconcile these conflicting valuations, I suggest, as the characters themselves reconcile their differences, through an abiding affection that has little to do with recognizing the limitations of others. Tristram's father happens to be right about Uncle Toby's preoccupation with warfare: it is exasperating, especially in a man who refuses to kill a fly. Yet Walter's chagrin at himself when he loses patience with Toby is, I suggest, appropriate; for the frustrating consistencies and inconsistencies in the behavior of those we love are less important than the fact that we do love them. Further, *Tristram Shandy* seems to me to share with Fielding's *Joseph Andrews* a delight in the eccentric and the imperfect that, while in part derisive, is fundamentally appreciative. Fielding complains in the *Covent-Garden Journal* number 56 that ill-breeding produces in England a great many "Characters of Humour" who make life in society often trying and unpleasant, yet he concludes "by wishing, that this excellent Source of Humour may still continue to flow among us, since tho' it may make us a little laughed at, it will be sure to make us the Envy of all the Nations of Europe" (Tillotson et al. 764). Considering Fielding's affection for Parson Adams, I take him at his word here, but for some students the possible irony in Fielding's remark tends to complicate rather than resolve the relation between character and satiric intent in the comic novel. Therefore, I encourage the interested to continue to explore the problem in the fifteen-page research paper due at the end of the semester, in their reading journals, or on the final exam. I suggest that for *Tristram Shandy* they begin with Melvyn New's *Sterne as Satirist* and John Stedmond's *Comic Art of Laurence Sterne* among the works I have placed on reserve to help them formulate their own readings of Tristram and his family.

The discussion of character and satire leads us into a more specific consideration of the novel as form. Using *Tristram Shandy* as an example of the genre, I have students identify the elements of drama and of poetry that the novelist found artistically useful. They discover character types familiar from the drama—the lusty widow, the military man who speaks the jargon of his trade—scenic representation, dialogue, stage directions, and costuming. To emphasize the intergeneric dialectic, I might have two students do a dramatic reading of the Shandys' bedtime conversation on breeches, or I might have them all stand and imitate Trim's posture of sermon delivery. A little more difficult is the identification of poetic conventions, but once I have pointed them out, students have no trouble seeing that Sterne's description of Toby after the Treaty of Utrecht would appeal to the same readers that relished Umbriel's visit to the Cave of Spleen:

> STILLNESS, with SILENCE at her back, entered the solitary parlour, and drew their gauzy mantle over my uncle *Toby*'s head;———and LIST-LESSNESS, with her lax fibre and undirected eye, sat quietly down beside him in his arm chair. (6: 35)

Students should recognize, too, that *Tristram Shandy* brings to full fruition what the periodical essay offered in inchoate form: the conversational and collaborative relationship between narrator and reader.

It is with the idea of collaboration that I end our discussion of *Tristram Shandy*. I point out that in spite of Tristram's eccentricity, his is not the isolated voice of the bard in the wilderness. Students of eighteenth-century literature will hear that voice in Collins, Cowper, and Blake, and it will dominate the next literary age; but Tristram is still talking *to* someone: his narrative is committed to sociability and conviviality in a way that links him firmly with the age that begot him. From the story of Yorick's ass, to the tale of Slawkenbergius, to the episode of Phutatorius and the hot chestnut, to the saga of Le Fever, to the final joke shared by the Shandy household and their friends, the novel celebrates community. The celebration is, admittedly, bittersweet; for there are problems as there is joy in living together, and for every moment spent in communication with another, there are many moments spent talking at cross-purposes or sitting alone. The students should recognize in *Tristram Shandy* the same sense of longing they will find in Johnson's *Rasselas* and his "Vanity of Human Wishes"—a longing that is inevitable when reality cannot answer the needs of the soul. Yet as limited as the possibility for real communication is and as short-lived as such communication, if ever achieved, may be, I believe Sterne would have us, like Tristram, turn our plains into cities by stopping as often as we can along the road of life to exchange stories, commend legs, or proffer pinches of snuff. Tristram's own experience suggests as much, for his flight from death in volume 7 is an obsession that is, as such, a flight toward death until he rediscovers in a dance with a "sun-burnt daughter of Labour" on the road between Nismes and Lunel (7: 43) what I hope my students will learn if they do not know it already: that life, however long, is not worth living without others to share in its joys and in its sorrows. This lesson is, to my mind, the most valuable lesson *Tristram Shandy* and Restoration and eighteenth-century literature in general hold for us and for our students.

NOTES

[1]For a discussion of Sterne's conservative view, which is basically a latitudinarian view, see Melvyn New, *Sterne as Satirist* 7–28.

[2]On the subject of Sterne and the Scriblerians, see John M. Stedmond 49–54 and D. W. Jefferson; for Sterne and Swift in particular, see Helene Moglen 28–29 and Melvyn New, *Sterne as Satirist* 53–69.

Tristram Shandy in a Restoration and Eighteenth-Century Course: Satire or Soap?

Deborah D. Rogers

Tristram Shandy does not exist in a vacuum. I teach Sterne in an upper-division period survey primarily for English majors. The organization of the course, which roughly follows chronological order by author, is designed to underscore the simultaneity of two contrasting (but overlapping) modes that run through the literature of the period: the satirical or neoclassical mode, which is characterized by suspicion of the growing Whig commercial world and by an emphasis on universality, community, reason, the ancients, and the theory of degeneration, and the sentimental or subjective mode, which is distinguished by support for the Whig commercial world and by an emphasis on individualism, originality, emotion, the moderns, and the theory of progression. Of course, the two categories are not always discrete—they admit many variations and combinations. This approach unifies Restoration and eighteenth-century literature by situating it against a background of the historical and cultural conditions that (reflexively) helped produce it. In addition, this scheme allows for the uniqueness of individual works, such as *Tristram Shandy*, where the two modes culminate, giving rise to difficult critical questions.

Although the section on Sterne spans only two classes, I lead up to it from the beginning of the course. In fact, since my teaching of *Tristram Shandy* depends so heavily on what precedes it, a brief description of the course is appropriate before I consider Sterne. The first weeks of class are devoted to the neoclassical mode, which is introduced with Dryden and further explored in connection with Swift. At the same time, however, the subjective mode starts asserting itself: in *Battle of the Books* and *Tale of a Tub*, I direct attention to the representation of the dichotomy in the ancient-modern controversy. And in *Gulliver's Travels*, perhaps the most famous satire of the period, the two major modes come clearly into focus again, not only in the parody of the moderns in book 3, but in the pervasive theme of the subjectivity of perception and in the very annihilation of emotion that comes with the total reason of the Houyhnhnms.

Next on the syllabus comes my hobbyhorse. Still observing chronological order, I assign—right smack between Swift and Pope—several subjective graveyard poems that were published during their lifetime but, unfortunately, are usually taught toward the end of the semester as "pre-Romantic" works, ostensibly because they fit in nicely with "new trends" like the odes of Joseph and Thomas Warton, James Macpherson's Ossian, and William Blake's visionary verse. The problem with this all too typical arrangement is that ignoring chronology in this instance invariably leads students to view the early part of the period as neoclassical and the second half as pre-

Romantic, even though such "pre-Romantic" works as the graveyard poems started appearing at the beginning of the century. These pieces, which enjoyed enormous contemporary popularity, include Anne Finch's "Nocturnal Reverie" (1713), Thomas Parnell's "Night Piece" (1722), Edward Young's *Night Thoughts* (1742–46), and Robert Blair's *Grave* (1743). To emphasize continuity and development, I reserve Thomas Gray's "Elegy" (1751) for later in the course. Such an arrangement may at first seem awkward, if not jarring. Encouraging unrestrained indulgence in emotion, graveyard poems represent a general shift in attitude from the neoclassical to the subjective mode. As such, these individualistic pieces may seem far removed from Tory satires. But the juxtaposition has a profound effect on many students. Indeed, contrast is the very vehicle through which students can be shocked into recognition of the simultaneity of neoclassical and subjective modes. By the time we reach our unit on Pope, which follows graveyard poetry, students readily recognize this subjective tone in such neoclassical poems as "Eloisa to Abelard."

Although I could continue to present the rest of my course in terms of the two modes, it is time to dismount. Suffice it to say that as the class proceeds, the contrast is even more dramatic since it gradually becomes apparent that the same period that saw the publication of such neoclassical works as *Absalom and Achitophel*, *Gulliver's Travels*, *Rape of the Lock*, *The Dunciad*, *Beggar's Opera*, and "The Vanity of Human Wishes" also witnessed the publication of such subjective works as the graveyard poems, *Spectator*, *The Seasons*, *Robinson Crusoe*, *Pamela*, *The Castle of Otranto*, and *The Task*.

It is with this frame of reference that we approach the section on Sterne, to my mind the pinnacle of the conflict between satire and sentiment. By this time students have already received study questions to guide their reading. These revolve around one major question, the still unresolved question that has been asked of *Tristram Shandy* since the work was published: Is it satirical or is it sentimental? Before we deal with this issue in class, however, students respond by defending a position in a two-page paper. (From the outset, to stimulate and somewhat shape or control discussion, the course requires such minipapers for each major author or section.) Instructions are as follows: "In a two-page paper, defend *Tristram Shandy* as a sentimental or satirical work. (You may wish to defend it as both.) Be prepared to argue your position in class. Since this is a short paper, begin to narrow your scope by focusing on a particular scene and doing a close reading." As previously mentioned, we devote two classes to *Tristram Shandy*. (Inevitably, we run over a bit.) We consider the definition and development of sentimentalism and the critical background of *Tristram Shandy*.

The class goes on to debate whether the novel is satirical or sentimental, and, finally, we do an in-class exercise.

After the minipapers have been written, I begin by discussing the meaning of sentimental(ism). We have, of course, previously defined and discussed satire. This stage is crucial because the term *sentimentalism* usually proves to be misleading. Most of the time the class readily volunteers the answer: sentimentalism is a pejorative term for the excessive/maudlin/unwarranted/affected/superficial indulgence in and display of emotion. When I bring up the notion that the eighteenth-century definition might have been different, it usually becomes obvious that the class has written papers on satire versus sentimentalism in *Tristram Shandy* without ever considering such a possibility. To remedy this situation (and to introduce some standard bibliographical sources along the way), I take to class my two-volume *Oxford English Dictionary* and my facsimile edition of Johnson's *Dictionary*. Using the *OED* we arrive at a revised definition, finding that in the eighteenth century, sentimentalism was, for the most part, a term for the display of refined/delicate/exquisite/lofty emotions. That Johnson does not have an entry on *sentimentalism* is a lesson in itself, since it may indicate that the term had not yet crystallized conceptually in public awareness.

To stress the interaction of literature and culture, I next provide some background information on the development of sentimentalism and the consequent legitimation of emotion. In the period under discussion this phenomenon begins with the Cambridge Platonists' association of virtue with benevolent acts. It can then be traced from Locke's insistence on subjectivity in his *Essay concerning Human Understanding* to Shaftesbury's theory of innate moral sense manifested by emotional display in his *Characteristicks* (and the similar emphasis on benevolence in Hutcheson, Hume, and Smith). I also discuss Addison and Steele's popularization of these trends and Addison's essays on imagination. Later these ideas are linked to Burke's *Sublime and Beautiful* and, in turn, to the Gothic novel.[1]

After outlining the development of sentimentalism and its underlying cultural assumptions in this manner, I move to a consideration of the dispute over whether *Tristram Shandy* is sentimental or satirical. Acknowledging that critics, from Sterne's time to our own, have never reached a consensus on this issue, I present a brief overview of the debate. From the beginning, *Tristram Shandy* has been described as sentimental. In the early 1780s, this view was encouraged by the publication of excerpts in an anthology called *The Beauties of Sterne*, which announced itself to be "Selected for the Heart of Sensibility" and to contain all Sterne's "Pathetic Tales" (Howes, *Sterne* 12). Later, much attention focused on the sentimental character of Uncle Toby and on nonverbal communication, which, in its substitution of gestures for words, is taken as one of the hallmarks of sentimentalism in literature. Similarly stressing sentimentalism, Herbert Read argued that Sterne "masked beneath his humour and licentiousness the kindly philanthropy of his age —the age of Shaftesbury and Hutcheson" (133).

But if Sterne's sentimentalism was praised from the beginning, it was also attacked: contemporaries not only called Sterne's sincerity into question, they accused sentimental philosophy in general of indulging in self-congratulatory benevolent feelings instead of engaging in charitable conduct, that is, of being all tears and no action. It is in this spirit that, in 1768, Elizabeth Carter, the well-known scholar, poet, and journalist, attacked Sterne:

> It is the fashion, I find, to extol him for his benevolence, a word so wretchedly misapplied, and so often put as a substitute for virtue, that one is quite sick of hearing it repeated either by those who have no ideas at all, or by those who have none but such as confound all differences of right and wrong. Merely to be struck by a sudden impulse of compassion at the view of an object of distress, is no more benevolence than it is a fit of the gout. . . .   (qtd. in Howes, *Sterne* 203)

From the start, however, some, such as Edmund Burke (Howes, *Sterne* 379–80), went one step further and answered such objections by responding that *Tristram Shandy* was satirical. More recently, Melvyn New, in what may be the most exhaustive argument for this reading, concluded that *Tristram Shandy* is firmly in the Augustan satiric tradition and is, like the *Dunciad*, a satire on "the triumph of the uncreating spirit in man, the celebration of chaos and confusion, destruction and death, whether in Toby's bowling-green, Walter's household, or Tristram's study" (*Sterne as Satirist* 203).

There is, of course, a third and middle position due, perhaps, to the inherent ambiguity of satire itself, where praise can always be interpreted ironically. It may be for this reason that from the eighteenth century to the present, this best-of-both-worlds view has persisted and *Tristram Shandy* has been read as a blend of satire and sentiment. More generally, John Middendorf and others have suggested that in the eighteenth century, satire and sentiment often went hand in hand, that satire awakens compassion. Although I try to play the objective umpire, these last views come closest to my own since I regard the century in terms of its overwhelming and uncanny tendency to "see double"—for example, to value the sublime for eliciting, like a roller coaster, fear from a position of security; to react to obviously fictional accounts as if they were factual (while at the same time sending letters to authors—Richardson comes immediately to mind—pleading that they alter the story); or, in the present instance, to read a work as simultaneously satirical and sentimental, as "digressive, and . . . progressive too,—and at the same time" (1: 22).

Each of the major positions in the controversy could, of course, be elaborated, but enough has been said to indicate the scope of the argument. In fact, since the work itself can reveal more about the issue of satire versus sentiment than can any secondhand generalizations, we turn directly to the text to begin our debate. Students may refer to their minipapers, and I encourage them to point to specific passages for close reading. If the class is not forthcoming, I ask several students to read their papers aloud. This usually generates much reaction and discussion. Students often focus on key scenes like the stories of Uncle Toby and the fly (2: 12), Le Fever's death (6: 6–7), Amandus and Amanda (7: 31, 40), the ass and the macaroon (7: 32), and the encounter with Maria (9: 24). (When appropriate I introduce similar episodes from *A Sentimental Journey* and *The Vicar of Wakefield*.) In addition, related matters—such as the character of Uncle Toby and the relationship between the Shandy brothers—inevitably arise. Predictably enough, the debate usually encompasses issues of genre, sexuality or bawdiness, and sincerity. We also investigate gestures that are invested with meaning beyond the ability of language to convey. My personal favorite here is the dropping of Trim's hat (5: 7) to represent the fleetingness of life, of which we are reminded throughout the work. In fact, death, a ubiquitous presence in *Tristram Shandy*, may be the very thing that gives human gestures and actions their double-edged meaning, making life both satirical and sentimental.

Finally, we come to the in-class exercise, a brief essay that is designed to demonstrate the value of adjusting and, one would hope, expanding personal reactions in relation to other critical views. Instructions are as follows: "In an addendum to your minipaper, you are invited to revise your previous opinion or to defend it, taking into consideration the arguments of others —in this case, your peers or critical tradition. Additional questions you should address are: How do you account for—and, if possible, reconcile— this diversity of opinion? How does *Tristram Shandy* fit in with your idea of eighteenth-century literature?" This exercise provides a valuable index of student comprehension of what is, after all, a difficult issue.

Continuing to use the framework of the satiric-sentimental dichotomy as the course progresses, we find that the subjective or sentimental mode becomes increasingly prominent and eventually dominant. Perhaps this is to be expected since, as William Saroyan put it much later, responding to the charge that he was too sentimental, "It is a very sentimental thing to be a human being."

NOTE

¹Besides the primary material pointed to in the text, useful sources for preparing such a background lecture include Frye, "Towards Defining"; Parnell; Hagstrum; Bredvold; Crane; New, *Sterne as Satirist* 29–49; Tuveson, "Importance," "Shaftesbury"; and Voitle.

Satirical Form and
Realistic Fiction in *Tristram Shandy*

Maximillian E. Novak

My title indicates the division of this essay according to the two ways that I teach *Tristram Shandy*: (1) as a satirical work coming at the end of a century of satire and (2) as a work of fiction. The first approach is undertaken for our graduate survey in literature from 1660 to 1800 and the second for an undergraduate course in early fiction. In the first, I talk of sources and background in looking for satiric models, and I search for attitudes toward satire not only in *Tristram Shandy* but as well in the English work that most closely approaches its satiric form, Jonathan Swift's *Tale of a Tub*. In thus pairing the works, I hope to suggest to students that Sterne and Swift were both responding in the same satirical fashion to the attempts of the age to build new systems out of the ruins of scholastic learning. And in treating *Tristram Shandy* as, in some ways, one of the more realistic novels of an age whose great contribution to fiction was to rescue it from the dreamy abstractions of romance, I want to suggest to students of early fiction that *Tristram Shandy* is less the precursor of *Gravity's Rainbow* than it is another experiment in the creation of a convincing fictional reality.

I should say at the outset, however, that I am one of those eighteenth-century scholars who regard *Tristram Shandy* as one of the great serious works of the period. This is not to say that I do not consider it a comic work, but I distance myself from those who prefer to see it as an example of pure play. From the first comment on "this Fragment of Life" in the dedication to Pitt to the ending on the failure of the Shandy bull, comedy is wrested from a view of life that is essentially sad. I use the term *sad* in class rather than, say, *tragic* deliberately, for there is nothing in the existence of those associated with Shandy Hall that pretends to anything so grand as tragedy. The action of the novel takes place in a world that forbids or mocks any aspiration to actions exceeding human limitations. The world of *Tristram Shandy* is a modern world, closer to the ambience of Chekhov's characters than to that of Shakespeare or Milton.

Uncle Toby's wound in the groin area is typical of Sterne's comic seriousness. We know of the pain that it causes, that Toby's "unspeakable miseries" last four years. Toby succeeds in saving himself through study of the science of warfare, study that amounts to a sublimation of sexual desire into an activity that contains all the symbolism of sexual experience with none of its physical involvement. In that sense I compare it to Walter's interest in books on noses or Tristram's pleasure in asses. Although Toby's mock battlefield shows an attraction to things rather than words, I remind students that in matters of warfare, Toby is as much a pedant as his brother Walter, that despite his preference for gesture over words as a mode of communication, he too is impelled into his world of battles by the words contained in the treatises on warfare. For him, the treatises constitute an endless quest for "truth" that, however different such quests may be, is generically the same as other human quests. For Sterne, like Freud, sees all humanity as merely passing time between birth and death in a variety of games that provide structure and interest to life. But such hobbyhorsical pursuits are invested with the utmost seriousness. As Sterne points out, they represent what amounts to everyone's pursuit of truth on earth, and only Tristram's wide-angle view allows us to see them as both crucial and absurd.

The sexual comedy inherent in our language and revealed in those unavoidable verbal associations carries the burden of this absurdity and betrays every pursuit of truth to a kind of sad laughter. Only great moments of human sympathy and kindness appear capable of creating states of seeming timelessness, states in which both views of human activity may be grasped simultaneously. Such moments aside, everyone appears to have mounted a hobbyhorse for a ride that must end in a darkness the presence of which, though usually banished to the margins of the text, the reader is ever aware. Whether I am treating *Tristram Shandy* as a satire or a realistic fiction, I begin with this sort of general overview of Sterne's text.

Words compose the medium in which Sterne and his characters move, and when I want to direct attention to the work as satire, I urge students toward some speculations on that whirl of words that leads the narrator of *Tristram Shandy* into seemingly endless digressions, the ever likely possibility that he will lose his way, and the promise that two volumes a year will pour from the presses as long as he shall live. Why is Sterne interested in such a subject or process, and where does it come from? I don't mean only what are his sources but also what is the situation that would create such an interest?

Sterne did not invent the obsession with language and linguistic indeterminacy that appears throughout his work. Rabelais's fascination with wordplay is as important a source for the verbal texture of *Tristram Shandy* as his having Panurge attempt to discover the answer to the key questions about love and marriage is significant for Sterne's plot. Robert Burton's quest for the secrets of the melancholy caused by love is a linguistic voyage into the kind of odd notions and authorities that must have delighted Sterne when he discovered them. But however much such writers influenced Sterne, I usually begin with the second half of the seventeenth century as the starting point for the most important attitudes that inform *Tristram Shandy*. This means not merely *A Tale of a Tub*, written mainly in the 1690s, but the milieu that produced Swift's work.

Although the scholastic philosophers may have contributed amusement to Rabelais, none of these writers was offering an entirely new epistemology or a new geology. But that was precisely what John Locke and Thomas Burnet afforded at the end of the seventeenth century. Burnet's *Sacred Theory of the Earth* provided a new theory of the deluge, and his description of paradise was only a prelude to what amounted to a rewriting of Genesis along highly imaginative lines in his *Archaeologicae Philosophicae*. And while John Locke's *Essay concerning Human Understanding* may not seem revolutionary to us today, it certainly appeared that way to many traditional thinkers of the time. Bishop Stillingfleet saw in it a radical departure and attacked Locke as lacking the authority of the past. Those who "write out of their own thoughts," he argued, "do it with as much Ease and Pleasure as a Spider spins his Web" (3: 563). But it is also notable that Locke overwhelmed Stillingfleet not only by the power and originality of his arguments but also by spinning out more words than his opponent. Locke's final response, *Mr. Locke's Reply to the Right Reverend the Lord Bishop of Worcester's Answer to His Second Letter*, is more than three hundred pages in the 1824 edition of Locke's writings. Stillingfleet, who wrote endlessly on theological subjects, seemed out of his depth and oddly reticent in his effort to combat the new world of thought and language.

In a similar fashion, Richard Burthogge, who dedicated his *Essay upon Reason* to Locke, moved rapidly from the Swiftian image of perceiving no object as it really is "but only under the Top-knots and Dresses of Notions, which our minds do put on them" (64) to the concept that everything that is in the mind, including dreams, provides us with the only key to reality we have. And from that point he proceeded to a most lengthy discussion of God as a great eye placed in the center of all things. If Burthogge's mixture of Locke and Neoplatonic notions seemed odd to some, even more strange was the outpouring of John Norris of Bemerton. Norris, of course, was one of the last of the Cambridge Platonists, a wholehearted admirer of Malebranche, and a believer in an archetypal world that existed in God's mind before he created the world known to humankind. He was, in brief, a man who seemed most comfortable when dealing with the incomprehensible.

And of course this was only the beginning. What often appeared first as a short treatise would grow to several volumes. Mandeville's *Fable of the Bees* started as a brief and clever fable in 1704 and by 1723 had grown to several volumes. Similarly, Mandeville's opponent, Shaftesbury, had his essays collected into the multivolumed *Characteristicks* by 1711. Anthony Collins's *Discourse of the Grounds and Reasons of the Christian Religion* (1724) was followed in 1727 by his work of four hundred and sixty pages, *The Scheme of Literal Prophecy Considered*, in which he commented on the more than thirty-five works written in opposition to his ironic advocacy of reading the Bible allegorically. Hume's extensive *Enquiry concerning Human Understanding* (1758) at least had the benefit of genius, but the same could not be said for John Brown's *Estimate* (1757), which spread over hundreds of pages an attack on luxury that might have been made in a brief essay. Who could have wished David Hartley's *Observations on Man* (1749) longer, and who could have wanted the Boyle Lectures to have gone on repeating the same thing year after year about the rational nature of God's creation in volumes of more than three hundred pages?

One cannot, of course, expect students to plow through all these tedious tracts today—and yet, if they are not at least made conscious of the existence of these writings, they will miss, I suggest, the seedbed of such satires as *A Tale of a Tub* and *Tristram Shandy*. The main point that I make about this outpouring of new systems of thought is that they did not appear without a general feeling of bewilderment among readers. Unlike the mass of learning that informed much scholarly writing, the new systems appealed to the process of thinking about thinking. When Swift was writing the volume that included *A Tale of a Tub*, *The Mechanical Operation of the Spirit*, and *The Battle of the Books*, this effort at philosophic system building had merged with the quarrel between the ancients and the moderns in the form of the quarrel between Sir William Temple and his adversaries, Wotton and Bentley. And by the time Swift's work was published in 1704, there had been added to these controversies those between Collier and the writers for the stage and between Blackmore and the Wits.

Now this kind of throwing about of words caused a flurry of works similar to Swift's exercises in the *Tale of a Tub* volume, the most curious of which was a parody of Norris's work with the title *An Essay towards the Theory of the Intelligible World, Intuitively Considered* (D'Urfey [?]). Among its other oddities it contained a huge table of contents and had a preface that appeared at the end. But the important point I make to my students is that within this tradition of parodying learned books, writers like Sterne and Swift learned their craft. Without attempting to search for one absolute origin of such jokes, I do like to use, most particularly, the writings of Antoine Furetière, especially his *Nouvelle allégorique*, first published in 1658.

Like Swift, Furetière has an allegory based on a war between the forces representing good art and those representing the bad. In Furetière, the bad includes romances, ironies, and allusions. For Swift it is modern taste. In Furetière a truce is arranged after the forces of Princess Rhetoric prove too powerful; in Swift's work the forces appear irreconcilable. But both writers depict the scene as a kind of warfare, and Furetière's fascination with the possible double entendres available in the vocabulary of fortifications and arms may have directly influenced Sterne.

Or again, a fine example of the fictional device of interrupted narrative, so carefully practiced by Sterne, appears in Furetière's *Roman bourgeois*, which breaks off in the middle to pursue the adventures of a relatively minor character, Charroselles. I talk about this work in my novel course as well as my satire course, but I might say, at this point, that I am not one of those critics who have been won over by Wayne Booth's arguments on *Tristram Shandy* as a completed work. The key issue is not Sterne's intentions concerning continuation of the book but rather his exploitation of the project's essential endlessness. In the satiric tradition to which so much of Sterne's work belongs, the notion of the fragmented and incomplete was standard. Writers on Sterne's debt to the concept of the *non finito* and his rhetorical use of aposiopesis reveal what are unquestionably important aspects of his art, but we should also realize that the satiric tradition took a positive delight in the chaotic. To the note in the Florida *Tristram Shandy* (3: 552) pointing to the possible connection between the cock-and-bull ending of *Tristram Shandy* and the French satiric tradition of the *coq-à-l'âne* with all its bawdiness and disorder should be added the tradition of the English bull and the fiddle, which also has no proper ending.

Tristram Shandy, like a *Vexierbild* that may change from a landscape on one glance to a portrait at a second look, shifts before our eyes even as we attempt to use it for various pedagogical purposes. As already noted, in my graduate survey classes in the eighteenth century, I tend to teach it both as satire (as Melvyn New has taught us to read it and as I have considered it to this point in this essay) and as a key to the thought and feeling of the period, or, in other words, as a playful treatise on eighteenth-century philosophy and as a representative work of sensibility. But *Tristram Shandy* can be the quintessential novel for Viktor Shklovsky and the last, genuine work of Renaissance rhetoric for Richard Lanham. In teaching it recently to a graduate class in the novel, I used it in the same way I might have used Italo Calvino's *If on a Winter's Night a Traveler*—as a novel about the process of writing novels. But the class in which I have taught Sterne's novel most frequently is my undergraduate survey of fiction from Defoe to Scott. Under these circumstances, Sterne's work inevitably follows some combination of Defoe, Richardson, Fielding, and Smollett. Although I assure the students that the class cannot cover all the developments in fiction, I try to draw connections between earlier and later writers. How, then, is one to explain the sudden emergence of what must seem to be a work extraordinarily different from everything that came before? Were there world enough and time, it might be possible to have students read selections from a novel of the 1750s such as Thomas Amory's *History of John Buncle* (1756) to demonstrate how the form of the novel had expanded to accommodate a jumble of disparate material drawn from theology, science, and contemporary events under an autobiographical format, but I am not certain that anything less than a year-long seminar devoted entirely to *Tristram Shandy* would permit so leisurely an examination of fictional models. Other methods are necessary.

Like every other teacher of *Tristram Shandy*, I attempt to demonstrate Sterne's play with narrative time and with the processes of cause and effect. But I also concentrate on what seems to me two essential elements in his work: his realism and his indebtedness to a tradition in fiction and in parodies of fiction devoted to subverting the epistemological bases for the creation of fictional works. Since the early novelists share an ability for creating a vivid and seemingly whole picture of the world in which their characters move, I attempt to show how the realistic elements in these works may be found to have a continuity in *Tristram Shandy*. And since all the major British novelists wrote with a consciousness of the forces undercutting the creation of a plausible fiction, I start with that consciousness and its effect.

As with my treatment of certain satiric elements in *Tristram Shandy*, I might begin with Swift's *Tale of a Tub*, since the influence of Swift's work on Sterne is obvious enough; but I would not want to do that without stressing the tendency of eighteenth-century readers to perceive that work as fiction with satiric elements rather than as we now tend to see it—as satire with those elements of fiction common to many satires. The evidence for this perception is everywhere apparent. For example, Charles Gildon, the contemporary critic and miscellaneous writer, could only think in terms of *The Arabian Nights* in his discussion of Swift's work, and Daniel Defoe's reaction to *A Tale of a Tub* was to write an imaginary voyage to the moon, *The Consolidator* (1705). I have already suggested as a source for Swift's and Sterne's odd method of storytelling Furetière's *Nouvelle allégorique* because Furetière, for the first time in a work of fiction, at least a fiction of ordinary life, steps in at a certain point to announce to the reader his doubts about the direction of his work and his decision to redirect it. He picks up a relatively minor character, Charroselles, drops the others, who do not interest him, and follows an entirely new narrative line. I do not argue for any direct influence on Swift or Sterne, however likely that may be, but I would want to insist that the methods of Furetière, widely influential as they were, could not but have reached Swift and perhaps Sterne through Swift. In seeing *A Tale of a Tub* more as interrupted fiction than as satire, Swift's contemporaries probably shared a position with Sterne. But Sterne's contemporaries (and my students in the novel course) could compare what Sterne wrote with the vivid representation of what the reader picked up as the "real world" in the fiction of Defoe, Richardson, and Smollett. Perhaps Swift's contemporaries would have demanded less help to fall into that metonymic process by which the reader reconstructs a kind of reality from details. The important point, however, is that *Tristram Shandy* operates very much in keeping with Richardson's world. We are given more real dates than Richardson provides in *Clarissa* and, except for some spectacular set pieces of realism, such as the description of Clarissa's prison room and of the prostitutes gathered about to witness the death of Mrs. Sinclair, just as much physical detail.

Since the reputation of *Tristram Shandy* as a model for the postmodern novel depends on Sterne's continually reminding the reader of the novel-writing process that is going on in the book's creation, it may seem unfortunate to bring up the idea of realism. Be that as it may, if we regard realism as a mode crossing over generic lines, Sterne's novel obviously represents a landmark in eighteenth-century fictional realism. Like Flaubert, Sterne selects a story about provincial life that has no intrinsic excitement. In a parody of realistic technique, Francis Kirkman, in his continuation of *The English Rogue*, devoted pages to the objects needed in preparing for a birth, but Sterne's focus on the day of birth, however much it may have sprung out of a parody of biographical and fictional methods, does not, in the end, emerge as parody. Comic as the scene with Dr. Slop and Toby may be, it presents us with a subject that was usually passed over by contemporary novelists. In portraying the hospital and the proprietess who is eventually to become Moll Flander's "Governess," Defoe devoted pages to the care that might be given to expectant mothers, but of the process of birth itself he says almost nothing. In part, *Tristram Shandy* is an extended discourse on a subject that was strictly forbidden to writers of romances. Similarly, Sterne treats the reader to detailed accounts of other topics usually banished from romances and even those fictions that attempted to follow in the tradition of Defoe, Richardson, and Smollett. Defoe's *Memoirs of a Cavalier* and Smollett's *Roderick Random* have their share of wounds, warfare, and death. But the focus on Toby's wound, with its details about the treatment and the anguish involved, represents a more concentrated realism than either Defoe or Smollett supplies on this subject. And the death of Le Fever, despite the control exerted over the emotion of the scene by comic devices, is depicted as a very real death.

Parody is never far off, but it never completely destroys the effect of the real. If, in its treatment of impotence, *Tristram Shandy* bears some resemblance to Petronius's *Satyricon*, one difference lies in Sterne's sense of the real. In the experience of the reader, the Shandy family appears to be, above all, a genuine family living within the confines of Yorkshire. However much Tristram may play with his role as a narrator, however much he may be puzzled by the nature of his true self, he never suggests that the story he has to tell is all invented for the purpose of entertaining the reader. Fielding may suggest something like this at playful moments in his role as narrator, but Tristram never offers the reader the chance to believe that uncle Toby,

Walter Shandy, and Corporal Trim are merely inventions. Even Mrs. Shandy, though shadowy as a character, becomes identifiable as a phlegmatic figure among a group of eccentric ideologues. Her desire to get to London, a place Walter detests as a monstrous economic growth absorbing the wealth of the nation, seems to be the one serious emotional drive of her life, and frustrated in that longing by a false pregnancy, she spends her life cultivating her curiosity about the intentions of her very odd family.

The doubts that Sterne expresses are about the conventional expectations created by narrative. Sterne's borrowing from Cervantes in having Trim tell the "story of the King of Bohemia and his seven castles" (8: 19) is the illustration I discuss most extensively in class. When Sancho Panza attempts to tell a story, he has trouble distinguishing fable and fiction from a true story and with remembering how the story develops. He wants to include all information in the tale, threatens to lose the story in an endless pattern of other narratives to which it is related, and, finally, has no ability to summarize the action. Each event is discrete to Sancho and must be narrated separately. Yet, despite all, he presents what would seem to have the pattern of a story on the familiar theme of the fickleness of love. Corporal Trim's story, by contrast, never gets beyond the first few sentences. Having raised all kinds of problems of geography and chronology in the mind of its particular audience, Uncle Toby, it falters entirely on the word *happening*—on the questions of cause, effect, and determinism. Trim is not prepared to answer such large metaphysical questions about destiny, and without some understanding on this issue how can a fiction proceed? By explaining his intentions and by shifting the direction of the fiction, Trim had managed to answer Toby's early objections, and up to that point, the major difference between Toby and Don Quixote as listeners involved the nature of the new associationism. Problems of time and place awaken chains of associations that make the narrative difficult. The word *happening* also involves its associations, as Toby broods over William III's theory that a man cannot be killed in battle until he encounters the bullet meant for him, but even more significantly, Sterne intimates that, once the ontology of action ("happening") within a work of fiction is questioned, the novel might be obliged to clarify its positions on such philosophic subjects as free will and necessity, chance and probability. Even were Trim capable of such an exercise, the result would be the loss of an entertaining fiction and the production of another nonsensical treatise on philosophy. Cervantes reads us a lesson about storytelling that demonstrates the absurdity of fiction imitating reality and that argues for the craft of the great writer as the solution to this dilemma. Sterne suggests that the conventions maneuvered by the writer of fiction are absurd and that life itself is merely a fragment.

Trim solves *his* problem quickly by entering into a different kind of narrative—one that the reader is asked to accept as an actual event—Trim's love for the fair Beguine. Like almost everything else in *Tristram Shandy*, that story has no clear ending, being interrupted by Toby's discomfort with sexual matters, but we are left without any doubt that it did have an end. It would seem, then, that if narratives of "real" events tend to become fragmentary, the attempt to tell what amounts to a piece of fiction dissolves almost immediately into improbability and doubt. In this scheme, incomplete narrative becomes the most realistic form of narrative. Whereas postmodernist fiction will hold up the narrative to assure readers that everything they are reading is a fiction, Sterne's most powerful effects are achieved by the assumption that the feelings of the narrator and the characters are part of a real world that is best approached through comedy and laughter.

Multistability and Method in *Tristram Shandy*

Stephen C. Behrendt

One of the most difficult aspects of Sterne's *Tristram Shandy*, for students and instructors alike, is the nature and purpose of Sterne's humor. Students tend to find the novel so disorienting—so frustrating to their expectations —that they generally either fail to see its humor or are simply annoyed by it, or put off, rather than amused. This understandable reaction creates difficulties for instructors who want their students to exchange the reader's customary role as spectator for the less conventional one of active participant in the "performance" of the novel, the role Sterne in fact assigns his reader. For reading *Tristram Shandy* is unlike reading virtually any other novel, and it requires of its readers a much different attitude and activity than does any other novel—indeed, probably any other verbal text—they are likely to have encountered. Particularly in undergraduate courses in the history and development of the novel, in which the class may be composed largely of nonmajors, the instructor has to be prepared for students to complain that the novel is "confusing," "directionless," even (worst of all) "boring." These complaints, of course, merely echo some of the leading opinions of two centuries of criticism and, to a considerable extent, the dismay of students and of their critical forebears arises from the same source: from a failure adequately to appreciate Sterne's intention to destabilize both the act of reading itself and the "content" or "meaning" readers typically set out either to discover or to construct when they read a "normal" text.

I have found that some preliminary class discussion of stability in the arts generally, and of how it is created, helps undergraduate students (particularly) to come to grips with some of the complexities of Sterne's text. In part this discussion involves assessing the relative reliability of Sterne's narrator, perhaps as opposed to the reliability of Defoe's or Fielding's narrators. But, more important, it involves exploring how the students themselves analyze the evidence of any given text in determining what they believe that text "means." For at least a short time, then, we focus on "truth" and how we perceive it, establish it, or construct it. Most readers see stability as a matter of security and dependability—of a sense of certainty that a rose is a rose is a rose and that two plus two equals, and will always equal, four. But in reading *Tristram Shandy* can we be sure that a nose is in fact a nose? For the student who finds *Tristram Shandy* perplexing, it is liberating to discover that the perplexity originates not in the reader's inadequacy (which the insecure student usually assumes) but, rather, in Sterne's deliberate intention. Once students break through to this recognition, they begin to understand what Umberto Eco means when he claims that any art work is both "closed" in its aesthetic, organic wholeness and uniqueness and "open" in its susceptibility to countless interpretations and that the act of reading is thus simultaneously both an interpretation and a "performance" (*Role* 49).

Because of their educational experience, our students often worry that a text may contain multiple meanings that implicitly challenge the one-to-one correspondence between question and answer (or text and "meaning") they have come to expect. And while they can easily appreciate that ambiguity is sometimes accidental and sometimes deliberate, their experiences with "objective" tests make them frightened of a calculated multiplicity of meanings—so frightened that they often mask their anxiety by accusing the author (or the text) of confusing or boring them. One method of overcoming this anxiety and releasing the students into the real fun of Sterne's procedure is to introduce them to the concept of *multistability*, a concept that accounts for the ability of images or "constructions" (whether verbal or visual) simultaneously to reveal, to "be," or to "mean" entirely different things.

In brief, multistability is the tendency of visual or (less commonly) verbal structures to suggest to the perceiver two different "meanings" or aspects without providing sufficient evidence to enable the perceiver to determine which of the two is "correct." A true multistable image forces the perceiver's mind to alternate between the two (or more) schemata that the visual image conjures; typically it is impossible to hold both images in the mind at once, a fact that becomes more and more apparent as the images increase in complexity. Multistable images "tease" the reader or viewer, alternately concealing and revealing something that is present all along.

Perhaps the most famous multistable image—and one that many students have already encountered—is Edgar Rubin's reversible goblet (see Gregory 16), which reveals both a two-dimensional goblet and a pair of silhouetted faces, depending on whether one focuses on the light or the dark areas of the image. A more complex, but also familiar, example is a picture of two women that first appeared in *Puck* in 1915 (Gregory 39). In both these images the viewer's focus—and comprehension or "interpretation"—alternates between two figures, focusing first on one, then on the other. And because nothing in the image tells the viewer which image she or he is supposed to "see," the viewer continues to shift back and forth, never coming to rest. Students have had a good deal of experience with pictures of this sort; as children many of them studied picture puzzles to find faces or objects hidden within landscapes. Sterne, likewise, undoubtedly was familiar with such images, whether in the form of well-known pictures by Giuseppe Arcimboldo (1527?–93) and his followers (like Arcimboldo's allegorical "portraits" of the seasons and the elements and his reversible pictures like *The Man and the Vegetables*) or in the still more common form of cartoons and prints in which the faces or silhouettes of political figures could be discerned within various landscapes or other topical constructions. Finally, there existed in the visual art of the later eighteenth century a tradition of anthropomorphic landscapes; these seemingly innocuous landscapes revealed, usually when rotated ninety degrees, unmistakable three-dimensional faces, faces that could never be fully eliminated from the picture once the viewer had glimpsed them and returned the pictures to their original position (Behrendt 47–51).

Sterne deliberately exploits the phenomenon of multistability in *Tristram Shandy*. His use of asterisks is one good example: in the window-sash episode, for instance, it is easy—given the context—to translate the series of asterisks attributed to Susannah into "piss out of the window" (5: 17), although these words are then our creations and not Sterne's (since he has supplied only asterisks that might—but of course do not—signify other words entirely). Moreover, in other crucial situations not even the contextualizing remarks supplied by Sterne/Tristram (the two being often virtually inseparable) provide sufficient information to enable us to decipher the asterisk puzzles (e.g., 5: 27; 7: 29). What this sort of literary trompe l'oeil reveals about Sterne's humor is instructive—and comprehensible—when applied to other aspects of the novel that appear to mean or to be now one thing, now another.

Other varieties of multistable phenomena occur when Sterne/Tristram gives his readers a blank page to draw their own portraits of the widow Wadman (6: 38): he does not intend, after all, that the reader should either take up the artist's pencil and actually, physically, draw her likeness in the blank space or pen in a verbal description; or when he inserts diagrams of Corporal Trim's stick flourish (9: 4) and his own plot lines (6: 40). The most striking example of this device in the novel is, I think, the "missing" ten pages in volume 4: "chapter 24," which the narrator tells us he has "torn out" (presumably from the printed book the reader is actually holding, as the gap in pagination is meant to suggest) and the "contents" of which he subsequently summarizes in the second paragraph of chapter 25. But such game playing with the reader's mind occurs elsewhere as well (as in the embedding within volume 9, chapter 25, of chapters 18 and 19, which had initially been left blank) and frequently enough to suggest a deliberate ploy of Sterne's.

Authors and artists use multistable structures deliberately to disorient and even annoy the reader or viewer, throwing that person off guard and calling into question both the reliability of the author or artist and the reliability of the reader's or viewer's own perceptions. Thus in teaching *Tristram Shandy* I encourage students to approach the novel with some sense of "fun and games" and to realize that what is perhaps most radically unconventional in Sterne's book is the playful manner in which the reader is forced to share with Tristram the perplexity elicited by Tristram's experiences themselves and by his attempts fully and adequately to convey them. If the instructor can help students to discover the method that informs this one aspect of Sterne/Tristram's "madness" and can offer them some visual analogies, they will fare better in reading the novel, will feel less threatened, and will stand a better chance of appreciating the mental gymnastics Sterne wishes to make them perform.

This last point also links *Tristram Shandy* to the larger issue of "open" texts generally, those works of multiple potential in which authors create formalities chiefly to outrage them (Adams 13, 164). Recent critics have claimed, for instance, that *Tristram Shandy* manages to destabilize everything from the common noun (Berthoud 25) to the Lockean view of the human condition (Day 76). Considered as book—as text—though, the novel also destabilizes the relationship between itself and its reader, as well as the relationships among its author, its narrator, and both its real audience (the reader who holds the book) and its internally imagined or invented narrative audiences (the succession of Sirs and Madams directly addressed in Tristram's narrative). I have used the concept of multistability to suggest that Sterne does not intend simply or exclusively to destabilize his reader's world, though that is part of his plan. Rather, he wishes graphically to demonstrate the dilemma confronting anyone who tries to determine the "meaning" of her or his own experiences: as with multistable images generally, the observable "facts" or data typically suggest many potential "meanings," none of which can be established with much certainty as "right" or even "most likely." Simply stated, things are almost always a good deal more than what they seem. Like Tristram, the reader is paralyzed not by a paucity of options but by an overabundance of them.

With this point in mind, I like to return the classroom discussion to the complaint about the novel's apparent formlessness. While Sterne appears to allow Tristram and everyone else blithely to ride their various hobbyhorses wherever they may go, on paths whose turns of association become increasingly bewildering, I like to remind students that this "directionless" narrative has been carefully controlled, or orchestrated, by an author who has, after all, created a formal, "made" thing in the printed book. Even the narrative itself involves multistability: Tristram is not just telling a tale—or gossiping (Stovel 116)—he is also writing a book, as he continually reminds his reader. Hence his attention to formal matters like chapter divisions, punctuation, and the like underscores the formally structured (or "closed") nature of the book as aesthetic object. Moreover, the novel's basic premise is also multistable. Writing the life and opinions of an imaginary character violates the presumed boundary between biography (or autobiography) as history (or "fact") and purely imaginative art (or "fantasy"). The book asks us to regard it as something that it is not. However, we only know it is not what it purports to be because of external facts (i.e., historical and biographical data that reveal the Shandys to be fictions). Within its own narrative framework the novel stays in character, maintaining—like *Moll Flanders*—an internal credibility as history. Sterne even heightens the illusion by drawing heavily on actual contemporary histories. The details of Uncle Toby's experiences at the siege of Namur, for instance, owe much to the extensive chronological account found in Nicholas Tindal's continuation of Paul de Rapin-Thoyras's *History of England*, the initial volumes of which Tindal had translated into English (Baird). To put it in a Shandyesque way, one could say that the novel is only fiction because we know it to be fictional, or at least partially fictional—a point that forces us to ask ourselves to what extent we are responding to the narrative itself when we read and to what extent to what we know ex post facto about the circumstances of that narrative. In terms of a multistable visual image, the distinction might be said to be between the figure and the ground, as in Rubin's goblet.

The concept of multistability enables students to attribute Sterne's admittedly eccentric procedure in *Tristram Shandy* to some demonstrable design, reassuring them about the validity of their ambivalent and initially alienated responses to the novel. It also helps them to appreciate why Sterne wishes to make it so difficult to distinguish between "real" and "false" meanings—or, more correctly, among diverse and often equally valid potential meanings. Most students, especially undergraduates, are not used to a text that manipulates them in this fashion, nor are they ready for such a text without some advance coaching or reassurance. The "transactional approach" to reading provides a useful point of reference in preparing the student for the nature and methods of Sterne's humor and of *Tristram Shandy* generally. Louise Rosenblatt's distinction between nonaesthetic—or "efferent"—reading (in which the reader's primary concern is with gathering information, finding solutions, discovering actions to be taken) and aesthetic reading (in which the primary concern is with what happens to and within the reader during the act of reading) is very helpful on this score (23–25). Most students approach works of fiction in terms of nonaesthetic reading, as "textbooks" to be read with an eye toward digesting and internalizing data, often for the short-term purpose of examination. *Tristram Shandy*, however, makes this procedure virtually impossible, forcing students into the aesthetic mode of reading. Indeed, Sterne makes his reader Tristram's coparticipant, his cocreator. In this sense, what happens to the reader in *Tristram Shandy* is not merely a subsidiary consideration, it is central to the book Sterne designed. Likewise, his humor—which is troubling because of its determination to keep the reader off balance and insecure—turns finally on the reader's ability to overcome the feeling of being threatened by the novel's multistability and to relax and laugh.

Instead of attacking the text as an endless series of potential multiple meanings—both decent and indecent (e.g., the countless sexual innuendoes)—that must be "figured out," readers of *Tristram Shandy* must learn to unbend, to recognize and even to relish the marvelously suggestive potential of language used with precision and particularity, for the express purpose of creating multiple, simultaneously viable meanings. Like multistable visual images, Sterne's multistable texts generate numerous meanings not because the author has carelessly used vague and imprecise language but, rather, because he has carefully and deliberately manipulated exact language to create two or more distinct impressions. Obviously, multistability is not the same as instability, and Sterne's primary intention is certainly not merely to undermine the text, as one might at first suspect. Sterne's humor derives much of its force from the fact that language is largely inflexible rather than slippery or amorphous. Because language generates its own determinate context within the reader's mind, Sterne can achieve some of his most striking effects by using particular words (like *nose*) as if they meant something else entirely, thereby creating a multilevel texture of suggestion and meaning(s) that makes virtually everything in *Tristram Shandy* appear simultaneously to be many things—or even nothing.

History and Theory, Literature and Criticism: The Two Knobs of Teaching *Tristram Shandy*

Joel Weinsheimer

I teach *Tristram Shandy* primarily in two types of courses, eighteenth-century novel and theory of narrative. Each course situates Sterne's novel in a distinctive context; each context makes it appear a somewhat different novel. Not surprisingly, when *Tristram Shandy* is introduced in the company of *Tom Jones*, contemporary aesthetics, and Locke's empiricism on the one hand, or of Shklovsky's formalism, Iser's phenomenology, and Barth's *Lost in the Funhouse* on the other, certain topics are emphasized to the neglect of others. Each kind of course has a place in the curriculum, as justified by its distinct function. A historically oriented course tends to place Sterne's work within an evolutionary sequence of precedents and consequents; a theoretically oriented course places it in a system of simultaneous variants. But I have found that taking one approach or the other in teaching *Tristram Shandy* makes less difference than one would expect (or at least less than I expected), and that particular nondichotomy between history and theory in my experience of teaching the novel is what I would like to talk about in these few pages.

Over the last decade or so, we have heard entirely too much about the incompatibility of the historical and theoretical approaches and about the dispensability of one or the other. Partisans of each camp have often simply ignored each other and, rather than admit laziness or lack of curiosity, have tried to pass off their narrowness as superior wisdom. A few such partisans still remain, no doubt, like the noble and pathetic soldiers on isolated islands who fought on, long after the war was over. But now that the battle of ancients and moderns has once again ended in stalemate, now that theory has become historical and history theoretical, it has become more evident that between the two approaches to *Tristram Shandy* there is no dichotomy and, in fact, a good deal of coincidence.

One of the theoretical essays that I have found most pertinent to *Tristram Shandy* is "The Reading Process: A Phenomenological Approach" by Wolfgang Iser. Iser was among the first reader-response theorists to argue that reading is active and productive. Where the formalists considered reading as, ideally, passive reception, Iser contends that literature evokes the reader's creativity: "literary texts transform reading into a creative process that is far above mere perception of what is written. . . . The product of this creative activity is what we might call the virtual dimension of the text, which . . . is the coming together of text and imagination" (54). If readers are to participate actively in cocreating the work, they must be left something to do. Some matters must remain indeterminate; some semantic gaps must be left unfulfilled; and it is just that incompleteness which invites creative reading. "No tale can ever be told in its entirety," Iser goes on to say.

"Indeed, it is only through inevitable omissions that a story gains its dynamism. . . . The opportunity is given to us to bring into play our own faculty for establishing connections—for filling in the gaps left by the text itself" (55).

Iser's metaphor of gaps has an immediate applicability to *Tristram Shandy* because there the omissions are forced on our attention. The blank page where we are invited to paint Widow Wadman in the image of ideal beauty; the "marbled page (motly emblem of my work!)" and the black page, behind which "truths . . . still lie mystically hid," (3: 36); the half-finished chapters over which a dark curtain is discreetly dropped; the endlessly interrupted and finally abandoned King of Bohemia story; the dashes and asterisks—all are so many invitations for readers to exercise their ingenuity and contribute to creating the novel. One citation must here serve in the place of many. Tristram repeats Jenny's words of comfort after a humiliating failure: " 'Tis enough, said'st thou, coming close up to me, as I stood with my garters in my hand, reflecting upon what had *not* pass'd——'Tis enough, Tristram, and I am satisfied, said'st thou, whispering these words in my ear, **** ** **** *** ****** . . ." (7: 29). What has been omitted, suppressed, or cut off is, in this novel, always important; and the reader is continually being enticed or commanded to remedy the omissions—or, in Iser's terms, to fill in the gaps.

Of course, any sufficiently general narrative theory is bound to be applicable to *Tristram Shandy*, as well as to a host of other novels. One might object that since Iser's hypothesis that omission engages the reader's imagination derives from Husserl and Ingarden, it has only an apparent relevance to Sterne and that to enforce it on a novel two centuries old amounts to the most naive kind of anachronism. There are many possible explanations of Sterne's gaps, and what we want is not just any explanation for them but rather Sterne's explanation. But this objection loses some of its force when we discover that Iser cites Sterne's explanation in support of his own theory:

> [N]o author, who understands the just boundaries of decorum and good breeding, would presume to think all: The truest respect which you can pay to the reader's understanding, is to halve this matter amicably, and leave him something to imagine, in his turn, as well as yourself.
>
> For my own part, I am eternally paying him compliments of this kind, and do all that lies in my power to keep his imagination as busy as my own. (2: 11)

There is, admittedly, no need to discuss Iser explicitly in a historical course in the eighteenth-century novel, but it is hard to keep him out altogether. His theory pertains to a wider domain than *Tristram Shandy* alone, and for that reason, once you begin thinking about Sterne in Iser's way, you begin picking up on similar things in other novelists, among them Sterne's contemporaries. And there's the rub for anyone who wants to insist on an antithesis between history and theory. Since these contemporaries compose the context for *Tristram Shandy* in a survey course, I am never quite sure whether my purportedly historical presentation of the eighteenth-century novel has or has not been contaminated by twentieth-century theory.

For example, to contextualize Tristram's comment indicating his intention to leave the reader something to imagine, I might point to similar passages in *Tom Jones* where the narrator sets the reader to "filling up these vacant Spaces . . . with his own Conjectures" (116)—or where he says, "thou art highly mistaken if thou dost imagine that we intended, when we began this great Work, to leave thy Sagacity nothing to do, or that without sometimes exercising this Talent, thou wilt be able to travel through our Pages with any Pleasure or Profit to thyself" (614). In his *Essay on Taste* (1759), Alexander Gerard likewise concludes that "even plainness and perspicuity becomes displeasing . . . [when they leave] no room for exercising the reader's thought"; the more enjoyable kind of writing, Gerard continues, "occasions a suspense of thought, and leaves the full meaning to be guessed at, and comprehended only on attention" (3–4). In *Spectator* number 411, Addison describes reading imaginative literature as "a Gentle Exercise to the Faculties, awaken[ing] them from Sloth and Idleness" (3: 539); and Locke, too, enjoins his readers to think for themselves: "*This, Reader, is the Entertainment of those, who let loose their own Thoughts, and follow them in writing; which thou oughtest not to envy them, since they afford thee an Opportunity of the like Diversion, if thou wilt make use of thy own Thoughts in reading*" (6–7). This background for Tristram's activist conception of reading seems perfectly appropriate for a purely historical treatment of Sterne's novel. Would it tarnish that historical purity, however, if it turned out that this material caught my attention only because of Iser's influence? Perhaps not, but that would mean, in this case at least, that no clear line could be drawn between a historical and a theoretical approach to the novel.

My experience with Viktor Shklovsky's well-known essay on *Tristram Shandy* brings me to a similar conclusion. This piece epitomizes the best and the worst of theoretical writing. Shklovsky opens with a very damaging admission: "In this essay I do not propose to analyze Laurence Sterne's novel; I intend to use it merely as an illustration to the general laws of novelistic form" (66); and he later explains, "I am not interested in [*Tristram Shandy*] but in plot theory" (87). At the distance of a half century, we can sense the dubious scientism involved in the search for "general laws" governing the novel. Even if any were to be found, they would not tell us what we want to know about *Tristram Shandy*. This novel, every novel, is singular, unique, unrepeatable; but *Tristram Shandy* is a great novel precisely because the interest excited by its particularity surpasses any interest the novel might have as an example of a rule or law or theory. Shklovsky's celebrated conclusion—"*Tristram Shandy* is the most typical novel of world literature" (89)—embodies not a paradox but a truism. Anyone looking for general laws will find nothing but typical cases.

This difficulty is not peculiar to Shklovsky; something similar is present in Iser's work, for it is implicit in all theoretical endeavor, whether in print or in the classroom. History particularizes; theory generalizes. As Geoffrey Hartman has written, when "a philosopher, or any generalizing intellect, uses texts as examples he subverts their exemplary power" (25). If any novel will do for an illustration, a course on plot theory is likely to teach students, inter alia, that plot theory is of more interest than *Tristram Shandy*.

Yet this objection assumes that *Tristram Shandy* belongs to one order of discourse and theory to another and that criticism and literature are defined antithetically. Thus when Shklovsky writes of Sterne that "the artist shows us the aesthetic laws which lie behind [his] compositional devices" (88–89), Shklovsky seems guilty of a basic category mistake. Isn't it true, I ask my students, that Shklovsky has confused Sterne the novelist with a literary theorist, for isn't it rather the theorist—indeed, Shklovsky himself—who wants to reveal these laws? Yet Shklovsky cannot mean that while the theorist formulates aesthetic laws, the novelist merely exemplifies them, because the heart of his argument is that the content of *Tristram Shandy* is a "reflection upon the form itself" (73). Surely it is hard to dispute Shklovsky's thesis that, among other things, *Tristram Shandy* is about its own devices, its own composition, and even its own interpretation. One could also say, however, that the content not just of Sterne's novel but of Sterne criticism—indeed, of Shklovsky's essay—is reflection on just these topics. What I try to show students is that when Shklovsky asserts that he is interested not in *Tristram Shandy* but in plot theory, his real mistake is to think that these are incompatible; for, as his own essay demonstrates, there is no categorical distinction between Sterne and Sterne criticism, no antithesis between *Tristram Shandy* and literary theory. To assert the contrary is merely to take the position that Sterne was not reflective, that he was not aware of what he was doing. But the great merit of Shklovsky's essay has been to make that position untenable. To include *Tristram Shandy* in a course on theory of the novel is, ideally, to consider it not as a mere example but as a source of narrative theory.

A serious historical anachronism results when one does *not* teach *Tristram Shandy* as if it were Borges's "Pierre Menard" or Barth's "Lost in the Funhouse," for all three of these metafictions call attention to the nondifferentiation of theory and practice, criticism and literature. One cannot even say that in the eighteenth century such distinctions are not recognized, while in the twentieth century they are recognized and denied. When in "A Digression concerning Criticks" Swift uses the word *digression* ironically, he simultaneously asserts and denies a division between the narrative and critical parts of the *Tale*. When Pope writes a poem called *An Essay on Criticism*, he labors under no confusion about the difference between poetry and essays or poetry and criticism. When Johnson includes in *Rasselas* a "Dissertation upon Poetry" that could as easily have appeared in his preface to Shakespeare, he is making no mistake about what properly belongs to a fable and what to a critical treatise.

This conscious nondifferentiation is one of the topics we talk about in both of my courses that include *Tristram Shandy*. There are still two courses; they have not melted into one. But in teaching Sterne's masterpiece I consider it important to insist on the complementarity of the two approaches: to show that as history without theory is blind, so theory without history is empty. In my view, and I think in Sterne's, *Tristram Shandy* itself demonstrates that literature and criticism are, like two knobs on the back of a chair, "indubitably both made and fitted to go together" (3: 20).

PARTICIPANTS IN SURVEY OF *TRISTRAM SHANDY* INSTRUCTORS

During the preparation of this volume a goodly number of teachers of *Tristram Shandy* participated in a survey for which they described their approaches to the book and the materials they used in teaching it. For their valuable contributions, the editor is most grateful.

Percy G. Adams, University of Tennessee, Knoxville; Jack Armistead, University of Tennessee, Knoxville; Jerry C. Beasley, University of Delaware; Stephen C. Behrendt, University of Nebraska, Lincoln; Sophia B. Blaydes, West Virginia University; Edward A. Bloom, Brown University; Patricia Brückmann, University of Toronto; George Butte, Colorado College; Max Byrd, University of California, Davis; Arthur H. Cash, State University College of New York, New Paltz; Alistair Duckworth, University of Florida; John A. Dussinger, University of Illinois, Urbana; Moira Ferguson, University of Nebraska, Lincoln; Robert P. Fitzgerald, Pennsylvania State University, University Park; Gerald M. Garmon, West Georgia University; Sidney Gottlieb, Sacred Heart University; Donald Greene, University of Southern California, Emeritus; Elizabeth W. Harries, Smith College; Frederick M. Keener, Hofstra University; Ira Konigsberg, University of Michigan, Ann Arbor; Elizabeth Kraft, University of Georgia; David H. Lindstrom, Colorado State University; Lawrence Lipking, Northwestern University; George E. McCelvey, Western Kentucky University; Brian McCrea, University of Florida; Maximillian E. Novak, University of California, Los Angeles; William Bowman Piper, Rice University; Irwin Primer, Rutgers University, Newark; Michael Raymond, Stetson University; Betty Rizzo, City College, City University of New York; Deborah D. Rogers, University of Maine, Orono; John F. Sena, Ohio State University, Columbus; William R. Siebenschuh, Case Western Reserve University; Robert D. Spector, Long Island University, Brooklyn; Susan Staves, Brandeis University; Philip Stevick, Temple University; George Winchester Stone, New York University, Emeritus; Sheila Ortiz Taylor, Florida State University; Leigh Ehlers Telotte, Smyrna, GA; Connie C. Thorson, University of New Mexico; James L. Thorson, University of New Mexico; Ian Todd, Pace University, Pleasantville-Briarcliff; Leland E. Warren, Kansas State University; Joel Weinsheimer, University of Minnesota, Minneapolis; Jeanne K. Welcher, C. W. Post Center, Long Island University; Samuel H. Woods, Jr., Oklahoma State University; Everett Zimmerman, University of California, Santa Barbara.

WORKS CITED

Editions of *The Life and Opinions of Tristram Shandy, Gentleman*
(in chronological order by publication date)

London: Dent, 1912; numerous rptgs.

New York: Random, 1928; numerous rptgs.

Ed. James A. Work. New York: Odyssey, 1940.

New York: Holt, 1950.

New York: Signet-NAL, 1962.

Ed. Ian Watt. Boston: Houghton, 1965.

Ed. Graham Petrie. Baltimore: Penguin, 1967.

New York: Airmont, 1967.

Sterne. Ed. Douglas Grant. Cambridge: Harvard UP, 1970. 25–524.

The Florida Edition of the Works of Laurence Sterne. Ed. Melvyn New. Vols. 1 and 2. *The Text of* Tristram Shandy. Ed. Melvyn New and Joan New. Vol. 3. *The Notes to* Tristram Shandy. Ed. Melvyn New with Richard A. Davies and W. G. Day. Gainesville: UP of Florida, 1978, 1984.

Ed. Howard Anderson. New York: Norton, 1980.

Ed. Ian Campbell Ross. Oxford: Oxford UP, 1983.

Books and Articles

Adams, Robert M. *Strains of Discord: Studies in Literary Openness*. Ithaca: Cornell UP, 1958.

Addison, Joseph. *The Spectator*. Ed. Donald F. Bond. 5 vols. Oxford: Clarendon, 1965.

Allen, Walter. *The English Novel: A Short Critical History*. New York: Dutton, 1955.

Alter, Robert. *Partial Magic: The Novel as a Self-Conscious Genre*. Berkeley: U of California P, 1975.

———. "*Tristram Shandy* and the Game of Love." *American Scholar* 37 (1968): 316–23.

Anderson, Howard. "Associationism and Wit in *Tristram Shandy.*" *Philological Quarterly* 48 (1969): 27–41.

Auerbach, Erich. *Mimesis.* Trans. Willard R. Trask. Princeton: Princeton UP, 1953.

Auerbach, Nina. "Engorging the Patriarchy." *Historical Studies and Literary Criticism.* Ed. Jerome J. McGann. Madison: U of Wisconsin P, 1985. 229–39.

Bacon, Francis. *Essays, Advancement of Learning, New Atlantis, and Other Pieces.* Ed. R. F. Jones. New York: Odyssey, 1937.

Baird, Theodore. "The Time-Scheme of *Tristram Shandy* and a Source." *PMLA* 51 (1936): 803–20.

Baker, Ernest A. "Sterne." *The History of the English Novel.* 10 vols. London: Witherby, 1924–1939. 4: 240–76.

Bakhtin, M. M. *The Dialogic Imagination: Four Essays.* Ed. Michael Holquist. Austin: U of Texas P, 1981.

———. *Problems of Dostoevsky's Poetics.* Ed. and trans. Caryl Emerson. Minneapolis: U of Minnesota P, 1984.

Bate, W. Jackson. *The Burden of the Past and the English Poet.* Cambridge: Belknap–Harvard UP, 1970.

Battestin, Martin C., ed. *British Novelists, 1660–1800.* Vol. 39 of *Dictionary of Literary Biography.* Detroit: Gale, 1985.

———. *The Providence of Wit: Aspects of Form in Augustan Literature and the Arts.* Oxford: Clarendon, 1974.

Baxter, Stephen, ed. *England's Rise to Greatness, 1600–1763.* Berkeley: U of California P, 1983.

Beasley, Jerry C. *English Fiction, 1660–1800: A Guide to Information Sources.* Detroit: Gale, 1978.

Behrendt, Stephen C. "Art as Deceptive Intruder: Audience Entrapment in Eighteenth-Century Verbal and Visual Art." *Papers on Language and Literature* 19 (1983): 37–52.

Berthoud, Jacques. "Shandeism and Sexuality." Myer 24–38.

Bleich, David. *Subjective Criticism.* Baltimore: Johns Hopkins UP, 1978.

Booth, Wayne C. "Did Sterne Complete *Tristram Shandy?*" *Modern Philology* 48 (1951): 172–83.

———. "Freedom of Interpretation: Bakhtin and the Challenge of Feminist Criticism." *Critical Inquiry* 9 (1982): 45–76.

———. *The Rhetoric of Fiction.* Chicago: U of Chicago P, 1961.

———. "The Self-Conscious Narrator in Comic Fiction before *Tristram Shandy.*" *PMLA* 67 (1952): 163–85.

———. "Thomas Mann and Eighteenth-Century Comic Fiction." *Furioso* 6 (1951): 25–36. Rpt. in *Now Don't Try to Reason with Me: Essays and Ironies for a Credulous Age.* Chicago: U of Chicago P, 1970. 273–85.

Borges, Jorge Luis. "Tlön, Uqbar, Orbis Tertius." *Labyrinths: Selected Stories and Other Writings.* Ed. Donald A. Yates and James E. Irby. 2nd ed. New York: New Directions, 1964. 3–18.

Boswell, James. *The Life of Samuel Johnson.* Ed. G. B. Hill. Rev. L. F. Powell. 6 vols. Oxford: Clarendon, 1934–60.

Brady, Frank. "*Tristram Shandy*: Sexuality, Morality, and Sensibility." *Eighteenth-Century Studies* 4 (1970): 41–56.

[Brandon, Isaac]. *Fragments: In the Manner of Sterne.* London, 1797.

Braudy, Leo. "The Form of the Sentimental Novel." *Novel* 7 (1973): 5–13.

Bredvold, Louis I. *The Natural History of Sensibility.* Detroit: Wayne State UP, 1962.

Briggs, Peter. "Locke's *Essay* and the Tentativeness of *Tristram Shandy*." *Studies in Philology* 82 (1985): 494–517.

Brissenden, R. F. "Sterne and Painting." *Of Books and Humankind: Essays Presented to Bonamy Dobrée.* London: Routledge, 1964. 93–108.

———. " 'Trusting to Almighty God': Another Look at the Composition of *Tristram Shandy*." Cash and Stedmond 258–69.

———. *Virtue in Distress: Studies in the Novel of Sentiment from Richardson to Sade.* New York: Barnes, 1974.

Brown, E. K. *Rhythm in the Novel.* Toronto: U of Toronto P, 1950.

Bruss, Elizabeth W. "The Game of Literature and Some Literary Games." *New Literary History* 9 (1977): 153–72.

Burckhardt, Sigurd. "*Tristram Shandy*'s Law of Gravity." *ELH* 28 (1961): 70–88.

Burthogge, Richard. *An Essay upon Reason, and the Nature of Spirits.* London, 1694.

Butt, John, and Geoffrey Carnall. *The Mid-Eighteenth Century.* Vol. 8 of *The Oxford History of English Literature.* Oxford: Clarendon, 1979.

Byrd, Max. *Tristram Shandy.* London: Allen, 1985.

Cash, Arthur H. "The Birth of Tristram Shandy: Sterne and Dr. Burton." *Studies in the Eighteenth Century.* Ed. R. F. Brissenden. Canberra: Australian National UP, 1968. 133–54.

———. *Laurence Sterne: The Early and Middle Years.* London: Methuen, 1975.

———. *Laurence Sterne: The Later Years.* London: Methuen, 1986.

———. "The Lockean Psychology of *Tristram Shandy*." *ELH* 22 (1955): 125–35.

Cash, Arthur H., and John M. Stedmond, eds. *The Winged Skull: Papers from the Laurence Sterne Bicentenary Conference.* Kent: Kent State UP, 1971.

Chandler, David. *The Art of Warfare in the Age of Marlborough.* New York: Hippocrene, 1976.

———. *Marlborough as Military Commander.* New York: Scribner's, 1973.

Conrad, Peter. *Shandyism: The Character of Romantic Irony.* Oxford: Blackwell; New York: Barnes, 1978.

Craddock, Patricia B. *Young Edward Gibbon: Gentleman of Letters.* Baltimore: Johns Hopkins UP, 1982.

Crane, R. S. "Suggestions toward a Genealogy of the 'Man of Feeling.' " *ELH* 1 (1934): 205–30.

Cross, Wilbur L. *The Development of the English Novel*. New York: Macmillan, 1899.

———. *The Life and Times of Laurence Sterne*. 3rd ed. New Haven: Yale UP, 1929.

Culler, Jonathan. *On Deconstruction: Theory and Criticism after Structuralism*. Ithaca: Cornell UP, 1982.

Damrosch, Leopold. *God's Plot and Man's Stories: Studies in the Fictional Imagination from Milton to Fielding*. Chicago: U of Chicago P, 1985.

Davis, David Brion. *The Problem of Slavery in the Age of Revolution, 1770–1823*. Ithaca: Cornell UP, 1975.

Davis, Lennard J. *Factual Fictions: The Origins of the English Novel*. New York: Columbia UP, 1983.

Day, W. G. "*Tristram Shandy*: Locke May Not Be the Key." Myer 75–83.

Dobrée, Bonamy. *English Literature in the Early Eighteenth Century, 1700–1740*. Vol. 7 of *The Oxford History of English Literature*. Oxford: Clarendon, 1959.

[D'Urfey, Thomas?]. *An Essay towards the Theory of the Intelligible World, Intuitively Considered*. London, [1701?].

Eco, Umberto. *The Name of the Rose*. Trans. William Weaver. New York: Harcourt, 1983.

———. *The Role of the Reader: Explorations in the Semiotics of Texts*. Bloomington: Indiana UP, 1979.

Ehlers, Leigh A. "Mrs. Shandy's 'Lint and Basilicon': The Importance of Women in *Tristram Shandy*." *South Atlantic Review* 46 (1981): 61–75.

Epictetus. *The Moral Discourses of Epictetus*. Trans. Elizabeth Carter. 1758. London: Dent, 1910.

Fetterley, Judith. *The Resisting Reader: A Feminist Approach to American Fiction*. Bloomington: Indiana UP, 1978.

Fielding, Henry. *The History of Tom Jones, a Foundling*. Ed. Martin C. Battestin. Middletown: Wesleyan UP, 1975.

———. *Jonathan Wild*. Ed. David Nokes. New York: Penguin, 1982.

———. *Tom Thumb: A Tragedy. Burlesque Plays of the Eighteenth Century*. Ed. Simon Trussler. New York: Oxford UP, 1969. 143–70.

Fluchère, Henri. *Laurence Sterne: From Tristram to Yorick: An Interpretation of Tristram Shandy*. Trans. Barbara Bray. London: Oxford UP, 1965.

Ford, Boris, ed. *The Pelican Guide to English Literature: From Dryden to Johnson*. Baltimore: Penguin, 1963.

Forster, E. M. *Aspects of the Novel*. New York: Harcourt, 1927.

Foundations of the Novel: Representative Early Eighteenth-Century Fiction. New York: Garland, 1973.

Frank, Joseph. "Spatial Form in Modern Literature." *Sewanee Review* 53 (1945): 221–40, 433–56, 643–53.

Frye, Northrop. *Anatomy of Criticism: Four Essays*. Princeton: Princeton UP, 1957.

———. "Towards Defining an Age of Sensibility." *ELH* 23 (1956): 144–52.

Furetière, Antoine. *Nouvelle allégorique*. Ed. Eva van Ginneken. Genève: Droz, 1967.

———. *Le roman bourgeois*. Ed. Georges Mongrédien. Paris: Club du Meilleur Livre, 1956.

Fussell, Paul. *The Rhetorical World of Augustan Humanism: Ethics and Imagery from Swift to Burke*. Oxford: Clarendon, 1965.

Garat, Dominique-Joseph. *Mémoires historiques sur le vie de M. Suard*. 2 vols. Paris, 1820.

George, M. Dorothy. *English Social Life in the Eighteenth Century*. London: Sheldon, 1923.

———. *London Life in the Eighteenth Century*. London: Kegan, 1925. New York: Harper, 1965.

Gerard, Alexander. *An Essay on Taste*. Ed. Walter J. Hipple, Jr. Gainesville: Scholars' Facsimiles, 1963.

Gibbon, Edward. *The Autobiography of Gibbon*. Ed. Dero A. Saunders. New York: Meridian, 1961.

Goffmann, Erving. *Forms of Talk*. Philadelphia: U of Pennsylvania P, 1981.

Graves, Patricia Hogan. "A Computer-Generated Concordance to Sterne's *Tristram Shandy*." 4 vols. Diss. Emory U, 1974.

Greene, Donald. *The Age of Exuberance*. New York: Random, 1970.

———. "From Accidie to Neurosis: *The Castle of Indolence* Revisited." *English Literature in the Age of Disguise*. Ed. Maximillian E. Novak. Berkeley: U of California P, 1977. 131–56.

———. "Latitudinarianism and Sensibility: The Genealogy of the 'Man of Feeling' Reconsidered." *Modern Philology* 75 (1977): 159–83.

Gregory, R. L. *The Intelligent Eye*. New York: McGraw, 1970.

Hagstrum, Jean. *Sex and Sensibility: Ideal and Erotic Love from Milton to Mozart*. Chicago: U of Chicago P, 1980.

Harries, Elizabeth W. "Sterne's Novels: Gathering Up the Fragments." *ELH* 49 (1982): 35–49.

Hartley, Lodwick. *Laurence Sterne: An Annotated Bibliography, 1965–1977*. Boston: Hall, 1978.

———. *Laurence Sterne in the Twentieth Century: An Essay and a Bibliography of Sternean Studies, 1900–1965*. Chapel Hill: U of North Carolina P, 1966.

———. *This Is Lorence: A Narrative of the Reverend Laurence Sterne*. Chapel Hill: U of North Carolina P, 1943. Rpt. as *Laurence Sterne: A Biographical Essay*. Chapel Hill: U of North Carolina P, 1968.

Hartman, Geoffrey. *The Fate of Reading and Other Essays*. Chicago: U of Chicago P, 1975.

Hazlitt, William. "On the English Novelists." *Lectures on the English Comic Writers*. London: Dent, n.d. 106–32.

Holland, Norman. *The Dynamics of Literary Response*. New York: Oxford UP, 1968.

Holtz, William V. *Image and Immortality: A Study of* Tristram Shandy. Providence: Brown UP, 1970.

Howes, Alan B., ed. *Sterne: The Critical Heritage*. London: Routledge, 1974.

―――. *Yorick and the Critics: Sterne's Reputation in England, 1760–1868*. New Haven: Yale UP, 1958. Hamden: Archon, 1971.

Humphreys, A. R. *The Augustan World*. London: Methuen, 1954.

Iser, Wolfgang. *The Implied Reader: Patterns of Communication from Bunyan to Beckett*. Baltimore: Johns Hopkins UP, 1974.

―――. "The Reading Process: A Phenomenological Approach." *New Literary History* 3 (1972): 279–99. Rpt. in Tompkins 50–69.

Jefferson, D. W. "*Tristram Shandy* and the Tradition of Learned Wit." *Essays in Criticism* 1 (1951): 225–48. Rpt. in Traugott, *Laurence Sterne* 148–67.

Johnson, J. W. *The Formation of English Neo-Classical Thought*. Princeton: Princeton UP, 1967.

Johnson, Samuel. *The Poems of Samuel Johnson*. Ed. David Nichol Smith and Edward L. McAdam. 2nd ed. Oxford: Clarendon, 1974.

―――. *Rasselas*. Ed. R. W. Chapman. Oxford: Clarendon, 1927.

Karl, Frederick R. *The Adversary Literature: The English Novel in the Eighteenth Century: A Study in Genre*. New York: Farrar, 1974. Pub. in England as *A Reader's Guide to the Development of the English Novel in the Eighteenth Century*. London: Thames, 1975.

Kestner, Joseph A. *The Spatiality of the Novel*. Detroit: Wayne State UP, 1978.

Kolodny, Annette. "Dancing through the Minefield: Some Observations on the Theory, Practice, and Politics of a Feminist Literary Criticism." *Feminist Studies* 6 (1980): 1–25.

Konigsberg, Ira. *Narrative Technique in the English Novel*. Hamden: Archon, 1985.

Lamb, Jonathan. "Sterne's Use of Montaigne." *Comparative Literature* 32 (1980): 1–41.

Lanham, Richard A. Tristram Shandy: *The Games of Pleasure*. Berkeley: U of California P, 1973.

Leavis, F. R. *The Great Tradition*. London: Chatto, 1948.

Lehman, Benjamin H. "Of Time, Personality, and the Author." *Studies in the Comic. University of California Studies in English* 8 (1941): 233–50. Rpt. in Traugott, *Laurence Sterne* 21–33.

Lipking, Lawrence. *The Ordering of the Arts in Eighteenth-Century England*. Princeton: Princeton UP, 1970.

Locke, John. *An Essay concerning Human Understanding*. Ed. Peter H. Nidditch. Oxford: Clarendon, 1975.

Loveridge, Mark. *Laurence Sterne and the Argument about Design*. Totowa: Barnes, 1982.

Loverso, Marco P. "Self-Knowledge and the Lockean 'Self' in *The Sermons of Mr. Yorick*: A Link with the Shandean World." *English Studies in Canada* 8 (1982): 138–53.

MacLean, Kenneth. *John Locke and English Literature of the Eighteenth Century.* New Haven: Yale UP, 1936.

Markley, Robert. "*Tristram Shandy* and 'Narrative Middles': Hillis Miller and the Style of Deconstructive Criticism." *Genre* 17 (1984): 179–90.

Maskell, Duke. "Locke and Sterne: Or, Can Philosophy Influence Literature?" *Essays in Criticism* 23 (1973): 22–39.

McClure, Ruth K. *Coram's Children: The London Foundling Hospital in the Eighteenth Century.* New Haven: Yale UP, 1980.

McKillop, Alan Dugald. *The Early Masters of English Fiction.* Lawrence: UP of Kansas, 1956.

Mendilow, A. A. *Time and the Novel.* London: Nevill, 1952.

Miller, J. Hillis. "Narrative Middles: A Preliminary Outline." *Genre* 11 (1978): 375–87.

Moglen, Helene. *The Philosophical Irony of Laurence Sterne.* Gainesville: U of Florida P, 1975.

Monkman, Kenneth. "The Bibliography of the Early Editions of *Tristram Shandy*." *Library* 25 (1970): 11–39.

Myer, Valerie Grosvenor, ed. *Laurence Sterne: Riddles and Mysteries.* London: Vision; Totowa: Barnes, 1984.

Nänny, Max. "Similarity and Contiguity in *Tristram Shandy*." *English Studies* 60 (1979): 422–35.

New, Melvyn. "The Dunce Revisited: Colley Cibber and Tristram Shandy." *South Atlantic Quarterly* 72 (1973): 547–59.

———. "Laurence Sterne." *British Novelists, 1660–1800.* Vol. 39 of *Dictionary of Literary Biography.* Detroit: Gale, 1985.

———. *Laurence Sterne as Satirist: A Reading of* Tristram Shandy. Gainesville: U of Florida P, 1969.

———. "Sterne, Warburton, and the Burden of Exuberant Wit." *Eighteenth-Century Studies* 15 (1982): 245–74.

———. "Surviving the Seventies: Sterne, Collins and Their Recent Critics." *Eighteenth Century: Theory and Interpretation* 25 (1984): 3–24.

———. "Whim-Whams and Flim-Flams: The Oxford University Press Edition of *Tristram Shandy*." *Review* 7 (1985): 1–18.

Noakes, Susan. "On the Superficiality of Women." *The Comparatist Perspective on Literature: Approaches to Theory and Practice.* Ed. Clayton Koelb and Susan Noakes. Ithaca: Cornell UP, 1988. 339–55.

Oates, J. C. T. *Shandyism and Sentiment, 1760–1800.* Cambridge: Cambridge Bibliographical Soc., 1968.

Owen, David. *English Philanthropy, 1660–1960*. Cambridge: Belknap–Harvard UP, 1964.

Owen, John B. *The Eighteenth Century, 1714–1815*. New York: Norton, 1974.

Parnell, Paul. "The Sentimental Mask." *PMLA* 78 (1963): 529–35.

Partridge, Eric. *A Dictionary of Slang and Unconventional English*. 7th ed. New York: Macmillan, 1970.

———. *Shakespeare's Bawdy*. London: Routledge, 1947.

Paulson, Ronald. *Hogarth: His Life, Art, and Times*. 2 vols. New Haven: Yale UP, 1971.

———. *Satire and the Novel in Eighteenth-Century England*. New Haven: Yale UP, 1967.

Piper, William Bowman. *Laurence Sterne*. New York: Twayne, 1965.

Plumb, J. H. *England in the Eighteenth Century*. Rev. ed. Baltimore: Penguin, 1950.

Pope, Alexander. *The Twickenham Edition of the Poems of Alexander Pope*. Ed. John Butt, et al. 11 vols. London: Methuen, 1938–68.

Pope, Alexander, et al. *Memoirs of Martinus Scriblerus*. Ed. Charles Kerby-Miller. New Haven: Yale UP, 1950.

Porter, Roy. *English Society in the Eighteenth Century*. London: Lane, 1982.

Poulet, Georges. "Phenomenology of Reading." *New Literary History* 1 (1969): 53–68.

Preston, John. *The Created Self: The Reader's Role in Eighteenth-Century Fiction*. New York: Barnes, 1970.

Price, Martin. *To the Palace of Wisdom: Studies in Order and Energy from Dryden to Blake*. Garden City: Doubleday, 1964.

Read, Herbert. "Sterne." *The Sense of Glory*. New York: Harcourt, 1930. 123–51.

Rev. of *Tristram Shandy*, vols. 3 and 4. *Universal Magazine of Knowledge and Pleasure* 26 (Apr. 1761): 189–90.

Rimmon-Kenan, Shlomith. *Narrative Fiction: Contemporary Poetics*. London: Methuen, 1983.

Rosenblatt, Louise M. *The Reader, the Text, the Poem: The Transactional Theory of the Literary Work*. Carbondale: Southern Illinois UP, 1978.

Rosenblum, Michael. "The Sermon, the King of Bohemia, and the Art of Interpolation in *Tristram Shandy*." *Studies in Philology* 75 (1978): 472–91.

Rothstein, Eric. *Systems of Order and Inquiry in Later Eighteenth-Century Fiction*. Berkeley: U of California P, 1975.

Ruffhead, Owen, and William Rose. Rev. of *The Sermons of Mr. Yorick*, vols. 1 and 2. *Monthly Review* 22 (May 1760): 422–25.

Sacks, Sheldon. *Fiction and the Shape of Belief: A Study of Henry Fielding with Glances at Swift, Johnson and Richardson*. Berkeley: U of California P, 1964.

Scholes, Robert, and Robert Kellogg. *The Nature of Narrative*. New York: Oxford UP, 1966.

Schweickart, Patrocinio P. "Reading Ourselves: Toward a Feminist Theory of Reading." *Gender and Reading: Essays on Readers, Texts, and Contexts.* Ed. Elizabeth A. Flynn and P. P. Schweickart. Baltimore: Johns Hopkins UP, 1986. 31–62.

Seidel, Michael. *Satiric Inheritance: Rabelais to Sterne.* Princeton: Princeton UP, 1979.

Shklovsky, Viktor. "A Parodying Novel: Sterne's *Tristram Shandy*." Traugott, *Laurence Sterne* 66–89.

Sherburn, George, and Donald F. Bond. "The Restoration and Eighteenth Century (1660–1789)." *A Literary History of England.* Ed. Albert C. Baugh. 2nd ed. New York: Appleton, 1967. 697–1108.

Showalter, Elaine. "Feminist Criticism in the Wilderness." *Critical Inquiry* 8 (1981): 179–205.

Showalter, English, Jr. *The Evolution of the French Novel 1641–1782.* Princeton: Princeton UP, 1972.

Stedmond, John M. *The Comic Art of Laurence Sterne: Convention and Innovation in* Tristram Shandy *and* A Sentimental Journey. Toronto: U of Toronto P, 1967.

Sterne, Laurence. "The Case of Elijah and the Widow of Zarephath Considered." *Works,* ed. Cross, 11: 69–95.

———. *Letters of Laurence Sterne.* Ed. Lewis Perry Curtis. Oxford: Clarendon, 1935.

———. *Memoirs.* Ed. Kenneth Monkman. Coxwold: Laurence Sterne Trust, 1985.

———. *A Political Romance.* Menston, UK: Scolar, 1971.

———. *A Sentimental Journey through France and Italy.* Ed. Gardner D. Stout, Jr. Berkeley: U of California P, 1967.

———. A Sentimental Journey through France and Italy, *with* A Political Romance *and "Journal to Eliza."* Ed. Ian Jack. London: Oxford UP, 1968.

———. *The Sermons of Mr. Yorick.* Ed. Marjorie David. Chester Springs: Fyfield, 1973.

———. "Sterne's Rabelaisian Fragment: A Text from the Holograph Manuscript." Ed. Melvyn New. *PMLA* 87 (1972): 1083–92.

———. *Works.* Ed. Wilbur L. Cross. 12 vols. New York: Taylor, 1904.

———. *Works.* 7 vols. Oxford: Blackwell; Boston: Houghton, 1926–27.

Sterneiana. 7 vols. New York: Garland, 1974.

Stevenson, Lionel. *The English Novel: A Panorama.* Boston: Houghton, 1960.

Stillingfleet, Edward. *Works.* 6 vols. London, 1710.

Stovel, Bruce. "*Tristram Shandy* and the Art of Gossip." Myer 115–25.

Suleiman, Susan, and Inge Crosman, eds. *The Reader in the Text: Essays on Audience and Interpretation.* Princeton: Princeton UP, 1980.

Swearingen, James E. *Reflexivity in* Tristram Shandy: *An Essay in Phenomenological Criticism.* New Haven: Yale UP, 1977.

Swift, Jonathan. *The Poems of Jonathan Swift*. Ed. Harold Williams. 2nd ed. Oxford: Clarendon, 1958.

———. A Tale of a Tub, The Battle of the Books, *and* The Mechanical Operation of the Spirit. Ed. A. C. Guthkelch and D. Nichol Smith. 2nd ed. Oxford: Clarendon, 1958.

Tave, Stuart. *The Amiable Humorist: A Study in the Comic Theory and Criticism of the Eighteenth and Early Nineteenth Centuries*. Chicago: U of Chicago P, 1960.

Thomson, David. *Wild Excursions: The Life and Fiction of Laurence Sterne*. London: Weidenfeld, 1972.

Tillotson, Geoffrey, Paul Fussell, Jr., and Marshall Waingrow, eds. *Eighteenth-Century Literature*. New York: Harcourt, 1969.

Tompkins, Jane P., ed. *Reader-Response Criticism: From Formalism to Post-Structuralism*. Baltimore: Johns Hopkins UP, 1980.

Traugott, John, ed. *Laurence Sterne: A Collection of Critical Essays*. Englewood Cliffs: Prentice, 1968.

———. *Tristram Shandy's World: Sterne's Philosophical Rhetoric*. Berkeley: U of California P, 1954.

Turberville, A. S. *Johnson's England: An Account of the Life and Manners of His Age*. 2 vols. Oxford: Clarendon, 1933.

Tuveson, Ernest. "The Importance of Shaftesbury." *ELH* 20 (1953): 267–99.

———. "Locke and Sterne." *Reason and the Imagination: Studies in the History of Ideas, 1600–1800*. New York: Columbia UP, 1962. 255–77.

———. "Shaftesbury and the Age of Sensibility." *Studies in Criticism and Aesthetics, 1660–1800*. Ed. H. Anderson and J. S. Shea. Minneapolis: U of Minnesota P, 1967. 73–93.

Van Ghent, Dorothy. *The English Novel: Form and Function*. New York: Rinehart, 1953.

Voitle, Robert. "Shaftesbury's Moral Sense." *Studies in Philology* 52 (1955): 17–38.

Warren, Leland E. "The Constant Speaker: Aspects of Conversation in *Tristram Shandy*." *University of Toronto Quarterly* 46 (1976): 51–67.

———. " 'Turning Reality Round Together': Guides to Conversation in Eighteenth-Century England." *Eighteenth-Century Life* 8 (1983): 65–87.

Watkins, W. B. C. *Perilous Balance: The Tragic Genius of Swift, Johnson and Sterne*. Princeton: Princeton UP, 1939.

Watt, Ian. *The Rise of the Novel: Studies in Defoe, Richardson, and Fielding*. London: Chatto, 1957.

Williams, Ioan, ed. *Novel and Romance 1700–1800: A Documentary Record*. New York: Barnes, 1970.

Wilson, W. Daniel. "Readers in Texts." *PMLA* 96 (1981): 848–63.

Woolf, Virginia. "The *Sentimental Journey*." *The Second Common Reader*. New York: Harcourt, 1932. 80–88.

Wright, Andrew. "The Artifice of Failure in *Tristram Shandy*." *Novel* 2 (1969): 212–20.

Zach, Wolfgang. " 'My Uncle Toby's Apologetical Oration' und die Politische Sinndimension von *Tristram Shandy*." *Germanisch-Romanische Monatsschrift* ns 27 (1977): 391–416.

INDEX